KNOWLEDGE, BELIEF, AND TRANSCENDENCE

KNOWLEDGE, BELIEF, AND TRANSCENDENCE

Philosophical Problems in Religion

James Hall
University of Richmond

HOUGHTON MIFFLIN COMPANY
BOSTON
Atlanta   Dallas   Geneva, Illinois
Hopewell, New Jersey   Palo Alto   London

To Herblock and Walt Kelly—
preservers of sanity in the land of the Bourbons
To Ann, Jim, Don, and Smitty—
students who made it worthwhile
To James Rachels—
friend, colleague, critic
And to Bonny—
without whom, nothing.

CONTENTS

PART TWO: THE LANGUAGE OF THEISM

PREFACE

Every instructor knows the agony of trying to find a text that fits his topic, and philosophy of religion seems harder to fit than most topics. One writer, knowledgeable and sensitive to the workings of ordinary religion, misses all the philosophical nuts and bolts. Another writer, bristling with philosophical expertise, fastens on the most arid reaches of intellectual theology and never reaches anything a student would recognize as religion. One book turgidly pursues the obscure through six hundred pages and a forest of annotations into oblivion. Another book, brilliantly honed, maps nature, man, God, and the history of the literature in eighty-three. So we keep looking, we use anthologies, we edit, we select, and we chafe. Of course we find some gems. I have my own—used to tatters. But, eventually, we try writing.

Decisions must be made at the very beginning to prevent the garden from coming up weeds. These decisions furnish guidelines for the whole project, and are a fair indication of what the writer is trying to do. Here are the guidelines that I reached:

1. To emphasize philosophy as a working discipline and as a natural extension of ordinary critical inquiry; to see philosophy as a tool for getting at issues, rather than as a "way of life" or compendium of "wisdom."

2. To use a problems approach, underscoring the importance of issues, arguments, and evidence over names, history, and resumés of opinion.

3. To start with absolute basics, illustrate each move with commonplace examples, and never leave the reader to cope with unexplained abstractions as the discussion moves into complex territory.

4. To keep a close focus on ordinary religion as the object of analysis, so as to throw some light on places where ordinary readers are apt to be.

5. To tighten the focus to a core problem, treat that with care and in detail, and leave other topics to other books.

While the conceptual puzzles in ordinary religion range from miracles to survival, *the* philosophical puzzle is (as usual) one of epistemology. If one gets clear on the nature and status of religious beliefs and claims-to-know, then the disposition of the other puzzles will ease substantially. Furthermore, with the religion that has had the impact in our part of the world, it is beliefs and claims-to-know about God (especially about whether there is one) that are at the core of the puzzles. This is the tight focus selected for this book.

I have carried the analysis beyond the classic sense/nonsense debate; but I have tried to keep that sense of evidence and objectivity missing in existential and fideistic views. The theory of use which I finally reach shows many influences, both positive and negative, which anyone familiar with the literature will instantly recognize. For such readers, this book could be considerably abbreviated. But, while I believe that my conclusions will be of use to philosophers, my main concern has been to make the issues and problems accessible to a more general public. Thus a full apparatus of preparatory, explanatory, and supportive material has been provided.

On the other hand, I have assumed that there will be sufficient interest generated to pursue the literature at many points. Suggestions are made in the notes. They should be pursued. However, since first formal exposure to philosophy of religion can occur at any time between the sophomore and second postgraduate years, there can be great variation in the amount and kind of added material sought by or urged upon any given reader.

The bits and pieces of the developing manuscript have been shuttled back and forth for several years between lecture, seminar, discussion group, and the writing desk. Every section has been revised, and revised again, in the light of repeated trial and feedback. Every part included has proved its utility and intelligibility in use. Neither the content, structure, nor style is accidental. Every effort has been made to show at each point just how the matters at hand relate to what has gone before and what is yet to come.

I am heavily indebted to many people whose articles, books, and lectures have nudged my thinking. Chief among these are John Hick, C. B. Martin, and John Wisdom. I must also acknowledge a debt to Maynard Adams, who first insisted that I think with care, and taught me what a philosophical problem looks like. Special thanks to James Rachels for his encouragement and illuminating criticism. I would like to express my sincere appreciation to John H. Lavely of Boston University and to Joseph Nystrom of Diablo Valley College, both of whom read and scrutinized the entire manuscript and provided much helpful criticism. The faculty research committee of the University of Richmond helped with stenographic expenses, and Joyce Stevenson supplied ever prompt and expert typing. Bonlyn Hall assisted tirelessly in the proofreading, as well as preparing the index.

If there is anything true in this book, it is surely common sense. The falsehoods that survive, and the errors, are due to my perverseness. True and false, I hope that it is clear. If I have produced enough light for the reader to see the issues and find his own way out, that is quite enough. If, in the process, I have provided a text that fits another instructor's topic, that is *lagnappe*.

Richmond, Virginia, 1974

J.H.

KNOWLEDGE, BELIEF, AND TRANSCENDENCE

INTRODUCTION

The enterprise of philosophy of religion no more requires a Bible or a prayer rug than the pursuit of philosophy of science requires a Bunsen burner and test tubes. Philosophy of religion is not religion. Some familiarity with religious phenomena will be useful, of course, for we shall be trying to locate some of the basic notions that religious devotees and theologians use, and to unravel them and see what their logic is. Thus, if we are perceptive and careful, we will achieve some clarification of religion's actual conceptual equipment. Ceteris paribus, that is exactly what we would do if we were doing philosophy of history, philosophy of art, philosophy of mathematics, or philosophy of whatever: locate the very basic and primitive ideas, notions, concepts, and presuppositions that occur when the subject enterprise is done, clarify them, and try to lay them straight. Analysis is our tool. Clarification and understanding are our goals.

Many people think that there is an especially close relationship between philosophy and religion. It is, they say, six of one, half-dozen of the other—a serious mistake. The two fields should not be identified or slurred together because, while their relationship is a natural one, it is not "special." The kinds of questions that philosophers have been asking since Socrates first posed "What is truth?" ("What does 'truth' mean?") are of a sort that can be asked about the language and concepts of any human enterprise, from politics and morals to astrology and bridge.

But since philosophers are as pinched for time as anyone else, they tend to focus their attention on concepts that are "basic." While they could, if they wished, raise philosophical questions about the concepts and logic of (say) baseball, they devote their attention chiefly to notions that are fundamental to more important subjects: morals, for instance, or science or law or art. Accordingly, it is easy to understand why philosophy and religion are so often linked. Religion, it is claimed, is as basic to human concerns as can be, and even if it were only half as important as its devotees and critics both affirm, it would still demand more than a little philosophical attention. Nevertheless, aiming philosophical attention at religion remains quite distinct from carrying on the religious enterprise.

Another serious mistake is to think of religion and philosophy as mutually antagonistic—as fundamentally "at odds." To be sure, philosophy can be abrasive. After all, what philosophers are trying to do is to get clear about things—to use their intelligence and speak unambiguously, consistently, and in an intelligible and well-ordered way about the notions they examine. When you do that with a topic as difficult as religion (and in the midst of the human community, which is not noted for its consistency and clarity of thought), things may get abrasive. But abrasion is not the point. The point is getting through the crust to whatever truth is under it. Except to those who are convinced that religion is all crust and no truth, there is nothing necessarily destructive about examining it philosophically. So, philosophy is no more the necessary adversary of religion than its twin. Religion is just one more occasion for philosophical probing—no more, no less.

Yet another commonly held view is that religion is especially privileged—it is so special that it should not be subject to unrestrained scrutiny. Someone might say, "Since religion is sacred, it is irreverent and impious to go after its ideas as you would go after quantum theory or manifest destiny. It is permissible to examine the theoretical foundations of the natural sciences or politics—no holds are barred; let the chips fall where they may. But when we turn to religion, we must remember the Creed, the Dignity of the Almighty, the sacrifices of the Saints and Martyrs, and that our own souls stand in danger," and so on. Stuff and nonsense. If religion is in any way informative, if some religious claims are in some sense "true," then clearly religion should stand up to scrutiny under the common rules of inquiry. If the only way in which an enterprise can be preserved intact is by changing the rules of inquiry[1] or by ceasing inquiry altogether, then there is *prima*

---

[1]The point here, of course, is not to exclude the possibility that the rules of inquiry can expand and improve in use. Nor is it to exclude the possibility that

facie evidence that something has gone awry. Any enterprise or ideology—economic, political, religious, or whatever—that cringes at straightforward investigation is in serious trouble: it cannot be relevant to the common circumstances of men unless the common circumstances of men are relevant to it. If you free religion (or any other enterprise) and its claims from all responsibility to everyday states of affairs (evidence), then everyday states of affairs are equally free from any application of the enterprise and its claims. If X has no relation to Y, it is idle to look for Y's relations to X.[2] So, since I am convinced that religion is not necessarily and systematically uninformative, we are not going to give it any special privileges in what follows. We are going to talk about it in the same way we would talk about any other human enterprise that we might try to unpack from a philosophical point of view. If it turns out that all is well, fine; and if it turns out that there are insuperable difficulties, so be it. I shall try not to load the questions either way; and you have a corresponding task.

The discussion that follows begins with two main issue-areas about religion. They are closely related. I work through them in the way I do in order to render a progressively difficult set of notions as digestible as I can. The best tactic is to work through from the beginning. There is no guarantee that you will agree with the conclusions I reach, or be content where I contend that no conclusion can be reached; but at least you will see your way to continue the inquiry on your own. And that, after all, is the point.

The first issue-area is what may be called the epistemology of religion.[3] We shall begin by looking at some questions about epistemology in general because, if we are going to examine religious concepts in terms of standard rules, it is necessary for us to have some clear idea of what the standard rules are. Consequently, we shall spend a little time on some rules of evidence, on what kinds of evidence there might be, on the difference between knowing and believing, and the like. Only then shall we turn to questions about the nature and status of religious

---

there exist techniques that are more (or less) suited to one area of thought than to another. The point is, simply, to avoid special pleading, redefinitions, and evasions that turn respectable inquiry into question-begging.

[2] You could, of course, claim that religious "knowledge" is just different and, hence, is not to be discussed along with or in the same terms as ordinary knowing. But, if so, why call it "knowledge"? Why not call it "*kabinett wein*"? The point is that such a retreat via redefinition fudges all the issues. We are interested in *knowledge*. Does it occur in religion? Mutatis mutandis for truth, etc.

[3] Epistemology is that branch of philosophy concerned with the theory of knowledge—its nature, sources, scope, and limits.

thought, and about the possibility of there being any such thing as
religious knowledge.

These inquiries will, as you will see, force us into the other main
issue-area: the language of religion.[4] There we shall ask how a variety
of religious utterances are used and what they could mean. We shall
focus our attention on specific claims. This part of the enterprise will
sharpen the aim of our exploration; and since these particular claims
are especially basic ones, it will also help us achieve some important
clarification at a fairly primitive level in the system.

In our initial examination of the epistemology of religion, we shall
concentrate on a particular item that some people claim to know, that
other people claim not to know, and that still others claim to know neg-
atively: whether there is a God. Then, on turning to the language, we
will find ourselves forced to ask whether "There is a God" is the kind
of utterance that can be a knowledge assertion.[5]

The excursion into language may puzzle you at first. It may seem
like an evasion of the real and basic issue. "What we want to know is
whether or not there is a God. What does language have to do with that?"
There are two replies. First, suppose that "whether or not" *is* the basic
concern for you (i.e., the most important). Even if it is, the only way
to get at it is to get clear on what "There is (or is not) a God" would
amount to; and basic to that (i.e., logically prior to it) is the primitive
question "What does saying 'There is a God' (or 'there is not') come
down to—what does this phrase mean?" The linguistic question, then,
is *logically* basic, even if it does not strike you as "most important."
There are two senses of "basic" operative here. Second, it simply must
be noted that, from a philosophical point of view, what is logically basic
is *basic* basic. The logically basic (basic$_1$) is of basic importance (basic$_2$)

---

[4]We are rarely in a position to decide whether a claim is true until we have some
clear notion of what it is being used to say. The particular kind of philosophical
inquiry that amounts to finding out what a claim is being used to say is very
basic. Indeed, in areas where we do not have clear notions of what is being said,
some kind of (formal or informal) philosophical spadework must be done before
the subject enterprise can effectively be pursued. You can hardly settle substan-
tive questions of theology, for example, if the very claims that express the questions are unintelligible to you, or if you have no notion of what would be germane
or significant evidence for weighing them.

[5]You may think now that this is a silly question. "People do assert that they
know there is a God, so the claim 'There is a God' must be the kind of claim that
can be a knowledge assertion. 'Do' presupposes 'can,' after all!" But some notions intrude which make it extremely difficult to spell out how one could utter
"There is a God" in an assertively successful way. The logic is rather confused
here. We shall have to wait and see.

to philosophers. That is part of what makes philosophy philosophy. So, from a philosophical point of view, "whether there is (or is not)" really is not the basic (basic$_1$ or basic$_2$) issue. This should no longer seem odd. Even though many would like to know "whether there is (or is not)," there is a prior question-set (questions that have to be asked first). What would be involved in knowing, either way? What would it be for the claim "There is a God" to be true (or false)? What does "There is a God" mean? What are we doing, precisely, when we say that there is a God? It is this question-set that arouses our basic interests as philosophers, even while other questions may arouse our basic interests in other roles. It is precisely because of our focus on this set that our task is distinctly one that concerns philosophy of religion and not religion.

You may think that you very well know what the claim "There is a God" means, and how it is used. You may regularly use it. But the use of an expression does not necessarily entail its comprehension. We can easily fall into conditioned patterns of talk and, when we have done so, talk to each other in apparent intellectual comfort. But that comfortable interchange may itself go far to conceal from us the actual dimensions of what we are doing in our language. In any case, we shall consider many options and interpretations of the meaning and use of religious locutions, in the hope that our comprehension may begin to catch up with our comfortable use.

Finally, I shall suggest a somewhat new approach to the understanding and use of religious utterances—one which I find both persuasive and helpful. But it will take many pages of chopping underbrush and looking through jungle before we get to the point at which we can begin to put things together. I will admit, frankly and at the beginning, that I am convinced that most of the questions we shall explore do have clear-cut and convincing answers that can be located. But, I must also admit, equally frankly, that I can make no guarantee of the truth of the theory which I will finally advance. I remain content to let you make your own final assessment, using your own intelligence and perseverence to push through to answers that you see as responsive to the arguments and the evidence. In the process, whether the evidence will finally support my own theory or not, you should obtain an increased understanding of the issues and their scope; and, having worked through alternative ways of dealing with them, should achieve a reasonably illuminated vantage point from which your own inquiry can be carried forward. I ask of you only an open mind and enough flexibility to entertain an unusual question or two.

I have little to help the inflexible. If, fixed in dogmatic faith, you cannot entertain doubt, or if, secure in the briars of atheism, you cannot entertain Eden, then there will be little here of much effect for you. But for the rest, there is the possibility of a little light in what has become, for many, a very dark room.

PART ONE

❧

THE
EPISTEMOLOGY
OF
THEISM

1

ON
KNOWING

In the next chapter we will be talking about knowledge theory as it applies to religion; but we must get some groundwork done so that when we talk about the nature of religious knowledge we will have our equipment in order. This chapter, then, is devoted to knowledge theory in general. We shall start very broadly, go only as far as is necessary, and raise the issues and draw the distinctions as simply as possible. Even so, since such basic matters are usually not easy, it would be wise to take the time and effort to get them firmly in mind now.

KINDS OF KNOWING

The Ambiguity of "Know" in Ordinary Talk

There are many different kinds of knowing; or, more to the point, there are many different uses for the word "know."[1] We use and con-

[1] Saying "there are many different kinds of knowing" suggests that there is one thing—knowing—that comes in many styles (rather like Chevrolet sedans that come with many different option groups but remain, unmistakably, Chevrolet sedans). But maybe there is no one thing at all. This is why it is better to say "there are many different uses for the word 'know.'" That avoids the not-necessarily-correct presumption that all the instances have something in common.

fuse them all too easily, for the uses are not (to use a good medieval word) univocal. They are, rather, equivocal. Consequently, unless we take care, an apparently single use may be ambiguous. Our purpose in this section is to call attention to a few of these uses before we focus on one or two that are especially germane to our purposes in the chapters ahead.

When I talk about knowing Martin Ryle, knowing my son, and knowing Plato, what appears to be the same word in each case ("knowing") obviously has changing force. (The force would change again if I talked about knowing God; but we shall keep that in reserve for a little while.) Different parts of what I mean when I say that I know Martin Ryle could be more precisely expressed in such statements as "I know what Ryle looks like," "I can often anticipate what Ryle is going to do," "There is some rapport between Ryle and me," and so on. None of these statements is a literal translation of "I know Martin Ryle"; but in most circumstances in which I might say "I know Martin Ryle," these are the sorts of things I would mean. (Even in this limited context, "know" could have at least four different emphases: familiarity, recognition and anticipation abilities, and even empathy.)

Probably the only difference between my knowing my son and my knowing Martin Ryle is one of degree, not of kind. I am so involved in what the boy does, and share with him so many experiences, that a remarkable degree of empathy is generated, and (from that) anticipation, understanding, and so on. You know people as a function of the extent and intensity of empathetic contact you have with them. Cases may vary, but they are of the same sort. But saying that I know a person who died before I was born seems rather different.

Of course, when I say "I know Plato," I do mean some of the same sorts of things just enumerated. It is not a case of no overlap at all.[2] But I cannot say that I know Plato in exactly the same sense that I say I know Ryle or my son. Ryle is alive and has an office down the hall in the history department. Plato is dead. I know Ryle out of shared experience, personal contact, and a whole network of sensations in which he figures. But I know Plato as a man only by inference and on "authority." It is rather like knowing a contemporary by reputation—you do know him, but it is not the same.[3] So, if someone asked me, "Whom do you

[2]If saying is a kind of doing, I can sometimes anticipate what Plato will do; and that is part of knowing Plato just as it is part of knowing Ryle. Knowing that Plato is likely to bring in a little transcendental business when he argues philosophy is not totally unlike knowing that Ryle is likely to buy a pipe whenever he is downtown.

[3]You could redefine "Plato" to make that word a label for a body of writings

know?" and I answered, "I know Martin Ryle, my son, and Plato," my reply wouldn't be a lie but it would certainly be misleading.[4]

But "know" has other, even more independent, uses as well. For instance, when I say, "I know the multiplication tables through 12," I am really saying that I have the ability to make a certain kind of recitation on demand. I am saying that I have a skill acquired by virtue of drill and reinforcement. But is being able to produce a recitation on demand quite like knowing Ryle (or Plato)? Not unless you are content to say that these cases, too, are drill-reinforced behavior skills.[5]

Further, while knowing the multiplication tables amounts basically to having a certain recitation skill, it also involves another element—remembering. Remembering plays an important role in a lot of our knowing. How do I know the 12 table? I remember it. How do I know Ryle at thirty paces? I remember what he looks like. In these instances, remembering appears to be the foundation on which the skill (recitation, recognition) rests. Thus, it seems to be a basis for knowing rather than a kind of knowing. But it is more complicated than that. Memory may be (part of) the basis here, but memory is not remembering. Memory is like a reinforceable skill or technique (you can take courses to improve your memory just as you can take courses to improve your golf). But remembering, as such, is more of an achievement than a skill. You may use many skills to get there; but, in the end, you either remember or you don't. Similarly, when I say, "Coming in first is how you win," I do not mean that coming in first is a good technique to use for win-

---

which I do know like I know my friend; but that fudges the distinction. We are talking about knowing *Plato.*

[4]However, saying that you know someone whom you have never met (who is dead, for instance) still involves a kind of familiarity with the thinking, the usual intentions, etc., of the person "known." Indeed, it is predicated on such great involvement with his historical remains and reputation that it really amounts to secondhand, inferential speculation that if he were alive, you would be able to anticipate his behavior, etc., in the same way you do that of your living familiars. He is dead, of course; so we cannot, in fact, verify the output of the knowledge we lay claim to except in his remains; but that does not stifle knowledge completely. (I am trading here on an important distinction between what is factually impossible and what is impossible in principle. It is because of this difference that I can talk about knowing Plato and cannot talk about knowing certain sorts of gods. I mention this now, but will defer further explanation. It is sufficient at present for you to start thinking about the de facto/per principium distinction in less obscure contexts until you have it clear. Compare holding your breath for an hour with drawing a circle with square corners.)

[5]Of course, if "I know Ryle" means only "I can identify Ryle at thirty paces," "I know him when I see him," etc., then you should be content to make such an equation. But when you talk about knowing a close friend, are you talking more about your own behavior skills or more about the rapport between you?

ning. Rather, I mean that that is what winning amounts to in the game in question. Sometimes, "remember" is very much like "win" is in this case. Thus, when Lola has accused him of forgetting her charms and Brute says, "I remember your kisses," his claim is simply that he knows and has not stopped knowing. The basis of his knowing is their kissing, not his remembering. That *is* his knowing.

So there are cases in which knowing amounts very nearly to the exercise of a skill (knowing the 12 table) and cases in which knowing amounts more approximately to the achievement that the exercise of skill attains (remembering Lola's charms). Over and above these skill-related cases, we have also suggested that there are instances of knowing that are less a skill than they are involvement-produced empathy (knowing Martin Ryle or, for that matter, knowing Lola), and that these instances may either be direct (knowing my son) or by evidence and inference (knowing Plato). It would appear, then, that quite a variety of forces may be meant when someone says "I know." Indeed, there are many more possible forces; but enough have been enumerated to indicate the need for care. In the next section we will take a closer look at two particular forces of "know" that have been much discussed in philosophical writing.

"Knowledge-How" and "Knowledge-That"[6]

The knowledge shown in reciting the multiplication tables, riding a bicycle, threading a needle, or tying your shoelaces is the sort of thing usually labeled "knowledge-how." Some writers have suggested that just about all knowledge (except, perhaps, the empathy or familiarity knowledge we looked at) comes down to one or another form of knowledge-how.[7]

There is considerable argument, however, over whether knowledge-how covers the kind of knowledge affirmed in such statements as "I know that Columbus discovered America in 1492," "I know that today is Monday," "I know that academicians are underpaid." When we claim to know in sentences like these, we seem always to be talking about knowing that such and so is true, knowing that a certain state of affairs obtains, or knowing that a certain fact is so. This sort of knowledge has

---

[6]The classic presentation of this distinction is in Gilbert Ryle's *The Concept of Mind,* (New York: Barnes & Noble, 1959), pp. 25–61.

[7]For example, see John Dewey's *The Quest for Certainty,* (New York: Minton, Balch, 1929). Relevant portions of it have been widely reprinted. See pp. 344–360 of M. H. Fisch, *Classic American Philosophers* (New York: Appleton-Century-Crofts, 1951).

been called "knowledge-that." While it may be clear that knowledge-that is distinct from being acquainted or familiar with a person (or place or thing),[8] it is not so clear that it is sharply distinct from knowledge-how. Perhaps it is only a peculiarly complex exercise of skill at a verbal level, and can be completely explained in terms of drill and reinforcement just like riding bicycles and threading needles. There is an *apparent* difference, however; and it will be helpful to make that difference clear even if there is a possibility of eventually explaining it away.

Suppose that we have two people, one of them an early-movie Tarzan and the other a professor of human physiology. The Tarzan that I have in mind is one of the greatest swimmers ever to enter competition. He is not, though, highly endowed intellectually. He can swim like a fish, but his "Me Tarzan, you Jane" is a fair representation of his brain power. The physiology professor I have in mind is extremely clever, well-read, and articulate, and has done extensive reserarch on all the biological processes involved when people swim. He knows which muscles move first, which nerves shoot stimuli in which directions at what time, and even all the details of training and diet. He is absolutely a world master of knowledge about swimming, swimming techniques, what goes on when you swim, and why. Our professor, however, is a dud when it comes to swimming itself. (He and I are very much alike here. I know a great many facts about swimming, have taken lessons, can go through all the motions, can sit on the bottom of the pool and hold my breath interminably. But there is one thing I cannot do. I cannot swim. When I get in the water I sink like a rock. Our professor is just like that.)

Now, no one would dispute that our Tarzan knows how to swim; but no one who knows him very well would ever claim that he knows very much about it (or about anything else for that matter), in the sense of having facts at his command. His knowledge is not a matter of his being smart or learned. He just has a motor skill acquired through practice, and good physical equipment. On the other hand, no one would dispute the fact that the professor knows virtually everything there is to know about swimming. Because he is smart and has done his

[8]It is possible that knowledge-that might be explained as a complicated instance of familiarity or acquaintance, viz., familiarity or acquaintance with a state of affairs. So: "I know that Paris is the capital of France" may equal "I am familiar with the state of affairs Paris-being-the-capital-of-France." But I do not think that this will work. Being familiar with the state of affairs Paris-being-the-capital-of-France involves at least knowing what that state of affairs amounts to, viz., that Paris is the capital of France. So this sort of explanation would generate an infinite regress. (For some elaboration of what an "infinite regress" is, see note 21.)

homework, he has lots of swimming knowledge on tap. But all you would have to do is throw him in the pool to discover incontrovertibly that he does not know how to swim. So Tarzan knows how and the professor does not; and the professor has a lot of understanding but Tarzan does not.

One way to underscore the apparent distinction here is to take note of the difference between what it would take to interfere with our two men's "knowledge." Knowledge-how can be blocked out by interfering with the individual's motor equipment, without ever touching his higher nerve centers (or, if your prefer, "attacking his mind"). Suppose, for example, that our Tarzan met with a grisly accident and became a quadraplegic amputee. He is now a torso with a head. He has all the brain and central nervous system he ever had. (If you prefer, he has all the mental capacity he ever had.) Yet it would be very strange to talk about his knowing how to swim any more, for knowledge-how is dependent upon motor skills and when the physiological equipment goes, surely the skills go with it. On the other hand, what we are more likely to label knowledge-that, cognition, or understanding is more directly connected with the central apparatus (or, if you prefer, the mind). Knowledge-that is disturbed, mainly, only when we begin to tamper with the brain—which, of course, we can do without disturbing any gross motor equipment at all.

Suppose, then, that we had one individual who was endowed with all the knowledge of the professor *and* all the knowledge of the movie Tarzan. We could mess him up either way. We could amputate his arms and legs and thus deprive him of his know-how, even though he could still regale us with facts-about-swimming at length. Or, we could do a little bit of brain surgery (if you prefer, tamper with his mind) and so erase the information he once had on tap, even though he could still "swim like a fish." With such a person we could deprive him of either the motor abilities or the cognitions, and so differentiate in practice between knowledge-how and knowledge-that.

There may be good reasons to say that all cognitions could be reduced to (i.e., explained in terms of) complex and subtle motor skills. There is controversy on this. The issue becomes particularly acute when we turn to man's specifically linguistic abilities. Whether this reduction can finally be brought off or not, though, a substantial apparent difference between know-how and cognition remains.[9]

[9]In our example, it may be that Tarzan and the professor simply have different knowledge-hows—Tarzan, knowledge-how to swim; the professor, knowledge-how to talk about swimming. But this depends on placing linguistic abilities on all fours with "behavior." There is the rub; and there is argument on it. (The argument as expressed by B. F. Skinner and Noam Chomsky even made *News-*

Summary

So far, we have glanced at several kinds of examples in which knowledge is affirmed with different forces—recognition, familiarity and empathy, description and inference, recitation and other skills, remembering, and assertion. Subtle and advanced epistemological analysis may show that all of these reduce to different complications of the same basic building blocks; but even if they do, they are not interchangeable in ordinary talk. "Know," in ordinary talk, remains ambiguous.

Of course, the ambiguity that we have discussed is not limited to the fact that when "know" occurs it may have any one of several forces. On many occasions it is used with more than one of these several forces (and others, too) present. Knowing the 12 table, for example, involves at least recognition, remembering, recitation skill, and (often) some understanding. We should keep the multiple complexity in mind.

When we turn our attention in the next chapter to religious knowledge, we will find examples there of all these forces. Certainly there are places where knowledge-how comes in. There are all sorts of things, for example, that the clergy (as clergy) "know how" to do—baptize people, celebrate mass, pray. We will find, however, for reasons that will become clearer, that the crucial instances of religious knowledge generally purport to be instances of knowledge-that. In any case, it is primarily the cognitions of religion that are of interest to us here; i.e., cases in which religionists say such things as "We know that such and so is true."[10] This is no different from the usual emphasis in philosophical inquiry. The knowledge that is the usual target of philosophical probing is at this "cognitive" level—the level of asserting and denying matters of fact, of explanation, and of description. Whatever area of philosophical labor we were going to pursue, then, we would need at this point to take a much closer look at knowledge-that.[11]

---

week several years ago.) This issue is crucial in philosophy of mind, has a bearing on moral philosophy, and (at least to the extent that religion involves notions of separable souls) is germane to philosophy of religion. The theories that I will advance here are compatible with both sides. I will cast them in terms of knowledge-that; but if the knowledge-how reduction is legitimate, the theories will carry over in the translation.

[10]If, in fact, all cognition will reduce to knowledge-how, then whatever we may say about religious cognition would be further reducible or explicable in those terms; but that is not our issue. See the preceding note.

[11]We will also see that many instances of putative knowledge-that in religion are presented as rooted in special cases of familiarity-empathy knowing (i.e., so "knowing" God). Because of this, we will look rather closely at how and whether familiarity-empathy knowing can give support to particular examples of knowledge-that.

COGNITION AND ASSERTION: NECESSARY
CONDITIONS OF KNOWLEDGE-THAT

Just what is involved when people claim to know that something is the case? More important, what is involved when people successfully make such a claim? What are they claiming and what does it take to make the claim go? There are three necessary conditions that any claim to knowledge-that must meet.[12]

Assertive Content

To begin with, if an item is going to constitute knowledge,[13] it certainly has to be the kind of item that *could* constitute knowledge. This seems so obvious that you may think there is no need to mention it; but there are good reasons why we should nail this down explicitly and not trust our sense of the obvious. To clarify this, let me introduce some useful vocabulary. I will use the word "cognitive" as an adjective indicating an item that *can* constitute knowledge, and the word "cognition" as a noun for items that *do* constitute knowledge. By this convention, my "obvious" claim is that every cognition must be cognitive (but not vice versa). It may help to look at this in terms of some sample statements or claims. As I am using the terms, "Pluto is solid cobalt" and "I will get a raise next year" are cognitive claims, while "January 21, 1974, was a Monday" and "Under standard conditions water boils at 212° F" are not only cognitive but are also (usually) expressions of cognitions.[14]

All it takes for a claim to be cognitive is the possibility of its being true. The affirmation of this kind of claim genuinely asserts something

---

[12]The necessary-condition/sufficient-condition distinction: Being able to read and write is a necessary condition of enrollment in most universities. That is something you have to know how to do to get in. But it is not enough. A lot of other conditions must be met as well. If we could make a list of all the necessary conditions, then all of them jointly would provide us with the sufficient conditions—a list of what is "enough." Curiously, the two kinds of conditions are sometimes confused.

[13]Hereafter, unless specified otherwise, I will use "knowledge" with the force "knowledge-that."

[14]Some of you are familiar with the term "cognitive" and probably all of you are familiar with "cognition"; but, perhaps, not in the way that I am using them. My use will become clear by the end of this section. For those of you who have read some history, I am using cognitive somewhat in the way the Logical Positivists used it; but I am not assuming that everything that is noncognitive is "nonsensical." And I am not assuming that every "sensical" claim is cognitive, either. "Close that door!" isn't nonsense; but neither is it cognitive. See the next note.

to be so—it "says something," it has assertive content. But it could very well be that when we subject such a claim to careful testing, we may find out that what it asserts is not actually so at all. But the falseness of the claim does not prevent it from asserting that something is so. It would still be cognitive, even though it would not express a cognition. For example, if I were to say, "Today is August 14, 1832," I would be making a claim that anyone alive today knows perfectly well is false. So no matter how confused I may be, I certainly cannot know that today is August 14, 1832. Nevertheless, my statement would still be a perfectly straightforward assertion; it has no flaws besides that of falseness. If the circumstances were right, I could know it. So it is cognitive. On the other hand, if I were to say, "The ergwhat quanifles somewhat on the kumquat," there would be serious question whether my statement is even cognitive, much less the expression of a cognition. That is, there would be serious question whether it actually asserts or denies anything to be the case. To find out, we would have to find out what in the world (if anything) an ergwhat is, how one quanifles, and whether that is the sort of thing one can do on a kumquat. Only when we got all of that straight could we decide whether the whole utterance was cognitive or not. And only when we found it cognitive (if we did), could we ask, "Is it the expression of a cognition?"[15] That this question has to come later in the argument is indicative of the fact that the necessary conditions of being a cognition are stricter than those for being cognitive. So: the first necessary condition for a claim to be a genuine, full-fledged knowledge[16] claim is that it be cognitive.

Knowledge and Belief It is interesting that this basic minimal necessity that a full-fledged knowledge claim be cognitive (have truth conditions of some sort, genuinely assert or deny something to be the case) is also a basic minimal condition for a full-fledged belief claim.[17]

[15]If, for example, we found that "quanifle" is Tamil for "weaves cocoons," and that "ergwhats" are a species of fruit-infesting moth, then the claim is cognitive (and maybe even a cognition claim). However, if "quanifle" means to discernibly transform the indiscernible qualities of a thing, then the claim is in trouble. Maybe it is just false ("You can't do that!"), but maybe it doesn't assert anything at all ("That doesn't make sense!"). Or maybe the whole phrase is Javanese for "Please forgive me." That makes sense; but it isn't true and it isn't false either. It isn't an assertion. It is an entreaty. Cognitive utterances assert. Cognition claims assert truly, at least.

[16]Reminder: "knowledge" is used for "knowledge-that" now, unless otherwise specified.

[17]Many say that belief itself is the first necessary condition of knowledge. Others disagree. I am only saying that belief and knowledge have the same first necessary

If the utterance "The ergwhat quanifles somewhat on the kumquat" turns out to be assertively empty, then I can no more believe it than I can know it. Take the statement from Lewis Carroll " 'Twas brillig and the slithy toves did gyre and gimble in the wabe." It is obvious enough that, without special information, you do not know whether Carroll's utterance here is true or false. It does not express a cognition for you. But we can take this a step further. Unless and until it is interpreted and filled in, it is neither true nor false as it stands.[18] It cannot be either one because it does not say (affirm or deny) anything. Unless and until it is interpreted and filled in, it may be a pleasant string of noises, and it may play an important part in the sort of verse that Carroll enjoyed writing; but you cannot know it and, consequently, cannot believe it either. If someone actually said " 'Twas brillig and the slithy toves did gyre and gimble in the wabe" to you, your appropriate answer would probably have to be "What do you mean?" If they asked, "Do you know whether slithy toves gyre?" you would have to answer, "No, I don't." If they pressed, "Well, what do you believe about them?" you would have to press back, "I don't believe anything about them; I don't know what 'they' are. What are you talking about?"

The point of this is simply that knowing and believing have something in common; namely, that what is known or what is believed is the cognitive content of the utterance expressing the cognition or belief. Knowledge and belief, then, both begin with having some genuine cognitive content. If a sentence lacks all such content, it cannot get any further as the expression of a belief than it can as the expression of a cognition. In many cases something is lacking, with the effect that we must retreat from a claim to know. In those lacking evidence, we may retreat to a simpler claim to believe. But if what is lacking is any assertive content, then such a retreat will not work. If we cannot, in principle, know X (because X has no content to know), then we cannot, in principle, believe X either (since X has no content to believe).

---

condition (i.e., possession of cognitive content)—a much weaker claim, but all that is needed for our purposes.

[18] I am not denying the law of the excluded middle (that every class, when taken with its complementary class, exhausts the options). That law holds. Example: everything is either a kumquat or a non-kumquat (most things are non-kumquats, of course). But "false" and "true" make complementary classes *only within the domain of cognitive utterances.* Every cognitive utterance is either true or false, just as every card played in a bridge game either follows or does not follow suit. But there are other domains of utterance, even as there are other games besides bridge. Following suit does not apply to taking your turn at bat. The rules and classifications of assertion do not apply to enterprises that are not assertive in the first place.

Truth

About all that is required for a statement to be believed at some time or another is that it have some cognitive content. People seem to be willing to believe almost anything they can believe, sooner or later. The content need not be obviously or even probably true for people to believe it. (At a county fair one time, I saw thirty-seven men pay a dollar each to see a girl in a glass tank who had "lived under water, breathing through the pores of her skin, for eleven years." Of course, the barker added that to prevent suffocation she could not wear clothes of any kind. That may have helped.) But while it makes perfectly good sense (and is unfortunately familiar to us all) to talk about "false beliefs," it does not make any sense at all to talk about "false knowledge." A second minimal condition of cognition is that what is "known" must, in fact, be true. Here belief and knowledge part company.

If a person were to say, "I believe that today is the day when Daddy Warbucks will give $1 billion to the University of Richmond—I may be mistaken, but I believe that this is the day," there is nothing at all wrong with what he says besides its improbability. But if he were to say instead: "I know that today is the day when Daddy Warbucks will give $1 billion to the University of Richmond—I may be mistaken, but even if I am mistaken and he does not give the money, I still know that this is the day," the utterance fails to jell because of a very serious flaw. Knowing does not admit of being mistaken. If Daddy Warbucks does not give the money today, then you cannot know that he is giving the money today.[19] The very best you could come up with would be a belief.

Of course you may believe that you know. Indeed, suppose that such an issue came up. You might (on strong grounds) have said: "I know that today is the day," only to discover that Daddy had given the money to the International Esperanto Society. At that point you would have to recant. You would have to say, "I thought I knew, but I was mistaken." You would not say "I knew, but what I knew was false." Rather: "I thought I knew but I did not know at all." At best you could go no further than "I believed; I had good reason to think that I was correct; within the limits of evidence available at the time, I was pragmatically justified in saying that I knew; but in final analysis, now that everything has been brought out in the open, I realize my evidence

[19]You might legitimately say that you knew he intended to give the money today, but that something came up to prevent it. But that fudges the issue.

was not good enough. I was led down the garden path. I really didn't know at all."[20]

This is precisely the kind of situation in which, on finding that knowledge has failed, we fall back on belief. It may be that in this sense knowing does "begin" in believing—that, typically, belief is what is left when some qualification goes unsatisfied and we discover that our strong conviction is not knowledge. In any case, while the first necessary conditions of believing and knowing are the same, we see that belief and knowledge promptly part ways because knowledge has a second necessary condition that belief lacks. Believing, by itself, is not enough to purchase knowledge, simply because a belief can be false. Our beliefs should be responsible to the truth, but even if they are not, they remain our beliefs. Our knowledge must be responsible to the truth. If it is not, then it is not knowledge at all.

Evidence

Cognitive content is a necessary condition. Truth is a necessary condition. But these are not enough, even taken jointly, because it is possible for a person to make a true claim under circumstances in which we would immediately deny that the person knows.

Suppose that one of the local stores is having one of those contests in which a bunch of beans in a jug sits in the front window, and you are supposed to guess how many beans there are in the jug, the person coming closest winning the prize. Suppose that Marcia plans to enter the contest. The night before she is going to submit her entry, she has a bizarre dream in which the figure 7,942½ is inscribed in the sky in flaming letters ten feet high. So she goes to the store the next day, enters 7,942½ on the blank, and tells all her friends, "You know, I believe I will win. My dream was an omen. I feel lucky. The jug has 7,942½ beans in it." Suppose, further, that one week later, when the jug is opened and the beans are counted, Marcia's entry is exactly right—

[20]There are occasions when, in trying to underscore our amazement over an unexpected turn of events, we might say, "I knew, I really knew; but I was mistaken!" But what we would be doing here is not so much the affirmation that we knew a falsehood to be true (which would be a contradiction in terms), as it is the use of a stylistic device to emphasize the fact that on discovery that our belief was mistaken (and that we really didn't know at all), we were completely bowled over. The force of "know" in this context is not the force of knowledge-that. It has, rather, the force of extreme conviction. As we shall see, the conditions for knowledge-that reach out to the affairs affirmed. But the conditions of this

7,942½ beans in the jug! Her assertion was certainly cognitive. Her assertion turns out to be true. She even believed it was true, for that matter. But barring further information (maybe she cheated), I think that we would be loath to say that she knew how many beans were there. I think we would say that it was a lucky guess or a coincidence. We might explain it in any of a dozen different ways, but not as a case of knowing. The reason is that we are not usually willing to say that a person knows something until they can incorporate some kind of evidence-connection into what they assert. What we are looking for here is not just the logical possibility[21] of evidence (which is tied up in the first necessary condition of knowing); but rather, for a link to some amount of actual available evidence, either in hand or readily accessible. Now, what kind of evidence is called for? How much evidence is required? Here a whole new network of problems opens up. But certainly evidence of some kind has to be forthcoming before we will be willing to jump from the verdict "correct guesswork" to the verdict "knowledge."

Summary

A full and adequate definition of knowledge would have to go way beyond anything we have said so far. But what we have said so far is where it would have to begin. Knowledge has three minimal necessary conditions: assertive content or cognitivity, truth, and evidence-connections. I have made no claims about its sufficient conditions.

One more basic area must be sorted out before we can go on; namely, what kind of evidence is there to which one can appeal when saying "I know"? Not only must we ask, "What kind of evidence could qualify?" but also, "On what grounds might that qualification be determined?" In the next section I am going to present five different kinds of evidence and a number of possible qualification tests. Once we have worked through them, we can move on to our proper business of religious believing and knowing, equipped with a basic set of useful tools.

---

kind of knowledge aim inward at the fervor of the subject. Perhaps those who seem to think that passionate commitment will make things so are guilty of a serious equivocation at just this point.

[21] Logical possibility is not the same as circumstantial possibility. Something is logically possible if its assertion involves no contradiction. So, many circumstantially impossible things are logically possible. Holding my breath for an hour is logically possible. Drawing a circle with square corners is not.

EVIDENCE

Consider the different kinds of evidence to which people appeal when they claim to know this, that, or the other. We want to weigh these different kinds of evidence to see whether or not they can, in fact, carry the freight they purport to carry. All of us are accustomed to the notion of weighing evidence. Weighing the evidence is something we not only expect a judge or jury to do; it is something we all do, every day. However, the weighing I have in mind here is slightly more complex than that—not weighing a specific piece of evidence on its merits as evidence of its kind, but rather, weighing kinds of evidence to see which will carry freight and which will not. But we cannot arbitrarily affirm that evidence of kind X is good and that evidence of kind Y is bad. Rather, it is necessary for us to have some objective and stable criteria against which different kinds of evidence can be measured, so that we can deem some kinds better than others *reasonably*. It is in terms of such criteria that we can decide which of the varieties of evidence people appeal to are worthy of our credence. Consequently, before we turn our attention to the several specific varieties of evidence we want to weigh, we must first consider the development of some such criteria to use in the weighing.

Criteria for Evidence

I have a number of such criteria in mind. Some of them are simple and straightforward. Others, perhaps, are subject to argument. However, I think that all of them can be pragmatically defended by appealing to the standard evidence-weighing moves that we all make in ordinary situations. This will have to be our court of appeal because we cannot engage in an interminable and infinite regress of criteria for criteria for criteria.[22] We shall use our evidence to weigh our knowledge claims; we shall use our criteria of evidence to weigh our evidence; and

[22]An infinite regress is a peculiarly sterile kind of explanation. If one said that to understand a state of affairs you must understand its causes, and also said that the causes of a state of affairs are states of affairs themselves, then understanding any state of affairs is impossible. It is impossible because, on this basis, understanding one state of affairs presupposes understanding an infinitely long list of others first. The result of this is either (a) we don't understand states of affairs at all, or (b) this explanation of understanding states of affairs is faulty. As an explanation of how we do understand states of affairs, then, this is a sterile account. It involves an infinite regress.

we shall use the practical day-in, day-out commerce of human activity,
dispute, and judgment, to weigh our criteria.

Relevance   Evidence of whatever kind must be relevant to the claim
which it is advanced to support. To say that evidence must be relevant
is to say that it cannot be completely detached. It must have something to do with what is at stake. That seems obvious enough; but when
we consider the number of ways in which evidence can fail to be relevant (and the frequency with which the "evidence" which people
offer does fail to be relevant), we are obliged to affirm this "obvious"
criterion explicitly. All of us are familiar with situations in which a
person finds himself losing an argument and turns, consequently, to
clouding the issue rather than trying to give bona fide support for his
position. Several years ago the North Carolina legislature debated
whether or not to continue capital punishment. One member of the
assembly took the floor to argue against the widely held view that
Capital Punishment is a Deterrent to Crime. He claimed that such a
view has been effectively disproved by many hardheaded scientific
studies. So, he argued, since capital punishment does not deter crime,
you must have a different reason if you are going to keep it on the
books and still claim to be reasonable men. He made his case rather
well, cited many impressive sources, and stirred a furious rebuttal. I
was eager to hear the rebuttal, because it seemed to me that he had
made a good case and I wanted to know if there were other studies
that might be cited to show that such a penalty does deter crime.
The rebutting speaker explicitly affirmed that he was going to prove
that capital punishment does have such a deterrent effect, so I settled
back to compare their cases. But the "argument" that the second man
actually advanced had nothing whatever to do with the announced
issue. Instead, his speech consisted of passionate and vivid descriptions
of the horrors of some crimes to which a capital penalty was attached—
child rape, malicious murder, and the like. When he had finished his
lengthy excursions on the evils of capital crime, he then shouted to
the galleries that North Carolina must keep execution on the books so
that such crimes will not run rampant in the Old North State! There
was thunderous applause, tears were shed, the continuance of capital
punishment was approved, and the original speaker (who had argued
that it didn't deter crime anyway) sat bewildered in his chair. He had
advanced a claim. He had supported it with documented studies. His
opponent had advanced a counterclaim and had "supported" it with

a string of unconnected facts and and an appeal to the passions of his audience.

The burden of this example is not that child rape is all right, or even that capital punishment is ineffective. Rather, it is simply that the grossness of the crime was not shown to have any connection with the deterrent effect of the legislation under debate. Evidence needs to be relevant to what we are trying to prove. In the cited case, the "evidence" was not relevant at all.[23]

Noncircularity   Effective evidence must not be too relevant to what is at issue. How could evidence be too relevant? Very simply: where the evidence offered in support of a claim is simply a reiteration of the claim itself. There is no question but that the issue at stake is relevant to the issue at stake. But there is considerable question whether such a reiteration is any kind of effective appeal in trying to settle the issue at stake. Logicians, debaters, lawyers, and legislators call appeals that are, in this sense, too relevant question-begging.

Suppose that in a Congressional hearing someone asserts that Distinguished Citizen Smith is a Communist. In reasonable times, such a serious charge would have to be supported by substantial relevant evidence. In the hearing, the witness might be asked, "How do you know that?" Suppose the witness replies, "His name is listed on Commie Poop Sheet No. 43, recently published by the Flaming Flag Society." At this point, all would be well and good if we had any basis for giving credence to CPS No. 43. It is, however, at least conceivable that we would carry the inquiry a step further. We would ask to see the document cited. Suppose that the document is hesitantly produced, and we discover that Smith's name is indeed listed, but that the list was drawn up by none other than the witness now before us. So the evidence for the witness's assertion is that Smith's name appears on a list; but the list, in turn, is simply the witness's assertion. The claim is relevant enough, but only one with a very weak sense of evidence would be convinced by it.

So, while we maintain our first criterion that evidence should be relevant to the issue at stake, we add our second: that evidence should not be question-begging. We want it connected but free of circularity. Only when this criterion is satisfied can we have evidence which carries the freight well enough to convince reasonable men.

---

[23]"Relevant" is elliptical. It is always an abridgment of "relevant to . . ."
Ignoring this makes trouble. Can a curriculum committee set up a "relevant" program of studies without deciding what the studies are to be relevant *to*? Many have tried.

Intelligibility   Good evidence is intelligible evidence. I shall consider two aspects of intelligibility: intelligibility in principle and intelligibility to the individual involved. Both are important.

Intelligibility in principle is also so basic and so obvious that we might overlook it. But, like relevance, it is often ignored in practice; and so, like relevance, it needs to be explicitly affirmed. For example, returning to our Congressional hearing, suppose that our witness has again affirmed that Distinguished Citizen Smith is a Communist. Again we pursue the matter. We ask, "How do you know?" and the witness replies, "Because the ergwhat quanifles somewhat on the kumquat!" Ludicrous? To be sure. His "evidence" makes no sense until it is interpreted and filled in (and, indeed, given the standard meanings of the English terms as they are used, may make no sense at all). No one, of course, would offer "evidence" so obviously unintelligible. However, from time to time, as argument goes on, evidence is advanced that is beyond the bounds of comprehension in principle. But what is beyond human grasp cannot constitute evidence for human beings. So, if evidence is a necessary condition of knowledge and the only "evidence" in a given case is beyond human grasp, then there is no evidence in that case and, hence, no knowledge either. Evidence of whatever kind must be intelligible in principle to those who would employ it to establish knowledge. Evidence for human knowledge must be intelligible in principle to humans. We do not have to employ this criterion often; but when we do, it is crucial.

More common is the question of intelligibility to the individual addressed. This criterion calls our attention to the fact that argument and demonstration are practical matters—aimed not only at theoretical or formal proof, but also at individual conviction (that is, at convincing the hearer). If an argument is going to convince us of a certain claim, it is going to have to be intelligible to us—not only "in principle," but also in the sense that it falls within the boundaries of our own actual comprehension. For this reason, vast areas of human knowledge cannot and do not constitute knowledge for some people. It is precisely for this reason that I do not know anything at all about five-dimensional geometry or plasma physics, to cite just two examples from the vast storehouse of my nonknowledge. I do not know anything about plasma physics because I do not understand what the plasma physicists say.[24]

[24]This is not to say, of course, that I cannot know anything about plasma physics. It is simply to say that I do not. Given the proper investment of time and energy, I would like to think that I could bring this area of inquiry within my comprehension, come to the point that the claims of the plasma physicist

So we want our evidence to be relevant, free of circularity, and intelligible in principle. But if we would know ourselves, we must also, in fact, have our evidence intelligible to *us*.

Nonambiguity   The effectiveness of evidence is a function of its degree of freedom from ambiguity. If evidence is going to support a claim sufficiently to demonstrate its content and convince the hearer, then that evidence must be substantially straightforward, clear, and unequivocal. Because ambiguity is difficult to eliminate entirely, complete unambiguity is best considered as an ideal limit against which our evidence can be measured. We cannot ask for evidence that is not subject to any interpretation at all. So we ask for evidence which, in the context of use, is sufficiently clear-cut for us to keep the possibilities of its interpretation within manageable limits.[25]

The trouble with ambiguous evidence is that it does not make clear the degree of support that it offers to the claim in dispute. If the evidence is subject to widely alternative interpretations, we may find that while under one interpretation it supports the claim in question, under some other interpretation it supports a rival claim (or, indeed, even supports the negation of the very claim we are trying to weigh).

Consistency   Evidence must be free of self-negation. It must be internally coherent. It should not shoot itself down. This, again, is extremely basic. Nevertheless, it is best made explicit, for we do find that certain individuals (for example, novelists and existentialists) heavily discount the desirability, indeed necessity, of such internal consistency. I shall assess such discounting later. Now I would simply note that the criterion of internal consistency is one we do maintain in most areas of human discourse. Indeed, if someone offers us a claim supported only by contradictory "evidence," we would find ourselves demanding again, with greater emphasis, that some *evidence* be advanced. This is because when we try to assess inconsistent claims, we find that they are without any net content.[26]

---

are intelligible to me, and come, consequently, to the point of having knowledge in this area. In contrast, when the evidence is unintelligible in principle, no amount of effort, no period of time devoted to study and inquiry, could bring me or any other man to the happy state of knowing.

[25] Even as it is obvious that ambiguity comes in degrees, so it is obvious that relevance and individual intelligibility do so as well. These, too, can best be considered limits toward which we try to elevate our efforts.

[26] A self-negating claim cancels itself out. This point, which comes from P.F. Strawson, is nicely used by William Blackstone in his *The Problem of Religious Knowledge*, (Englewood Cliffs, N.J.: Prentice-Hall, 1963), now deplorably out of print. (Also, see below pp. 58-9)

Publicness Effective evidence must be open, in principle, to public confirmation. Repeatability (or publicness) is just about basic for scientific inquiry. A scientist who, when asked for evidence to back up a claim, asserted that the only possible evidence is available exclusively to him, would be in very bad straits. We would not be inclined to give him any credence at all.

You may remember that several years ago a Dr. Schmidlap supposedly discovered a "cure" for cancer. The medicine was a very odd one: when Dr. Schmidlap analyzed it, it contained many mysterious therapeutic ingredients; but when the National Institutes of Health analyzed it, only an uninteresting combination of two parts hydrogen to one part oxygen could be found. The doctor then claimed that the analyses done at the NIH were "insufficiently refined." My point is not to try to pass any judgment on the medicinal merits of the material in question. Rather, it is simply that we tend to be very suspicious (and are entitled to be so) when someone comes along with evidence that no one else can duplicate, even using techniques, devices, and tools of great refinement, virtually unlimited time and money, and no lack of trained scientists to devote to the experiment.

A few years ago there was another very interesting case in which a young man informed the president of his university of certain policies and procedures that would, he claimed, put the institution on a sound footing. He further affirmed that these proposals had been audibly delivered to him by Aristotle. It seems that in the late afternoons, he would often hear Aristotle's voice through the return grille of the library air conditioner—outlining plans, not only for the university but also for the American economy, the structure of Western society, and the general conditions of human life today. Most of us are so biased that we discount this kind of claim immediately without checking it. But if we were tempted to give it any credence, we would certainly know what steps to take to confirm it. The very first would be to go to the library and listen. If we did not hear Aristotle's voice, our natural suspicions would be somewhat increased.[27]

[27]What we check at the library is not the merits of the young man's proposals, but the credibility of the claim that they came from conversations with Aristotle. The actual content of the proposals was not necessarily without merit. A proposal may well have tremendous merit, regardless of where it comes from. This is why ad hominem is a fallacy. The point of the example is simply that he claimed to know on the basis of information received; but the "information" was received in such a way that it was inaccessible to everybody except him. Maybe Aristotle did tell him, but we have no way of knowing. (Ad hominem is attacking the virtue or position of a man instead of his arguments, when his arguments are what is at stake. A scoundrel can tell the truth. We can have true opinions [not knowledge] even with no evidence at all.)

If we are going to give credence to the testimony of an individual in a court of law, in a scientific laboratory, in a political argument, or in any of the other ordinary affairs of human commerce, we expect (indeed, we insist) that the evidence he offers be accessible to our own inquiry. We do not, however, always go ahead to check it out for ourselves. What we demand is the possibility of public access. There is no need for each beginning biology student to redo every biological experiment that has ever been done. The very fact that he could do so, if he wanted to take the time and exert the effort, is sufficient to give weight to the evidence that he finds in his textbooks and in his professor's lectures. Were it not for the fact that we do not have to carry through on public verification, there would be no progress in human knowledge at all. We regularly rely on the mere possibility of public verification in order to go on to new researches and new questions and the discovery of new truth. But if the possibility of a public test of the evidence is blocked, then a presumption of doubt is placed upon the claim supposedly being supported.

Perhaps, if all the other criteria of evidence were satisfied at a high level (if there were no questions of evidential weakness on any other grounds), we might retreat somewhat on the question of repeatability and publicness. But this is not likely. Further, we want always to be on guard against (and discount for) the possibility of bias or conflict of interest in the person who is offering the evidence we weigh. It is largely because bias and conflict of interest are so common (and so fatally infective when they do occur) that we insist so adamantly on repeatability and publicness of evidence under scrutiny. As long as there is the possibility (and there always seems to be) that a person's claims may be an exercise in bias, prejudice, self-fulfillment, the feathering of his own nest, special pleading, and the like, then surely we must insist that whatever evidence we accept must be evidence which we could collect and test ourselves.

I am not denying the fact that the evidence-gathering and evidence-using capacities of individuals vary. They do. Some people, for example, are blind. (If I were blind, I would say, "Some people can see.") It would be impertinent in the extreme for a blind man to deny the possibility of sight-funded knowledge on the part of others on the mere grounds that he does not have such input. That would be epistemological bigotry. But it would be foolish to affirm the existence of some putative knowledge on the bare grounds that somebody might have the relevant input. That would be epistemological naiveté. We have perfectly good ways of telling who has what modes of input. How does the blind man know that I have experiences that he does not? By my

behavioral capacities, which exceed his. I can dodge bricks when he
cannot. While avoiding the epistemological bigotry and naiveté mentioned, we must also avoid the conceit that one can obtain for oneself
the knowledge of others (on appeal to their expertise, secondhand)
simply by recognizing the input discrepancies. If I am blind and you
can see, the most I can know is that you do not share one of my limitations. I can modify my behavior to suit your more-informed vantage
point (duck when you say "Brick!"), but I cannot share your knowledge (ducking bricks isn't seeing bricks!). So, if one would fund a
special body of knowledge by appeal to a special (and restricted) mode
of input, we should realize that he is also affirming that those who
lack that mode of input do not and cannot have the body of knowledge
in question. Exactly the same thing may be said for gradations in our
ability to utilize the input we do receive. If I am not intelligent enough
to utilize certain information, while you are, then knowledge predicated on such intelligence is quite unattainable to me.

Controlled Limiting Conditions   The sources and channels of our
evidence must be free of limiting conditions or at least such conditions
must be noted and compensated for. In a case of secondhand evidence,
we want the witness free of defects. If the evidence is firsthand, we
want the process of its collection similarly free. This needs no lengthy
elaboration, but we should note the variety of limiting conditions
that are possible: bias, conflict of interest, stupidity, lack of experience
and expertise, sensory flaws, environmental interference, and so on
and on. Limiting conditions are the possibilities of error. They must
be eliminated or at least located and controlled.

Viable Theoretical Setting   Effective evidence must be formulated
in terms of a viable theory. The description and explanation that may
be offered for some event that is going on is inevitably formulated in
terms of one or another broader theoretical arrangement of the facts.
Often we find that a given set of events can be described, explained,
and so on, in terms of more than one such arrangement. We want to
use the best arrangement possible.[28]
     For example, a particular phenomenon that occurs in the labora-

---

[28]Later, when we turn our attention to language as such, I shall argue that every
descriptive claim is cast in terms of some theoretical framework and that, consequently, it is impossible to assert or describe anything "theory-free." When we
get to that point, I shall give close attention to the ways in which such theories
are expressed and how their own theoretical viability can be assessed.

tory—say, some water is boiling in a pot—might be explained in terms of several alternative theories, one of which appealed to such matters as the "natural place" of the elements in the universe, and the "yearning" of these elements to be where they "belonged." Earth, water, air, and fire were deemed, in this early theory, to be of such a nature that, if left to their own devices, air would find its way above all save fire. In these terms, it was thought that the heating of water liberated the air that was trapped within it; and that, upon being so liberated, the air struggled upwards toward its natural habitat. Thus the boiling. Nowadays we have a slightly different view. The point is that both the ancient and the contemporary explanations of boiling water are cast in terms of a theory, and that, consequently, part of our evaluation of a particular account of what is happening is, necessarily, the evaluation of the theory in terms of which it is formulated. To the extent that everyday descriptions, assertions, etc., do gain their structure from some sort of theoretical framework, we must—if we are going to make a final assessment of those assertions as evidence—make some assessment of their theory-frame as well. If evidence is advanced in a broken-backed theoretical apparatus, it is seriously flawed.[29]

Summary

When we consider a particular piece, or a whole kind, of evidence for effectiveness, we will look for relevance to what it "supports," absence of circularity, intelligibility (both in principle and in local fact), relative freedom from ambiguity, the absence of self-negation, coherence, the control or elimination of limiting conditions on source and media, the possibility of open and public confirmation, and a foundation in terms of a theory that is itself viable on pragmatic grounds. With these criteria in mind, we can now turn our attention to the kinds of evidence people do appeal to, and see which (if any) fare well, and which (if any) fare ill. We will consider as evidence the raw data of pure experience,

---

[29]The grounds on which we would make this kind of assessment would take us into a whole new area of inquiry—an important part of knowledge theory which we shall examine later on. (See the previous note.) Suffice it to say here that the sort of theory criteria that I have in mind (and will discuss) have to do with fertility, self-correctiveness, internal coherence, external mesh, and the like. If we find that the theory in terms of which evidence is structured is fertile, self-corrective, internally coherent, meshes with other theories in use, is not ad hoc, etc., we will deem the theory viable. It may be noted that these criteria are distinctly pragmatic. When we turn to the assessment of theories, I will argue that the only possible criteria that could be used at this level are pragmatic.

the free exercise of pure reason, assorted combinations of experience with reason, appeals to authority, intuition, revelation, and faith.

Possible Kinds of Evidence

Pure Experience The notion that experience is crucial to the settlement of arguments and issues is so much a part of the era in which we live that you may be surprised that it could be called into question. But appeals to experience as a basis for our knowledge do have problems, as has been pointed out by skeptics for many years. Experience can be unreliable, misleading, and very troublesome. So we have to establish some kind of canon of rules for appeals to experience in order to avoid at least the lesser difficulties. We want more than a single experience, if possible; and we want experience that is reinforced through more than one sensory mode or capacity, if possible. We know that the single experience (or what we take to be the content of the single experience) may be hallucinatory, deluded, or interfered with in any number of obvious ways—hypnosis, drugs, fatigue, the position of the observer, perspective, disruptions to the media through which the stimuli are projected, and the like. While we know this, we do not common-sensically dismiss all experience as a way of backing up our knowledge claims. Rather, we make every effort we can to protect our appeals to experience from being flawed in these ways. Having seen something once, we look again; if we have any doubts about the testimony of our senses, we appeal to other witnesses who are there; when some physical risk is involved (like crossing a railroad track), we use multiple senses (we look *and* listen) to get a cross-check internally. So, in our era, even recognizing the many difficulties, we simply apply all the checks and controls we can, and go right on using experience as a basic court of appeal.[30]

But, while we live in an empirical era, few would claim that experience taken by itself would be a complete basis for all the knowledge to which we lay claim. We would do well, indeed, to hesitate at the notion that experience taken neat is a complete basis for any of our claimed knowledge, for we find that such "pure" experience does not pass the tests we have enumerated above. Indeed, the criterion of relevance alone is enough to cause insuperable trouble for "pure" experience.

---

[30]The point of this paragraph is not to "handle" skepticism. It is, rather, to say something about the role of experience in ordinary affairs.

Certainly experience is frequently relevant to the claims that we make; but that relevance does not come clear unless and until the experience is structured in some way. As a matter of fact, the experience to which we do appeal is always structured in terms of organizations, principles, presuppositions, and theories (of which we are often unaware). That it is so structured prevents it from being "pure" experience, even though we may not realize it. As soon as we give any attention to the process of argument, judgment, and decision, we quickly realize that there is far more involved in it than any bare appeal to simple sensations (or other sorts of experience, for that matter) as they occur.

"Pure" experience (i.e., experience free of all imposed structure or other independent elements) would be utterly unintelligible to the one who had it. (A report of it would not be utterly unintelligible, of course, because a report of it would be structured. Reported experience is not pure experience.) Pure experience is something which, at the very best, would be completely limited and held within the confines of the individual encounters of a particular organism. If I would tell you my experience, I must structure it in language at the very least. Indeed, in most instances, if I would even remember my own experience, I must structure it for myself in language. I think there is little prospect, then, for the notion of grounding our knowledge in experience alone. This is not to say that knowledge can be grounded free of experiential connection altogether. It is simply to say that experience is not sufficient by itself.[31] The extent to which structured experience will work, and the sorts of structure there might be, remain to be seen.[32]

Pure Reason   Our era is not so much one of reason. In our everyday hierarchy of evidence, we do not place nearly so much stock in the exercise of reason as has been placed there in times past. Consequent-

[31]Here I part company with some phenomenologists. An attempt to get "behind" the conceptual apparatus to raw experience is futile because unless and until experience is structured, we cannot even bind it to our memory, much less investigate it at a public level.

[32]I am not supposing that all structure is imposed. To the extent that we perceive in gestalt fashion, we must allow that some structure is a constituent of experience. Whether we do so experience is not my issue either way. If we do, it does not alter the point.

The structure of the perceived gestalt must be remembered and classified if it is to contribute to what we know (knowledge-that). Perhaps there is an inexplicable capacity to recognize a pattern of iterated experiences, but this is another sense of "know" (recognition). Whether there is discovered structure in ex-

ly, it sometimes surprises a student that anyone ever claimed that
reason by itself is sufficient to deliver up knowledge and truth. The
notion that we may discover truth and substantiate knowledge via
pure reason is, however, one that has been seriously maintained.
While I would allow that the exercise of reason has a part in the establishment of our knowledge (as you might suspect, I think that
reason is the primary device by which we give structure to the experiences we have), I do not think that reason by itself is ever adequate
to yield knowledge about "matters of fact." Rather, I am convinced
that we are able by the devices of reason only to manipulate, maneuver, extract, take apart and put together, structure, and interpret data
that has already somehow been given.

For example, the exercise of deductive reason cannot yield output
information that is not in some form part and parcel of the input on
which the deductive process begins. Indeed, a deductive argument
that purported to yield output that was in no way included in the
premises with which it began would be invalid on its face. To be sure,
not all exercises of reason are deductions. But I think it can be safely
said that deduction, generalization, theory formation, or any other
forms of rational enterprise are all at best devices, techniques and
means for extrapolating, sorting out, interpreting, and making sense
of data which the rational process itself did not supply. This is to assert
that reason is sterile when taken alone.

The criterion on which "pure" reason fails is also, curiously enough,
that first and most elementary one—relevance. Our exercises of reason
have to be connected with the claims that we are attempting to support. Insofar as a claim is about matters of fact, an exercise of reason
that is to be relevant at all must be connected to them. The exercise
of reason that is empty of any and all such connections cannot (by
failure of relevance) yield information about states of affairs. Reason
by itself is as sterile of content as experience by itself is lacking in
form.

Perhaps one reason why it may have been thought that pure reason
is an adequate basis for knowledge about matters of fact is that pure
reason is an adequate basis for knowledge of a different sort. When we
turn to formal systems of thought (like logic and mathematics), we
find ourselves in an area in which it is usually deemed possible to know
a priori (i.e., independent of experience). I have no objection to this,

---

perience or not, knowledge-that waits upon the structuring of experience. This
structuring is where language begins; and language is where knowledge-that
begins. (see note 47.)

but can only point out that what we know a priori in such systems is simply the form of the system itself. We can know that the formula $2 + 2 = 4$ is a mathematical truth, given standard definitions of the symbols; but to know this is simply to understand the standard definitions of the symbols. It remains a contingent fact that such an arithmetic applies to our world, is useful in counting apples and oranges. We do know that it is useful in counting apples and oranges, but we know this because we have used it and found it to work. Our knowledge of the application of such systems is a posteriori (i.e., not a priori). It comes with an experiential involvement.

Perhaps because this peculiar formal knowledge is available to us via reason alone, men have often aspired to factual knowledge by the same route. But I am convinced, on the basis of the criterion of relevance, that factual knowledge, while it may be structured, implemented, extrapolated, analyzed, synthesized and maneuvered in countless ways by the superimposition upon it of formal systems through the exercise of reason, cannot be generated from reason alone. It comes only when our formal inquiry is brought to bear on facts; and that requires fact input.[33]

So, I am arguing that pure reason (like pure experience) cannot furnish an adequate basis for claims to knowledge about matters of fact (states of affairs), although it can furnish an adequate basis for knowledge about its own formal constructions.[34] I will consider below certain possible combinations of reason and experience, as more likely means to carry the freight. First, however, let us consider some other putatively independent forms of evidence that we encounter from time to time.

[33]Some might even argue that our formal knowledge itself is a posteriori, that it, too, presumes experiential input, viz., the experiential acquisition of the formal system. This, however, misses the point. We are not arguing the genetics of what we know. We are arguing the logic of what we know. A formal system is, in principle, intelligible without any appeal to field studies, experimentation, data collection, and the like. Given the definitions of the terms in the system, its structure is transparent. Factual knowledge, on the other hand, does necessitate a beginning in experience. We should try to avoid confusing questions of genetic priority with questions of logical priority. Indubitably, genetically speaking, experience of some sort is prior to all we know (i.e., we have had experience of some sort—*in utero,* if need be—before we know anything). But in terms of logical priority, a formal system stands or falls in terms of its own structure internally. A formal statement within it is true or false in terms of its structure. And all of this is independent of what may or may not, has or has not been, the case "in the world."

[34]There is another sense of "reason" available—the sort of thing we associate with Platonic rationalists. This is the putative ability of the individual to know certain states of affairs (universals, abstract ideas, etc.), independent of the usual

Authority Many of our claims to know are supported by appeals to authority. Even as our era is, broadly speaking, empirical, so it is also anti-authoritarian and anti-authority. But authority comes in two important styles.

Charles Goren is an authority. Gerald Ford and the local police are also authorities. When we say, "Charles Goren is an authority," we seem to be speaking elliptically ("Charles Goren is an authority on . . ."). The statement calls for completion of some kind. Goren, of course, is an authority on contract bridge. He is not, to my knowledge, an authority on plasma physics, international law, or the gradations of venial and mortal sins.

Is there anything wrong with accepting the testimony of an expert witness? It depends. It depends on what you are accepting the evidence about. "He is an authority," in this use, is always elliptical. No one is an authority simpliciter. So, while there would be no good reason for accepting Goren's testimony as evidence to support a claim about plasma physics, there is every kind of good reason for accepting his testimony to support a claim about the strategy, play, and rules of contract bridge. Why? Simply because in accepting his statements "on authority," we are not actually introducing any new kind of evidence at all. For, what does it mean to say, even elliptically, "Charles Goren is an authority (on bridge)"? Simply that by virtue of his experience, actions, and exercises of mind, he knows enough about bridge that ordinary people are justified in deferring to his judgments, advice, and interpretations. He is an authority by virtue of his expertise. So, in accepting his testimony, we are simply deferring to his experience and exercise of mind. Our evidence is simply his evidence—secondhand. Furthermore, we are accepting it, if our wits are about us, subject to possible outside tests under the assorted criteria of relevance, intelligibility, and the like. If, upon subjecting his advice, recommendations, etc., to test, we find that they fail, not only would we reject his claims— we would demote him. He would be an authority no longer. I shall call such an expert an Authority$_1$.

---

five sense modes. (We do not see, taste, smell, feel or hear Justice or the paradigmatic Horse.) Some (maybe all) of these notions may be handled as constructions from what we do sense; but Plato, of course, suggested that we have such knowledge by "recollection" from direct encounters between the mind and such "in another world." So seen, it seems to me that such "rational" knowledge (if it occurs) is not so much nonexperiential as it is superior-experiential—to be dealt with as an additional way of experiencing (subject, of course, to tests as usual), rather than as some experience surrogate. So while this kind of "reason alone" might bear fruit (if it occurs), it is still not "reason without experience." In this case "reason" is experience (plus recollection).

On the other hand, when I say to the gang occupying the campsite next to mine on Mont Tremblant, "Either turn down the hillbilly music or I will report you to the authorities," I do not intimate that I am about to inform some nearby hillbilly music expert. The authorities I have in mind are the Mounties. Such authorities are people who occupy positions of assigned power—people who have been granted the responsibility and the devices for enforcing rules. They exist in virtually all social organizations. Even the university has some, and so does the church, the Kiwanis Club, and the National Football League. I shall call such an individual an Authority$_2$.

Some Authorities$_2$ might even be Authorities$_1$ on something. But to confuse, for example, the authority$_2$ of the "man in blue" with the authority$_1$ of a legal-social expert would be grotesque. An appeal to the testimony of an Authority$_2$ by virtue of his authority$_2$ is very different from any appeal to the testimony of an Authority$_1$ by virtue of his authority$_1$. One is an appeal by virtue of role assigned. The other is by virtue of knowledge held. We can appeal to Goren on bridge precisely because he is an Authority$_1$ on bridge—he has knowledge which we can fruitfully utilize secondhand.[35] But an appeal to the local policeman on law and equity is footless if it is made because he has had authority$_2$ assigned to him by the community. For, while such assignments of authority$_2$ are essential to the operation of a community, and while the policeman may have acquired some expertise on one topic or another in the course of his work, he does not have any knowledge that accrues to him solely by virtue of the role to which the state has assigned him. A claim made by an Authority$_2$ might be correct, but it would not be correct by virtue of his authority$_2$. It would be correct by virtue of whatever authority$_1$ he may have picked up in practice. There is, of course, no guarantee at all that he has picked up any.

Authority, then, is not an independent way of knowing because in its first sense it is only an appeal to experience and reason secondhand, and in its second sense it is not a way of knowing at all. Of course, we would go awry if we were to appeal to an Authority$_1$ in an area which his expertise does not cover.[36] But as long as we stay within his area

---

[35] Goren's bridge claims may not all be correct, but their probable truth can be assumed—subject to test as necessary—because they have been tested successfully so often before. The point is not that his words are infallible; only that they come out of reason and experience, and can, therefore, be tested in standard ways.

[36] This would be a classic *ad vericundiam* fallacy: "Nine out of ten Hollywood stars prefer Vigoro." The fallacy here is not in appealing to an Authority$_1$, it is in failing to do so.

of expertise, our appeal is quite legitimate—subject to test. When we turn to an Authority$_2$ for knowledge, however, because of the "authority" which he bears, we are pursuing irrelevance through a swamp of equivocation.[37]

Intuition   People sometimes base their claims to knowledge on what they call intuition. But the word is used in several ways. For one, we label a person's opinion intuition when we do not have any insight or understanding of how he came to hold it. So we say, "Aha! Intuition!" because we are extremely uncomfortable with unexplained phenomena. In this use, the word is a catch-all term for unexplained information.[38] In another use, "intuition" indicates that some special sort of comprehension or understanding has occurred. In this sense it is sometimes claimed that particular individuals are highly intuitive, or that women are possessed of more intuition than men. Still, there is no indication of what the intuition amounts to. It may be a special source of information, but the implication remains that it is an unknown special source.

I must admit that I tend to be less than satisfied when intuition is all the evidence that is offered in support of a claim to know. For, on its face, it does not satisfy the criteria of repeatability and publicness. It also tends to be highly ambiguous. Most crucially, it appears to be not so much a kind of evidence as a label for the lack of evidence.[39]

[37]I suspect that much of the opposition to "authority" on the part of the college set is reinforced by the fact that the boundary between Authority$_1$ and Authority$_2$ has not been maintained in the public eye. Persons who have been assigned positions of responsibility and power in the society are commonly (and wrongly) seen as thereby possessed of such expertise that their opinions and statements can be deemed correct without test. One mistake is made when "authority" is thus misread by the public at large. Another is made when people reject all authority, even when it is supported by a network of public and open tests, because this confusion is so common in the marketplace. But only by appeals through experts to experience and reason at secondhand we are able to build upon the experience and the thought of the past. We should not sacrifice the possibility of progress to the confusions of those who think that insight is acquired with political assignment, that knowledge can be funded by office held. Neither should we abandon the notion of Authority$_2$ as a social functional role simply because some people confuse it with Authority$_1$ and elevate its possessors to fraudulent heights of "expertise." Both kinds of authority are useful if we keep them straight.

[38]There is a strong possibility that the word "knowledge" in such contexts does not have the force that we have stipulated (knowledge-that). It may, rather, have the force of "thoroughly persuaded," which depends more on psychological causes than on evidence. Whether one "knows" in this sense is a genetic question. See notes 20 and 33.

[39]There is, of course, the common fallacy of mistaking a label for an explanation. There is something odd, however, about taking comfort, when you have

Sometimes, however, intuition is used to represent a particular kind of inference and judgment-formation that is open to analysis and is justifiable. But in such cases, it is in no sense independent of the processes of experience and reason. Is it amazing that Einstein, after a lifetime of scientific and mathematical inquiry, was able to formulate mathematical judgments without any necessarily self-conscious or overt exercise of mathematical labor? Unless you find it amazing that most people over thirty don't count on their fingers and toes, you shouldn't find this amazing at all. For the processes of mathematical inference, which would be tortuously difficult and involve great application of self-conscious attention for you or me, became, to him, through familiarity and practice "second nature." Similarly, consider the fictional Dr. Doolittle. We all remember his "intuitive" ability to perceive what was wrong with sick animals. After a lifetime of work diagnosing their ills, the gamut of symptoms had become "second nature" to him. His diagnoses did not require self-conscious exercise, but rather, they flowed naturally out of his experience and out of the great number and variety of judgment-formations he had made up to then. To cite another example, closer to home: all of us can look at a bunch of bananas and "see" that there are three of them without stopping to count. Ours is no mystical ability. We have counted lots of bananas before. But we would be surprised indeed if Dr. Doolittle had intuitions about calculus and n-dimensional geometry, or if Einstein had had intuitions about canine melancholia and the heaves.[40]

In cases like these, the evidence to which the intuition alludes is not of an unknown and mysterious kind. Careful analysis would show that the operative evidence here is nothing more or less than a no-self-conscious-attention-required kind of inference that is based on a vast network of prior experience and reflection. If, at the peak of their careers, Bertrand Russell could not follow *modus ponens*[41] and Dr. Mayo could not diagnose measles; if, in 1974, Scoop Jackson could not read an

---

an irritated throat, in the "explanation" laryngitis. "Why is E-Z Kramp Shortening so good?" "Because it contains Esophogene-Q!" "Thank you. Now I understand." Television watchers should be Authorities$_1$ on such things.

[40] I am not discounting intelligence of varying degrees and differing focus as an important part of such knowings. Intelligence of appropriate degree and focus is as essential to calculus or animal diagnosis as is a strong pair of legs to running cross-country. But we do not say, "He ran the mile by using his running-the-mile faculty." We say that he used his legs (etc.) effectively. So, too, Einstein solved problems by using his brain (etc.) effectively. "Intelligence" would be a useful word here, behaviorally defined, I think. "Intuition" is either a blind or is superfluous in such contexts.

[41] *Modus ponens:* If P then Q. P. Therefore Q.

audience; and if I could not tell when my wife is angry—here would be amazing cases that would need a special label. The conclusions of the experienced logician, physician, politician, or husband, who do understand what is going on, can be called intuition if we like; but all that the label indicates is that a kind of non-self-conscious shorthand process of inference and judgment-formation is going on. It is nothing new. It is a complex of the reason and experience with which we are endowed.

Of course "ESP" remains. Formally, this is not unlike the Platonic reason-as-encounter-of-mind-and-abstract-entity.[42] That is, ESP occurs (if it does occur, which is not my issue) as an additional package of experience modes, and can be dealt with in the usual way on standard tests. If the Russian lady does read the newspapers with her elbows (a delightful summertime news fraud a few years ago), well and good. Does she? We know how to find out. The same goes for telepathy, blind-card reading, and the like. The only ESP-ish notion that raises real issues of principle is foreknowledge. (All the rest can stand or fall on standard tests.) Since knowledge presumes there is something to be known, then foreknowledge is either inferential and hypothetical, or else our whole conception of what-there-is needs an overhaul to include what-will-be-but-isn't-yet. Such a move has many fancy entailments for action, responsibility, process, identity, and so on. It should not be lightly made. I would prefer to take all of this out as hypothetical and inductive inference. "Ceteris paribus, the chance of rain in Richmond tomorrow morning is 37 percent" poses no problems of quasi-existent future facts. Unless we treat seers' pronouncements ("The President will be assassinated next spring") in parallel fashion, then they do pose such problems and we are in epistemological chaos. We should leave the door open here; but until there is strong reason (independently) to posit the existence of things that have not happened yet, we should not walk through it. A theoretical apparatus of not-yet beings not only smells ad hoc (that is, "made to fit"), it also fails on mesh, coherence, and parsimony.[43]

Revelation   Many persons reject out of hand the notion of knowledge based on "revelation." Others accept such a notion uncritically, without any attempt to place it under objective public appraisal. I would not do either. If revelation is to be admitted as a kind of legitimate evidence, then either it should pass the standard canons (relevance,

[42]See note 34.
[43]See note 28. The troubles that I allude to here all have to do with the criterion of viable theoretical foundations.

intelligibility, etc.), or there should be independent demonstration that this kind of evidence does not need to pass them. If one reflects on the question "Does revelation pass the standard canons?" substantial trouble soon appears. Some of the greatest difficulties are with the criterion of relative unambiguity. Revelations (or supposed ones) of the sort I have read about tend to be subject to considerable and flexible interpretation. It has not been very difficult through the years for those who have received "revelations" to have confidence about their precise content and force. But, unless and until some kind of unambiguous and forceful interpretation can be placed upon a "revelation" at a public level, then that "revelation" cannot stand as evidence in support of any specific claims to know for the population at large. But seeking that public force throws us into chaos in the face of the multitudes of conflicting "revelations" to which assorted individuals lay claim.[44]

I have two reasons for disagreeing with the view that revelations should not be subjected to standard tests of evidence. One has already been discussed in the Introduction (see page 3), where I argued that if any body of affirmations cannot stand on its own feet according to standard canons of public dispute, it is in severe trouble on a charge of systematic irrelevance. Because there is no point in examining any view at all if it is systematically irrelevant to human affairs, we must either dismiss it flat out or invite it to stand examination. The other reason why I hesitate to excuse revelations from meeting the standard canons of evidence is simply that I do not see any compelling reason to think that they are different in any relevant way from the sorts of data, information, and evidence that we have already been talking about. After all, revelations come in relatively straightforward ways: a message in the sky or a voice in the night. The person receiving the revelation reaches some inference through the exercise of his mind. That is to say, he has an experience of a certain sort, and he exercises his reason on it in a certain pattern. Revelation can readily be classified as a particular variety of reason-experience complex. But why should one man's experience and reason have the tests of evidence waived while those of another are held under careful scrutiny? That would not be fair. Indeed, if religion is as important as it is supposed to be (and that, after all, is where the revelations happen), then there is all the more reason to in-

---

[44]The ambiguity of a revelation may not be immediately apparent. Suppose it is "revealed" that God loves us "like a father." We all know what that means. The trouble is that when we take it at face value, we are told that that isn't what it means. The question then arises, "What does it mean?" At this point the equivocation becomes obvious. This sort of thing is surveyed below in the discussion of one-legged analogies on pages 119–120.

crease our demands for rigor. Should we expend less care on "God" and "the meaning of life" than we do on "beans" and the "Democratic Party Plan"? Further, unless good independent reasons can be given, any request for waivers is an exercise in special pleading. It begs all the questions.

Therefore I would insist that, while revelation should not be ruled out of court, it ought to be weighed for what it is—a particular family of (usually religiously structured) experiences and rational inferences. Once so classified, its instances should be weighed in terms of the standard weights and measures for experience and reason. To the extent that revelations pass such tests, well and good. To the extent that they do not, then they do not constitute a basis for knowledge.[45] We owe them epistemological due process; but we do not owe them any more than that. In no case do they constitute a new kind of basis for knowing. They have no unique status in the commerce of human inquiry.

Faith We also find instances in which people claim to know "by faith." This is rather ambiguous on its face, for the notion of "faith" is not a clear one. Perhaps "I know by faith" means "I know by virtue of the fact that I am committed to my belief's being true," or "I know by virtue of the fact that I believe," or "I know by virtue of the fact that I have placed this notion at the center of my world view." But the fervor of commitment is not evidence. The centrality of a claim in a world view (religious or not) is not evidence. The fact that one believes is not evidence that what one believes is true. It may be that knowledge begins in a kind of faith; that is, it may be that knowledge begins in belief. (We have already indicated that the first necessary conditions of knowing and believing are the same, anyway.) But knowledge does not *end* in belief. For, if the fact that one believed made knowledge, then there would be no distinction between believing and knowing. And if the passion with which one believed made knowledge, then there would be no distinction between fervent truth and fervent error. Faith may be an occasionally necessary and valuable *alternative* to knowledge—it may be that there are areas of human concern where knowledge is not possible and faith is the best that we can do; but faith does not make knowledge because people can believe what is false.

There remains another possibility. It may be that when one speaks of "faith," one is speaking not of belief in a proposition, but rather of

[45] Again, revelation may come as a kind of "surrounding apparatus" for our ordinary experiences, rather than as the "source" of particular experiences. If so, it stands as one of those theoretical frames that need scrutiny on pragmatic grounds. Is it ad hoc, does it mesh, is it fertile?

confidence in the one who has propounded the proposition in question. Thus, one might claim to know that a certain proposition is true by virtue of one's faith (i.e., confidence) in the proposition's utterer. For example, someone might claim to know that one is under an obligation to render to Caesar the things that are Caesar's, by virtue of his confidence in Jesus of Nazareth (who said it). But this is no help. Nowhere else would we suggest that our confidence in a speaker purchases the truth of what he says, or even when what he says is true, that our confidence in him purchases our knowledge of that truth. Now, it might be that in the context of many claims uttered by a single speaker, large numbers of which we had independently found to be true and well evidenced, we might come to feel a high degree of confidence that even his untested claims are so. Still, unless and until we have independent evidence bearing on the individual question (or bearing on the claim that the person who made the claim is incapable of error), our confidence in the claim would be insecure. And the independent evidence we would seek (either of the truth of all the claims he has made, or of his inability to be in error) would have to be sought in our experience and rational examination of the individual in question, his claims, pronouncements, and thoughts. So again, faith, as important as it may be in the pattern and organization of our lives, does not stand as a way of knowing, or as a basis for knowing, or as a kind of knowledge-yielding evidence. It stands, instead, as a form of belief—as one of the steps through which we may pass before knowledge is gained. And it calls (as does belief in general) for evidence itself, in order that our affirmtion of conviction might be reasonable and so stand a chance of becoming something we know.

Reason Coupled with Experience   I have already argued that neither experience nor reason is a sufficient basis for knowledge when taken by itself. My contention is that, as we attempt to support a knowledge claim, both experience and reason are necessary components of the network of evidence to which we must turn.[46] Experience, one of the two components, would furnish the input—the content, the data to be utilized by the exercise of thought. Reason, the other, would furnish the structure—the organization in terms of which we weave something intelligible out of the experiences that occur, in terms of which (at the very least) we impose the structures of language on the content of our

---

[46]Unless the knowledge claim we are attempting to fund is one that has solely to do with the formal structure of some formal system, in which case (at least in principle) an appeal to reason alone will be sufficient.

experience so as to render it memorable, describable, and useful in further thought.[47]

Reason and experience can interact in many different ways. It is not our task at this point to try to enumerate, analyze, and appraise all of them. But it would be useful to mention several that seem crucial to cognition. First and foremost, there is that initial imposition of language on experience, which converts the maelstrom of random events into a structured whole. This occurs initially as we utilize the memory capacity of the mind to classify and to impose some taxonomic[48] pattern on the experiences that we have in our earliest days and weeks of life. At a more and more complex level, this same pattern continues as our use of language grows,[49] and as we steadily and inexorably bring the content of our experience under the structure and rubric of the mother tongue. It is in this process of classification and mapping, and the imposition of linguistic structure, that we first convert the raw input of our experience into that which we conceptualize as experience of this, that, or the other. It is here that the distinguishables within our experience-stream are first described and consistently named and referred to.

At a more complex level, once the language itself has been gained, new patterns of interaction between reason and experience appear: generalization (the construction of general descriptive principles, which we build by process of extrapolation out of the particular experiences we have), deduction (the inference of statements asserting states of affairs from those generalizations that we have already constructed, or accepted,[50] out of our experience content),[51] and the hypothetical-deductive pattern of inference in terms of which we construct hypotheses (funded with the content and patterns of the lin-

[47]I keep saying that knowledge begins in linguistic structuring of experience (see above, note 32). I have a very broad concept of language here, viz., any semantic apparatus. Some such apparatus is physically necessary. You cannot use elephants to think about elephants. It is too clumsy. You may not use words, but you will use some semantic apparatus or else you will not think. Thinking is an important constituent of knowing-that.

[48]Taxonomy is a kind of classifying or mapping of types. Taxonomy is what Linnaeus did for botany.

[49]I would hypothesize that it grows by route of mimicry of, and positive and negative reinforcement from, those in our environment who already have its use. But this is arguable. How we gain the use of language is an empirical (psychological) question.

[50]That is, as found in gestalt experiences.

[51]This is a more traditional notion of deduction than is found in current technical definitions, which are given in terms of logical necessity.

guistically structured experience that has been had thus far and the formal systems that have been invented thus far), and from which we may infer predictions, explanations, and assertions that are confirmable in the broadening network of our continuing (and continually restructured) experience.[52] It is at this last level of hypothesis construction, deduction of inferences, and confirmation through test that we find the standard pattern of "scientific" inquiry going on. But "scientific" inquiry is not confined to science. It is the stuff of everyday curiosity, assertion, and explanation.

Summary

Among the kinds of evidence to which people can appeal, there survive, as distinguishable forms, assorted complexes of experience and reason both first- and secondhand. Of these, particular instances survive only to the extent that they pass those tests which other putative kinds of evidence have failed; that is, only to the extent that they can stand the rigors of at least those few criteria we have named. If we would then know, we would confine our claims to those which are cognitive, among them those that are true, and among them those we can connect in the pattern of our thought to the structure of experience and reason that constitutes evidence as it is available to man. To the extent that a claim does not satisfy the necessary condition of cognitivity, it is not even a claim, much less knowledge. To the extent that it does not satisfy the necessary condition of truth, it is at best a false belief. To the extent that it satisfies all else, but does not satisfy the criterion of evidential connection, it is at best true belief. Would we know, we must go on from true belief to true cognitive assertions that are enmeshed and confirmed in the open network of relevant, intelligible, unambiguous, coherent, repeatable public test.

KNOWLEDGE AND CERTAINTY

You may believe that an adequate sketch of knowledge should also include its certainty. I have already said that what we know must be true, that if it is not true then we do not know it. Can we, then, seriously claim to know something that is not absolutely certain? But to say

---

[52]See Carl Hempel's *Philosophy of Natural Science* (Englewood Cliffs, N.J.: Prentice-Hall, 1966) for a thorough survey of this "hypothetico-deductive" method.

"X is certain" may mean either "I am certain that X is true" or "It is not possible that X is not true."

The first alternative makes "X is certain" a piece of psychological autobiography. I suppose that no one ever (seriously) claims to know without implicitly affirming his own psychological certainty. But one's psychological certainty does not guarantee the truth of what one claims to know. Indeed, as evidence, it is totally irrelevant. So this sort of certainty is, even if always present when knowledge is claimed,[53] thoroughly irrelevant to whether such knowledge is achieved.

The second alternative has been a continuing source of trouble to philosophers who try to analyze knowledge. Descartes, for example, seems to have been convinced that the impossibility of error was a condition of genuine knowledge.[54] To alleviate the trouble here, we must first note the difference between saying, " 'If *XYZ* is known, then *XYZ* is true' is necessarily true," and saying, "*XYZ* is necessarily true." The first statement is correct, and merely makes explicit the fact that truth is a necessary condition of knowledge. That is, if *XYZ* is cognitive, true, and evidenced, then certainly *XYZ* is true. But the "necessary truth" attaches to the entire "if . . . then . . ." statement, and is no more perplexing than the fact that "if *P* and *Q* and *R*, etc., then *P*" is also necessarily true. It is true by virtue of its logical form and the definitions of the logical operators within it.[55] It has nothing at all to do with what might be substituted for *XYZ*, *P*, *Q*, or *R*. The second statement might be correct, but it can be correct only if *XYZ* is true by virtue of the logical form and the definition of the logical operators in it. But if *XYZ* were logically true, then its force (like that of the first statement) would be essentially hypothetical as far as any application to matters of fact is concerned. Thus, for example, Descartes could have claimed that "If I think then I exist" was necessarily true, if the antecedent of that conditional could be analyzed to show that think-

---

[53]Those who say that belief is a necessary condition of knowledge may have something like this in mind.

[54]This is why Descartes struggled so to find an indubitable basis on which to reconstruct the superstructure of human knowledge. That he thought he had found it and that he did not find it have been an unending source of philosophical discussion. See his "Meditations," in *Philosophical Essays* (Indianapolis: Bobbs-Merrill, 1964); and Alexander Sesonske and Noel Fleming's *Meta-Meditations* (Belmont, Calif.: Wadsworth, 1965).

[55]That is, it is true by virtue of the meaning of "and" and "if . . . then" and by virtue of the arrangement of the variables (*P*, *Q*, and so on). "If ([if *P* then *Q*] and *P*) then *Q*," for example, is true whatever *P* and *Q* mean. Its truth is "a priori" or "formal."

ing includes existing; but he could not conclude his existence without independently asserting that he did, in fact, think. But the assertion of that is not the assertion of a logical truth (whether it is the assertion of an autobiographical psychological certainty or not).[56] Truths of logic do not yield truths about the world unless and until they are coupled with some such truths about the world to start with. This is where experience gives its input.

But can we not begin with some "necessary truths about the world"? If we could, they would also be essentially hypothetical; so an infinite regress is generated—hypothetical behind hypothetical in the search for one plain statement of what is so. As an inevitable consequence, this second kind of certainty about matters of fact is not possible within any finite span of time. So, our first sense of certainty shows itself to be irrelevant; the second, to be unobtainable. If, then, certainty (of a relevant sort) were a necessary condition of knowledge of states of affairs, it would follow that we do not know anything about the world at all. We have, then, a choice between total skepticism and the exclusion of "certainty" as an essential part of such knowing. That is why I have not included "certainty" in my sketch of knowledge-that.

Why not affirm total skepticism? Because we are analyzing the notion of knowledge as that notion occurs. Should we decide on a definition of it that entailed its never having legitimate use (i.e., a definition that forced the conclusion "we never know anything"), we still would have the notion's working use to take into account. For, even if (under some definition of "know") we never know anything, we still find the notion employed to draw practical distinctions (e.g., between Dr. Ginott, who "knows what he is talking about" and Mary Worth, who "is just a windbag"). So, even if we abandoned the term "know," unless we are willing also to abandon the practical distinctions, we would have to invent a whole new vocabulary to perform the same tasks. But this would be silly. The vocabulary we have works very well indeed. So we conclude that knowledge is not quite what some have thought it was— i.e., that knowledge does not entail certainty—and keep our working distinctions, rather than concluding that we have no knowledge, and then make up new terms to perform old tasks.

Other reasons for skepticism have been advanced, too—the essential privacy of experience, the uneliminable possibility of error both in sensation and reflection, and so on. The net effect of these arguments

---

[56]There are other ways of taking the *cogito*. See, for example, J. Hintikka's brilliant essay, reprinted in the Sesonske and Fleming anthology, cited in note 54.

is that maybe we are mistaken all the time, and so, since knowing does not admit of being mistaken, maybe we don't know anything. At least two things are wrong with this. First, there is equivocation on "knowledge never being mistaken" that exactly parallels the equivocation on "certain" which we have just explored. We are torn between the irrelevant and the unobtainable. We have said enough about that. Second, the very notion of "maybe being mistaken all the time" is a bogey. We may be mistaken in any given instance, but only in contrast to other instances in which we are not. The notion of a "mistake" is a parasitic notion. It cannot be defined except in the context of some stipulated veridical experience. Skepticism that is predicated on the possibility of all-inclusive error is nothing more than a pious fraud.[57] So one does not affirm total skepticism.

The net effect of the argument in this section, so far, is the relativizing of our notion of knowledge. This is a dangerous step, for there are always those who will leap to the conclusion that such relativizing obliterates the knowledge/opinion working distinction. But that leap is a mistake. What is diminished is not the distinction between knowledge and opinion. Rather it is our tendency toward smugness in applying the distinction. My purpose has not been to elevate all opinion to the status of knowledge, for mere believing does not make things so. Rather, I would encourage us to realize that first, we have often claimed knowledge unjustifiably—some of our "knowledge" really is just opinion; second, knowledge is best seen as a limit toward which inquiry moves, which is approximated rather than guaranteed by our labors; third, the route toward that limit can be clearly specified; fourth, the realization of the danger zones on that route implement rather than stifle our attempts to approximate the limit; and fifth, knowledge is not just "relative" simpliciter—it is relative to the facts and a whole network of tests and procedures. The quest for knowledge is neither footless nor self-guaranteeing. It is goal-directed and pragmatic. We are entitled to say "we know" when our claims carry the freight of use and stand the pressures of controlled test. If, later, they break down, we then say, "Well, we thought we knew" and make the

---

[57]Hospers, Scriven, and Cornman and Lehrer all have useful explorations of systematic skepticism in their introductory texts. They cover it in more detail because it is one of their main topics. If your interest is quickened here, do not stifle it. Hospers is best, but Scriven is more readable. See John Hospers, *An Introduction to Philosophical Analysis,* 2d ed. (Englewood Cliffs, N.J.: Prentice-Hall, 1967); James W. Cornman and Keith Lehrer, *Philosophical Problems and Arguments* (New York: Macmillan, 1968); and Michael Scriven, *Primary Philosophy* (New York: McGraw-Hill, 1966).

needed adjustments. Knowledge is not an edifice built on eternal foundations. It is a plot of clear and ordered ground hacked out of the jungles
of opinion. It takes constant work to keep it up.

SUMMARY

I have tried in this chapter to develop a little bit of background for what
is to come by asking such questions as "What is it to know something?"
"What are the bases on which we do claim to know things?" "Which
of these are any good?" "How can we decide?" and so on. We have
only skimmed the surface; but now we must turn our attention to some
claims that are made in religious contexts, and see what can be said
about them in terms of the background we have laid out.

There are many religious claims: "At the ringing of the bell, the
elements will transubstantiate into living flesh and blood . . ."; "The
return of the Lord will precede rather than follow the Thousand
Years"; "The Rapture will be split"; "And the bush burned but was not
consumed, and Moses heard a voice saying . . ." It would be interesting
to spend a chapter simply listing and trying to catalogue the varieties
of religious claims. Since I cannot do that, I will focus our attention on
a particular claim that is obviously central: "There is a God" (or "God
exists").

I do not intend to deny the occurrence of religions that do not advance any such god-claim (e.g., classical Buddhism). Nevertheless, it is
rather standard for religions to affirm the existence of one or more
gods. Indeed, those that fall within the realm of our usual contacts seem
to agree not only that the class is not empty, but that it has exactly
one member. Islam, Judaism, and Christianity (by courtesy, perhaps,
in its trinitarian forms) all make such a monotheistic affirmation. Indeed, the affirmation is central to everything else they affirm, endorse,
and propose. The centrality of this claim is, naturally, the reason why
we shall focus on it. If we can get it clear, then we can branch out.

There are many different notions of God, of course, but the notion
that we will be examining here is the one with which we are familiar—
the notion of an omnipotent, omniscient, benevolent creator of everything from nothing—the notion that men in the street, at revival meetings, at mass, and in arguments with their parents have in mind when
they affirm or deny that God exists. We might begin with the question
"Does anyone *know* God exists?" We could then try, "*Could* anyone
know God exists?" Many people have claimed to know it, but what
sort of evidence is appropriate to support such a claim? We shall have
to see.

2

ON KNOWLEDGE
OF
DIVINE EXISTENCE

In this chapter we shall examine a variety of views on whether a God could be known to exist. Many say they know One does, many that they know One doesn't, many say they do not know, and some say nobody can know; and there are several possible alternative stands that can be taken within each of these options. We shall take up the main ones in sequence, keeping at the center of attention the question "Is the existence of a God the sort of thing one *could* know?"

KNOWLEDGE THAT A GOD EXISTS

Many have claimed that men can (and that some men do) know that a God exists. While their reasons are not at all the same, we would find Saints Thomas and Anselm, Descartes and Billy Graham, John R. Rice and the Apostle Paul in the group. While their appeals run the full gamut of the "varieties of evidence" examined above, our attention will be more restricted. We shall not, for example, consider a "pure faith" posture, for we are interested at present in knowledge, not belief— however important, influential, or intense that belief may be. Nor shall we now consider appeals to authority, revelation, and intuition as such: as shown in the first chapter, these can be dealt with as subspecies of reason and experience. Rather, we will focus our attention on the basic a priori and a posteriori arguments.[1]

A Priori Appeals and Rejoinders

The first appeal we shall try to unravel contends that (a) we know that God exists, (b) the basis of this knowledge is found in our exercise of reason, and (c) this exercise of reason is one of "pure" reason. While we have already argued that "pure" reason is inadequate to deliver facts-about-things, we shall still examine this position with care because it is so venerable and, further, is widely held and seriously argued by numerous religionists today. Some think that it is particularly appropriate to support claims about God's existence with reason rather than experience because they feel that an appeal to the content of our sensations, emotions, and so on, would somehow cheapen or demean the status of the Divinity. There is a strong dose of mind-body dualism in such an attitude, rooted in a rather Pauline separation of flesh and spirit. The notion is that God quite transcends the physical-experiential world, and that (hence) only the mind (which is more "spiritual") is appropriate to the pursuit of Him.[2] For all the problems of relevance[3] this notion poses, such "ontological"[4] approaches have had many advocates.

The Anselmian Approach   Saint Anselm's argument would go more or less like this: Even a fool who denies the existence of God remains caught in the limits of logic and good sense. Either he is making an intelligible assertion or he is not, for there are no other alternatives. But, in order for "There is no God" to be intelligible, its conceptual constituents must be intelligible too. So the *concept* "God" must be

[1]Each position could be presented by simply repeating or abridging the stated argument of some famous writer. I choose, however, to go at it another way. I shall try to stylize each type of argument, exercising a great latitude of interpretation and expression, in an attempt to get across what I see as the core force of each. You should then read the classic arguments in their classic form, of course. They are all available in economical paperback editions, which will be cited in the chapter notes.

[2]The merits of such a dualism are not my issue, though, frankly, I think it is a theoretically sterile approach. For every duality you need a mediator, and for every mediated duality you need two demimediators, and so on, ad infinitum.

[3]See above, page 33.

[4]From the Greek "ontos" or being. *The Ontological Argument,* edited by Alvin Plantinga and published in paperback by Doubleday, Anchor (1965), is an excellent single-topic source book on this whole approach.

intelligible for the fool to use it in his denial-claim. Indeed, it must not only be intelligible in principle, it must, to the fool, be intelligible in fact. One must conceive of God to deny His existence. If not, then either one conceives of something else or of nothing at all. If the latter, then the "denial" has no force at all; and, if the former, it is no denial of *God's* existence. So, logic forces point one: to deny God's existence one must conceive of God.

From an Anselmian point of view, God is "that than which no greater can be conceived." Anything such that something greater (than it) can be conceived just is not *God* (by definition). Nothing greater than God can be conceived, for "God" *means* "that than which no greater can be conceived." So, definition fixes point two: any concept of an *X* that you can conceive of a *Y* greater than, is not a concept of God.

Now, assume that we have two concepts identical in all respects save one: one of them has a counterpart in reality, the other does not. Given this, it is claimed that the designatum of the former concept is fuller (more complete and substantial) than that of the latter. The latter may be perfect and perfectly real *"in intellectu,"* but the other one has all of that *plus* existence *"in re."* So, point three, an arguable assumption: to be perfect and real in-the-mind-and-in-the-world is greater than to be (merely) perfect and real in-the-mind-alone.

Now we have already seen that the fool must conceive of God to deny God's existence, and accordingly that he must have a concept of that-than-which-no-greater-can-be-conceived if it is God's existence he would deny. Now, could that possibly amount to no more than having a concept of that which is perfect and perfectly real in-the-mind-alone? Certainly not. For it is possible for him to have in mind a different concept—namely, one identical in all respects save that it has a counterpart in reality—and, consequently, the designatum of that concept would be greater. So, you see, if the concept that the fool has in mind when he says there is no God is not a concept that actually has a counterpart in reality, then it is not a concept of God. It is not a concept of God because it is a concept of that which is inferior (by virtue of non-existence *in re*). In that it is not a concept of God, then he is not denying God's existence. Indeed, he isn't even talking about God at all! That is point four.

So: the only way for a fool to significantly deny God's existence is for there to be a God. Even the denial of God presupposes the existence of God. So God exists, and the argument has appealed to nothing besides logic, reason, and the consistent use of language. The argument never touches "the natural order," our "experiences," or even our "mystical" encounters.

While I would grant that it is rather persuasive (on its face, and given its assumptions about language),[5] I still balk. Rather than turning back to our general principle about the sterility of "pure" reason, however, consider this question: if this argument is valid, then will it not work in other disputes, too? Anselm's antagonist, a monk named Gaunilo, gave it such an analysis, and gave rebuttal by analogy.[6]

The analogy that he used has to do with a perfect island. Might not some unromantic soul say, "There is no perfect island"? If he did, could you not run an Anselmian argument through, replacing "God" with "perfect island" throughout? If the argument is valid at all, it should work here, too: a really perfect island is that island than which no greater island can be conceived . . ., and so on. So you are driven to the same choice. Either the denial of the existence of the perfect island is empty (i.e., when the unromantic denier has no concept in mind), or it is irrelevant (i.e., when he has some other concept in mind), or else it shoots itself down (i.e., when he has the right concept in mind— the one that has a counterpart in reality). So when the unromantic denier seriously and intelligibly denies the existence of the really perfect island, he demonstrates its reality in that act! But this is madness.

Imagine what the world would be like if this thought-into-reality gambit worked. I shall immediately start denying the existence of the perfect diamond-in-my-pocket. Think your way to wealth! But, unfortunately, my pocket stays empty. Even after feverish and repeated

[5]The argument gains force because the first option seems to have been lost in the wash. Maybe the concept of God is not intelligible to begin with. Maybe the statement "There is no God" is not an assertion at all. By ignoring this option and holding the limited position that it is an assertion and is only either true or false, one is driven to the point of allowing that in order for it to be such, it must be significant; and in order to achieve that, there must be a God. Strictly speaking, the claim so interpreted is not assertively contradictory. Rather, what the utterance, so taken, denies, the utterer performatively affirms. As an assertion, then, it is not felicitous at all. The question would then become: "If it is not an assertion, what is it?" We shall return to this question at some length in later chapters.

[6]Refutation by logical analogy: taking a questioned argument and constructing another with exactly the same form that has obviously true premises and an obviously false conclusion. Since the force of logical validity depends on the form of the argument, a form that can have true premises and a false conclusion must be invalid. The analogy simply makes it plain. The Americans for Democratic Action support guaranteed income. The Dirty Reds support guaranteed income. So the ADA are Dirty Reds. But, cats have fur. Dogs have fur. So cats are dogs. Both arguments have the same form. Many a man was suckered by the first; but nobody would buy the second. So the first is refuted "by logical analogy."

intelligible denials, all I would have is (in Albert's deathless prose in *The Pogo Sundae Book*) "a greasy pocket and my memories."

But of course there is a reply: How infamous it is to use an argument that is appropriate only to sacred contexts to argue about islands and diamonds! Of course the ontological argument will not work with mundane things—it only works with God.

I do not find this convincing. Why should it work with God and not with islands? Three reasons have been advanced: (1) because God has the special property of being ontologically provable (which is question-begging in the extreme); (2) because the logic that applies to God is not the same as the logic that applies to things (which is self-defeating because the whole point was to prove God's existence through an appeal to ordinary logic); and (3) because, God being infinite, we have no right to "confine" him with our finite thought (which is again self-defeating, for—if it is true—it obviates the whole enterprise of divine "knowledge"). The notion that God is above logic is advanced often enough; but unless one is willing at that signal to suspend all theological reflection, it is pointless.

One could try this: Existence is a perfection in God's case, but not in the case of ordinary things. Something that does not exist cannot be a God; but something that does not exist can be an island or a diamond. I am not at all sure that we can treat existence so loosely. It would be at least as difficult to spend a vacation on a nonexistent island as it would be to communicate with a nonexistent God. Certainly a nonexistent God is not God; but a nonexistent island is not an island either. Maybe it is an "imaginary" island; but imaginary islands are not islands. My point, however, is not that the argument works for God and islands—just that if it works for one, it works for the other.

Finally, isn't there a vicious shift in the argument from the notion that a concept of God must be a concept of God-as-existing (which may be the proper conceptualization) to the notion that a God does exist (which begs the question)?[7] There may be some force in ontological argument, but this formulation, at any rate, is inadequate.

A Cartesian Formulation This has a very different apparent foundation. It begins with an appeal to an area of knowledge which all admit is purely rational—geometry—discovering there a valid pattern of argument and transferring it to theological issues.

Geometrical figures are defined in terms of their geometrical proper-

---

[7]That is, from the idea that existence is part of being God (no nonentities are Gods) to the idea that there actually is one. But "*P* only if *Q*" does not entail "*P* and *Q*."

ties. A triangle, for example, may be defined as a closed three-sided figure, uniquely determined by three nonlinear points in a plane. From these characteristics, taken with the axioms of the system, other characteristics may be deduced—for example, that the three interior angles of a Euclidean triangle always add up to 180 degrees[8] regardless of how the three determining points are arranged in their plane. So, while the possession of 180 interior degrees is not the defining characteristic of such a triangle, it is a necessary characteristic, known prior to and independent of any field research. Each and every Euclidean triangle will be so arranged; and this is known (by inference from a set of definitions) a priori. Similarly, God is defined in terms of His properties (the totality of all perfections). From this definition, in turn, we can deduce further Divine attributes-in-specific; for example, that God exists. Existence is part of the meaning of "God," even as "180 degrees" is part of the meaning of "Euclidean triangle." "God does not exist" is just as contradictory as "The interior angles of this Euclidean triangle add up to 193 degrees." So we know a priori that God exists.

This is still the ontological argument (that the denial of Divine existence is contradictory), but in new and more persuasive dress: (a) a strong analogy is drawn to a valid case of "similar" reasoning, and (b) the putative contradiction is a straightforward one rather than an indirect conflict between logical and Moorean implications.[9] But the argument still will not carry the freight. What, after all, does it prove? It proves that even as all Euclidean triangles have 180 degrees, so do all Gods exist. But both of these conclusions could be sound even were there no Euclidean triangles and no Gods. Whatever Euclidean triangles there be will have the property specified; so, too, whatever Gods there be. If you ever run into a Euclidean triangle, you may be sure that it

[8]We must, of course, specify *Euclidean* triangles now, for we are aware these days that there are other kinds of geometries and other kinds of triangles (which, distressingly, have sometimes more and sometimes less than Euclid's 180 degrees—as a function of the warpage of the space which they subtend). Euclidean triangles are safe, though. This does, however, reinforce the suspicion that you should be feeling: that such inferences only inform us about the structure of our own conventional systems, and not about "reality." They achieve the latter only when we discover empirically that there is some segment of facts which the conventions fit. Euclid is fine for tobacco allotments, but clumsy for stellar displacement in high-gravity fields.

[9]Moorean implication is what is implied not by a proposition but by the fact that a proposition is uttered in a speech act in a certain context. It is the force of the fool's denying that sets the argument in motion in its Anselmian guise. More neatly, in the Cartesian mode, the inconsistency resides in the utterance and not in the melding of utterance and uttering.

will fit the definition and its entailments. (If it didn't, then it is not a Euclidean triangle. It may look like one, but if it has 180.001 degrees it is a fraud. It is still there and still deserves inspection and classification, but it is no Euclidean triangle.) So, too, if you ever run into a God, you may be sure that It exists. If on your tours, you do not run into anything, you may be assured that you have not encountered any Gods. But, even if all Gods exist, there still remains the question "Are there any?" The argument does not tell us.

There is a further, deeper (Kantian) difficulty, subtle but quite serious. Existence may not be a property at all. But if it is not a property at all, then it certainly cannot be a necessary property. Thus, while we might list all of the properties of some X, including, of course, its necessary properties, existence would not be on the list. For, existence is *the occasion of having properties.* Thus, in listing all of the necessary characteristics of the perfect island (the presence of palm trees, lagoons, native girls, or whatever else), we would not list existence. Though we may spell out rationally what the nature of the perfect island would be (were there one), whether there is one remains a question whose answer must be sought elsewhere. Nor can we do more[10] for God— all Gods are awesome, majestic, loving, wise, and so on, but whether those characteristics are actually occasioned in fact cannot be settled by reason alone.

Part of the problem here is the ease of confusing existence with necessary existence, and the easy conflation of several senses of "necessary existence." Even if existence is not a property, at least one sense of "necessary existence" makes *that* label a property-marker. Among the properties of some X, we might find that of being noncontingent, of having aseity (i.e., depending on nothing external for being, nature, or essence). Further, it is customary to grant that this is one of the defining characteristics of any God. So we may grant readily that all Gods are noncontingent. We may even grant, further, that we know this to be true a priori. But we still have no a priori grounds to suppose that the class of noncontingents has any instantiations. To suppose that we do is to make a specious shift from "no Gods are unnecessary" through "all Gods are necessary" to "necessarily there is a God." Even if one sense of "necessary existence" designates a property, the argument still does not carry through.

I think that the assorted rebuttals to these formulations of a priori

[10]And maybe not this much. If "transcendence" is stipulated as His first property, it is difficult to see how we could get at any others. We will sort this out with care, later.

argument for the existence of God are substantially correct. Of course
we may decide, there being no particular problem involved in this,
that when we speak of God, the concept in use is of some all-perfect
One among whose attributes would be independence, autonomy,
necessity, superiority over all else, and so on. Anything else wouldn't
be God. No God is petty, limited, inferior, or contingent in any way.
But this is to talk about the characteristics that may be conceptually
attributed to a God whose existence is being presupposed (or at least
hypothesized). But: is that presupposition true? (Is that hypothesis
legitimate?) Is there anything that possesses these virtues? Reason cannot tell us by itself. It can tell us that among all the many things we
encounter, all those that are contingent, limited, petty, and so on, are
not Gods. This is an excellent ontological argument *against* idolatry.
But we still have seen no effective ontological argument *for* theism.
Still, the argument survives, a number of contemporary philosophers
finding it persuasive when reclothed yet again, and offering assorted rebuttals to the notion that a priori argument is factually sterile. Let us
consider one such recent treatment.

A Contemporary Formulation   In his introductory essay to Alvin
Plantinga's collection, *The Ontological Argument,* Richard Taylor says:
"[Those] who have deemed it obvious that one can never legitimately
pass from the mere description of something to any conclusion con-
cerning the existence in reality of the thing described have simply failed
to note that this is not only a legitimate inference but a very common
one when it is the nonexistence of something that is inferred."[11] He
cites as an example the well-known case in which "from one's clear understanding of what is meant by a plane four-sided figure, all of whose
points are equidistant from the center, one [concludes] with certainty
that no such being exists in reality."
   Implicit in this contention is the corollary notion that affirmative
inferences from idea to thing are possible, too. Indeed, Taylor focuses
on the ontological argument for the existence of God as an instance
of just this kind of affirmative inference, arguing that the traditional
objections to it are misguided.[12] But if negative inference of this pattern is not only "very common" but also "legitimate," there is no

---

[11] Alvin Plantinga, ed., *The Ontological Argument* (Garden City, N.Y.: Doubleday, Anchor, 1965), p. xv.
[12] Taylor is not claiming that the ontological argument is unobjectionable. He is
only insisting that it cannot be deemed bad solely on the ground that it is an
idea-thing inference.

need for diffidence: if the negative move will work, then the affirmative one can be validly deduced from it.

1. In discussing Anselm on necessary nonexistence, Taylor says: "We can apply this notion to anything, such as a square circle, which is nonexistent by its very nature. It exists *in intellectu*, [but] from one's very understanding of it he can be certain that no such thing exists *in re*."[13] But, consider the phrase "square circle, which is nonexistent by its very nature." This use presumes that a locution like "square circle" has a designating function and that what it designates has a "nature." But can one designate nonexistents? Indeed, do "they" have a "nature"? (I once read that the notable thing about square circles is not that they all have the property of nonbeing but, rather, that there aren't any. This still seems apt to me.) What *is* clear is that the expression "square circle" is an inconsistent description-attempt. Being inconsistent, it fails to describe, necessarily. " 'Square circle' fails to describe, by definition" is much more straightforward than "Square circles nonexist by their very nature," and it avoids a serious material mode/formal mode confusion.[14]

Nevertheless, if such description-attempts do fail necessarily, then their negations (call them tautological description-attempts) will succeed necessarily. If "square circle" is inconsistent, then it *cannot* designate anything; and if an adequate descriptive unpacking of "God" shows it to be tautological, then that term *must*.[15] But the reason why such tautological "descriptions" must have counterparts is nothing more surprising than the fact that they (like any and all tautologies) are individually and collectively compatible with any state of affairs whatever. The truth conditions of a tautology are satisfied whatever happens to be the case. Consequently, if a description ever is tautologi-

---

[13]Plantinga, p. xvi.

[14]This is a distinction well worth looking up. Cats have four feet; but "cats" has four letters: the use/mention distinction is a good place to start being careful. But it does not end there.

[15]The thesis is that if a contradictory "description" cannot have a designate in reality, then a tautological "description" must have one. Assuming that the notions of contradictory and tautological "descriptions" are somehow not problematic: Let d represent any specific description, $-d$ its negation, V the logical property of being tautological, and Λ the logical property of being contradictory. It is clear that if Vd then Λ-d, and if Λd then V-d and vice versa. So: $Vd \equiv \Lambda$-d, and $\Lambda d \equiv V$-d. Further, let $!D$ indicate that a state of affairs, D, which is designated by d, obtains in reality, $!$-D that $-d$ has its counterpart, $-!D$ that a situation designated by d does not obtain, and $-!$-D that $-d$ lacks a counterpart. It is clear that if $!D$ then $-!$-D and vice versa; and if $!$-D then $-!D$ and vice versa.

cal, then it has a counterpart in reality no matter what specific character of reality happens to obtain. But, this being so, reasoning from
tautological "descriptions" to reality is without any informative point.
It does not tell us which of the very many possible characters of reality,
all of which equally satisfy the tautology in use (or any other one, for
that matter), does in fact obtain. In order for the "description" to be
tautological, it must be so informatively vacuous that it places no constraint whatever on the shape of the facts. So, for example, if some
unpacking of "God" turned out to be tautological, it would follow that
there was such a God. But the theological efficacy of such a move would
be dubious because such a "God" would be equally compatible with a
reality of terror or delight, a cosmos of justice or infinite iniquity, a
world-order or a world-chaos.[16] So, inferences *ab intellectu ad rem*
are allowed in the affirmative, but they are informatively sterile.

2. For that matter, are contradictory "descriptions" really the bases
of legitimate inferences *ad rem*? Even if the affirmative form yields no
useful statements, can we still endorse the notion that the basic negative pattern is unobjectionable and productive? In fact, the very notion
of a contradictory "description" is entirely misleading. Whether affirmative, negative, or mixed, the descriptive force of an utterance resides in
the fact that it is the vehicle for the more or less explicit assertion that
some distinguishable state of affairs obtains. We do expect a description
to convey *something* solid about reality, whether what it conveys turns
out to be so or not.

As has been indicated already, a tautology does not operate effectively

----

So: $!D \equiv -!-D$ and $!-D \equiv -!D$. Now, the claim that a contradictory description
cannot have a counterpart in reality can be symbolized for the description d: $\Lambda d \rightarrow$
$-!D$. However, since $\Lambda d \equiv V-d$, and $!-D \equiv -!D$, we can obtain, by simple substitution of equivalents: $\Lambda-d \rightarrow !-D$. But since every contradiction has a tautology for its
negation, the same could be done in any given case. Consequently, for each contradictory "description" that has no counterpart in reality (i.e., all of them),
there is a tautological "description" (its negation) which does have a counterpart
in reality. And, since every tautology is the negation of some contradiction, it
necessarily follows that every tautological "description" has a counterpart in
reality. Q.E.D.

[16]Many theists, of course, would readily allow that God so transcends the dimensions of contingent things that their character places no constraint upon His
dimensions. The theologically unfortunate consequence of that, as indicated
previously, is that then His character places no constraint upon theirs either.
Such a move is not viable for any theist who conceptualizes God as having a
character delineable in any regard (e.g., as being to some degree beneficent
rather than sadistic).

in this role because it does not pick out or identify any distinguishable state of affairs. A contradiction is flawed for the task of describing in a closely related way; that is, an inconsistent claim, insofar as it is inconsistent, advances and then withdraws the same assertive content. It commits "self-erasure."[17] Its net assertive content, then, insofar as it is inconsistent, is nil.

So a contradictory "description," one that offers and withdraws the same "descriptive" freight, retains as a whole no descriptive force. Broken-backed, it is a descriptive cipher. Consequently, the notion that we ever have a clear comprehension *in intellectu* of the descriptive force of such a cipher is confused—even though the inconsistent expression is intelligible to the hearer. When a logic teacher says, " 'All round squares are triangular' is true because its logical form is that of a conditional with a false antecedent," his statement is intelligible; but whether his students have a clear conception of what is "described" in the conditional is rather problematic. Understanding a descriptive utterance *qua* description requires much more than simply getting the words laid straight. It involves capturing the net descriptive force of the words as they are jointly used for a descriptive purpose. But "round square" as a paradigm inconsistent phrase has no net descriptive force. Consequently, there is no clear conception to be captured *in intellectu*. But one cannot reason from a clear conception *in intellectu* to matters of fact when there is, in fact, no clear conception *in intellectu* from which to reason. To go from Chicago to Detroit, there needs to be a Chicago.

A claim like "There are no round squares" is not a claim about matters of fact in the first place. It is a metalinguistic claim revealing or affirming the conventions implicit in the use of ordinary language. The conclusion of an "inference from idea to thing," however, has to be a claim about things. But this is not a claim about things. Therefore, this is not the conclusion of an inference from idea to thing, and the claim that we regularly and legitimately reason in the negative mode from idea to thing, in the fashion that Taylor says we do, is a mistake.

When we go beyond the error of misreading the descriptive failure of inconsistent utterances as an instance of logical necessity working its will on the world, and reason in a parallel fashion from formal or definitional truths to claims about "necessary being," we are guilty of a parallel mistake—thinking again that logic is describing reality for us, when, in fact, it is only locating those claims that are so vacuous that they fit any and all worlds whatever.

[17]See Chap. 1, n. 26.

A Posteriori Appeals and Rejoinders

Upon reflection, it seems fairly obvious that there should be difficulty
with pure rationalist approaches. After all, barring extreme transcendentalism, whether there is a God seems a question of fact; and the
very notion of trying to settle a question of fact by means of arguments
that do not appeal to matters of fact is strange on its face. Human
understanding of the nature of the reality we confront must begin with
that confrontation. Any argument that is going to have results germane
to the human condition is obliged to begin within the dimensions of
the human condition. So there is good reason to move away from the
pure-reason business, for all of its elevated tone, toward more down-
to-earth, empirically based arguments. If it is still contended that the
existence of God can be demonstrated, these demonstrations will begin
in experience.

There are several such empirically connected arguments. They have
technical names (just like the ontological argument did), and include
the cosmological argument, the teleological argument, and the axiological argument. The axiological argument is an argument from value
("axios" is a Greek term for value or worth); the teleological argument
is an argument from (or to) design or purpose ("telos" is Greek for
purpose or end); and the cosmological argument takes several forms,
all of which have to do with the ground, source, or nature of the universe as a whole (the Greek root here is "cosmos"—the only one of
these roots commonly preserved in our contemporary language). All
three of the argument-types just enumerated are special instances of
the large family of arguments from "sufficient reason": *Nothing occurs
unless the sufficient conditions for its occurrence have occurred; Therefore, if we can discover what the sufficient conditions are for some
state of affairs (which we do discern), then we can reasonably conclude
that those conditions have obtained (even if we do not directly discern
them.* In order for such an argument to work, we must presume that
every event has a set of sufficient conditions and that there is a way
of figuring out what the sufficient conditions of a specific event may
be. Even if both of these presumptions were secure, which is far from
obvious, another problem arises if there is more than one set of conditions sufficient to bring about the event we are trying to explain.

For all of the attendant difficulties, however, the "sufficient reason"
maneuver is a common one in everyday affairs. For example, if we
discover the highway strewn with corpses and the wreckage of automo-
biles, we have little difficulty understanding the probable source of
the carnage—on the basis of our previous experience and the principle

of sufficient reason. Our immediate assumption would be that it didn't "just happen"—conditions preceded it that were not unconnected from or irrelevant to it. We could go on (indeed, the police *will*) to collect quantities of evidence and, eventually, to formulate a detailed explanatory hypothesis. If we discover one of the upended vehicles on the wrong side of the median; and if, when we open one of the doors, the odor of gin assails us; and if, when the corpse of the apparent driver is subjected to chemical analysis, we discover that its tissue-alcohol level is 4 mg/cc; we can begin to hypothesize a fair account of what probably occurred. In such cases, we are appealing to (what we take to be) the standard pattern of cause and effect,[18] based on our already accumulated experience-as-interpreted. It is not a simple pattern of explanation, nor is it presumption-free. Still, in ordinary affairs, if an event occurs, there must have been a set of antecedent events sufficient to set it up.

It would be counter to all the bias of our era to suggest that some event had no cause at all. (Of course, the bias of our era is not self-guaranteeing.) The more practical problems, however, are that (a) we may not be able to figure out the sufficient reasons in a given case, (b) we may be able to figure out too many sufficient reasons in a given case, and (c) the actual reason in a given case may not be among the assorted sufficient reasons that we have figured out. This pattern of inquiry will almost always provide the investigator with several alternative accounts. This is the main source of practical difficulties. After all, our experience clearly shows that there is usually more than one way by which things could have arrived at their present state; and the argument from sufficient reason, insofar as any of these alternatives would be sufficient, is not adequate to designate which of them is most likely to have occurred. Consequently, if very much depends on a question (as, for example, in a court trial), we take great pains to press the matter beyond "reasonable doubt." We do not insist that the argument drive us through to one and only one solution, all others being conclusively eliminated; but we do insist on as much, and as precise, elimination of options as "due process" can provide.[19]

But in many cases, a really credible alternative is readily available.

[18]Or the standard correlations of statistically associated events. "Cause and effect" is not empirically transparent.

[19]Such notions as "reasonable doubt" and "due process" are, of course, imprecise. How much is "reasonable" or "due"? This has to be settled pragmatically. This is just one more reason why sufficient-reason explanations are not coercive or definitive. This is also why, in court, we provide avenues for appeal.

For this reason, if for no others, the argument from sufficient reason is, while helpful, only rarely conclusive. Maybe, here, we have not figured out any sufficient reason. Maybe, even, in some instances, there is no sufficient reason! In any event, the location of a "sufficient reason" means not "here is what happened"; rather, *either* "Here is what happened" *or* "This is the best explanation our ingenuity can produce." As long as our ingenuity is to any degree subject to possible limitations, then the sufficient reason argument is inconclusive.[20]

Let us examine some of the particular forms that this argument-pattern takes, theologically.[21] We shall begin with the cosmological argument for the existence of God—the simplest, broadest, and most basic of the lot.

Cause   Every event has a cause. No event "just happens." This is the premise with which the cosmological argument begins. From this point on, the argument can be run on two channels—one dealing with the individual events of history, the other dealing with the entire body of history as a single "world-event." The former is simpler and we shall take it first.

If we trace back in history, event behind event behind event, every event having a cause behind it, we are confronted with only two alternatives: either the sequence of events and their causes goes back infinitely without ever stopping, or the sequence of events and their causes goes back eventually to some cause which is not itself an event and, hence, does not itself require a further cause. In the latter alternative, this ultimate nonevent which requires no cause may be called the "uncaused cause" or the "unmoved mover."[22]

"But the first alternative," say the Aristotelians, "is absurd." It presumes the (temporal) infiniteness of natural history, while all of the

[20]Perhaps those who think that it is conclusive are failing to observe the difference between sufficient and necessary conditions. If we could find (and know) the necessary conditions of an event, we would be in business.

[21]*The Cosmological Arguments,* edited by D.R. Burrill (Garden City, N.Y.: Doubleday, Anchor, 1967) is a good one-volume survey.

[22]"Unmoved mover" is far more specific than "uncaused cause." When we say "unmoved mover" we are presuming that the ultimate nonevent caused motion. There is no overwhelming reason to make this presumption. Perhaps the ultimate nonevent caused the materialization of static geometrical structures ex nihilo. The Aristotelian tradition, of course, traces all events back to primal motions; but I think that forces too many dubious specificities on the whole argument. So I will settle for "uncaused cause" and not worry about what the "uncaused cause" caused.

evidence that we have makes clear that we are dealing with a finite system of finite things. So there must be an Uncaused Cause.

The second form of the cosmological argument, the one that takes
the entire body of history as a single world-event, allows that this
world-event either has *no* cause, is *self*-caused, or has an *external* cause.
In this case, the first two alternatives are dismissed as absurd because
the notion of an event without any cause at all, and the notion of an
event that causes itself, are just as much outside the pale of our experience as is the notion of an infinite event-system. So, given the occurrence
of the world-event, its only intelligible explanation must be a cause
wholly external to it.

We might like to think that the acceptability of an argument de-
pended entirely on its logical merits. There is much more involved,
however, because argument is a pragmatic affair. When the output of
an argument is labeled "absurd," it may mean that the argument is
invalidly formed, it may mean that the conclusion is simply false
(which is possible, even in a valid argument, if the premises are false),
or it may mean simply that the conclusion is incredible to the hearers.

The last is a purely pragmatic affair, and has nothing to do with the
actual validity or soundness of the argument. It has only to do with
the degree of acceptance that the argument gets; and this depends
to a great extent on the psychology of the individuals to whom it is
addressed. That, in turn, depends on the common way of looking
at the world that is packed into their culture and their era—their
time, their mores, their values, and their biases. It would be neater
if the verdict "absurd" were always reserved for strictly inconsistent
conclusions—if the "incredible" and the "inconceivable" were kept
clearly and precisely distinct. They are not, though.

Whether statements like "The world-whole causes itself," "The
course of history is an infinite sequence of causally linked events,"
or "Some events are not caused at all" are internally self-negating is
arguable. (They do not seem so to me.) Self-negating or not, however,
they have been judged absurd again and again. Those who so judge
them clearly take them to be incoherent.

To an Aristotelian, the notions that the world was either uncaused
at all, self-caused, or caused by a series of events that goes back infinitely, are all unintelligible barbarisms. These options simply do
not fit the mind set that the world is fixed, finite, comprehensible,
controllable, and subject to man's examination and rational mastery.
Everything that we ever encounter is finite; so, by inductive reasoning,
we have long since come to the conclusion: *everything* is finite. In
this manner the infinite-regress-of-events alternative is dismissed as

absurd. The notion that the world as a whole is either uncaused or
self-causing is rejected because everything that we ever encounter
is externally caused. The same inductive inference holds. So these
alternatives are dismissed as absurd. In all these cases, the final argument
pattern is the disjunctive syllogism. If it is the case that either *P* or *Q*
and if, further, it is the case that Not-*P*, then all that is left is *Q*. So,
if we accept the premises and the only alternatives left are (a) infinite
regress or uncaused cause, (b) self-caused or uncaused cause, and (c)
not-caused-at-all or uncaused cause, and if infinite regress, self-caused,
and not-caused-at-all are to be dismissed as "absurd," then an uncaused
cause is all that is left.

The problems so far are numerous: Are the alternatives listed all
really "sufficient"? Have we left out any alternatives that are also "sufficient"? Is the elimination of some of the ones we have listed really
legitimate? And so on. A further problem is added, when the uncaused
cause, so perilously established, is given the label "God." But the label
is given, and the argument is then taken to stand as a demonstration
of the divine ground of true religion, based on simple intelligence
and experience. But can one reasonably accept this identification of
the conclusion? Even supposing that all the enumerated problems
could be solved or dismissed, on what credible grounds do we call this
"prime cause" God?

Proving, were it possible, that there is an uncaused cause, has about
as much to do with proving the basic premise of theism as proving that
America had a first president has to do with proving that the first president was George Washington (or Louis XIV or Caligula). One can
envision all sorts of uncaused causes, perhaps even the Great Demon in
the sky—infinitely evil, totally depraved and maniacally chortling to
itself in its Transcendent Madness. The move to an uncaused cause
is simply a move to an uncaused cause. "Its" character remains wholly
indeterminate.

And what does one do with an uncaused cause? How do you deal
with a cause that is not an event? How do you address it? "I believe
in the Uncaused Cause, Mover of All Moves"? Perhaps for a *very* dispassionate Aristotelian this sort of thing would be sufficient; but I
can hardly see it for a Saint Francis, a Bonhoeffer, or a Ferré. The content and force of theism centers on a God of righteousness and virtue,
justice and mercy, love and wisdom. Proving that somewhere "back
down the line" there is/was an uncaused cause is, on these standards,
religiously inadequate if not simply irrelevant.

The charge of inadequacy, however, has point only if the "proof" of
the uncaused cause is, itself, effective. Frankly, I do not think it is.

Why dismiss the infinite regress alternative out of hand? *Is* it "absurd"? We may want to grant that no specific event in history is infinite, but why must we balk at the notion that history as a whole might have no intelligible limit? Is it any easier to comprehend the notion of an infinite God than it is to comprehend the notion of infinite History? Why? Reflection on these questions would oblige me to conclude that while the historical sequence may go back to an uncaused cause, it just as easily may not.

Further, have we considered all the options? Maybe there is an uncaused cause. Maybe there is an infinite sequence of temporal events. Maybe there are five uncaused causes, or ten, or 513. Even if the infinite sequence seems difficult, there is nothing to force our attention on one terminator. The very best that one could conclude would be that *perhaps* there was a first cause. You could not carry through to the point of showing that there was until you could refute all the alternatives. To do this you would have to enumerate all the alternatives, and then find adequate grounds for dismissing each one until only the uncaused cause remained.

This problem is common, of course, to all sufficient-reason arguments. In court, it does not prove insuperable because the optional explanations are fairly few in number and we have a massive fund of experience of events of like kind, in terms of which we may make the eliminations. When we are talking about the origin of the cosmos, however, our fund of experience is nil. We have no experience on which to generalize, no analogies on which to draw, because we have had no experience of a cosmos originating and, consequently, have no idea what the range of options is and no effective way to dispose of any intelligible and consistent alternative that anyone might suggest.

So, with the cosmological argument, as with sufficient-reason arguments in general, we have the (radical) "no cause" option, and we also have (if "no cause" is too radical) the practical problem of selecting *the* cause from among the sufficient causes we have thought of. Unlike sufficient-reason arguments in general, we find ourselves operating in this case without any experiential fund on which to draw. Consequently, as even Saint Thomas saw, this argument cannot function as a coercive proof that an uncaused cause is or ever was. It is suggested, rather, that it serves to reinforce belief with reason—to encourage and sustain those who are already committed. It is not even really effective at the reinforcement task. How many people need reinforcement for belief in an uncaused cause? A great many people may need reinforcement for belief in God, but that is a different affair.

The cosmological argument, then, is not coercive; and whatever effect it does have reinforces a particular view of cosmic history—not theism. Can the axiological and teleological versions of the sufficient-reason maneuver do any better?

Design   The teleological argument for the existence of God is more specific than the cosmological argument. While also an example of the sufficient-reasons approach, the teleological argument begins by drawing our attention to specific characteristics of the world in which we live. It then offers, as a sufficient reason for those specific characteristics, the occurrence of a *designer*.

Consider what would happen on one of our Apollo moon jaunts if, upon embarking on the EVA to collect moon samples, the astronauts discovered, among the rocks and dust, a stainless steel Hershey bar, a cathode-ray tube, a block and tackle, and a sundial. The community would, of course, be startled by these discoveries; but, more than that, the community would immediately conclude that there must have been, at some time, intelligent, civilized, and productive beings on the moon to have left these obvious artifacts behind. If anyone were skeptical, we would simply call attention to the obvious differences between such things as rocks and dust and such things as cathode tubes and sundials. The latter are distinguished by the fact that they have a structure which is peculiarly adapted to a function. (Sundials are so constructed that they apportion the lapse of time into roughly equal segments. Blocks and tackles are designed so as to ease the physical labors of men in moving heavy objects.) Dust and rocks might, perhaps, be *put* to some use, through the ingenuity of men; but dust and rocks have no apparent use for which they are organized or intended. The point, of course, is simply that man has the ability to distinguish artifacts in terms of their characteristics (specifically in terms of their adaptability to function) and, further, that upon the discovery of an artifact, he immediately infers the occurrence of some maker, some designer, who determined its function and fabricated it to fit.

We would be little less than astounded if we found television sets, laser generators, and linotype machines in a situation in which it was demonstrable that there had never been a designer or maker of any kind. Just so, it is argued, if we examine the "natural world" (i.e., the world independent of human design and purpose), we must see the occurrence of a designer and maker *there*. For, it is claimed, even the "natural world" reveals a structure adapted to function, sufficiently like that of artifacts, to make the inference of a Designer inescapable.

Many different examples could be given.[23] Consider the human eye,

---

[23]Probably the best source of examples is William Paley's *Natural Theology*

the opposable thumb, the turn of the seasons, the exquisite arrangement of the celestial furniture. The human eye alone, in its intricate mobility, range of signal sensitivity, self-maintenance and defense apparatus, is far more analogous to locomotives and TVs than to rocks and dust. The thumb, for its location[24] if nothing else, is far more analogous to a block and tackle than to some nonstructured and nonfunctional lump.

So an analogical inference is drawn: even as recognized artifacts make necessary the occurrence of a designer (because of their adaptation to function), so, too, the myriad objects of the natural world make necessary the occurrence of a designer (because of *their* adaptation to function). The design of recognized artifacts may be more obvious; but the fact that the design of natural objects is there to be seen, if we will merely take the pains to look with care and precision, is all that is needed to purchase a designer for the natural order analogous to man-the-maker-of-machines.

But our examination of man and his history is sufficient to demonstrate that no man is adequate in skill, intelligence, or resources to be this grand designer. So grand a compendium of design demands a sufficiently grand source. That source we shall call "God." Thus the teleological argument moves from the specific character of specific features of the natural order, by analogy and sufficient reason, to a God who is the Designer and Maker.

All of the standard replies to sufficient-reason arguments are germane here, as you might expect. Is this particular sufficient ground for the world being the way it is the correct sufficient ground? Have we even considered the full variety of sufficient grounds there might be? Even if this argument does establish a designer adequate to design the world we have, is such a designer justifiably called "God"? Further, additional difficulties arise because of the way analogy is here employed. Consider:

1. The argument does not eliminate all the known alternatives. The whole point of evolutionary theory is to account for adaptation to

---

(London, 1802). A convenient excerpt can be found in Burrill, ed., *The Cosmological Arguments,* pp. 165–170. His account is inventive, often charming, and strangely persuasive.

[24]My high school biology teacher once told me that, given only a thumb, the whale would have ruled the earth in lieu of man. I misunderstood her, of course, and used to imagine all sorts of fanciful locations where a whale might sport such an appendage. The location, however, is the whole point. The opposable digit enables art and industry as well as written language. As Paley recognized, a thumb on his elbow would be of no use to man (or whales). The incomparable wisdom of the Maker, then, is shown even by the fact that our thumb grows where it does instead of some place else.

function in terms of random change and competitive "selection" instead of intentional design. Given the option of evolutionary explanation (and we certainly have that option today, even if Paley did not), we must have some grounds for eliminating it in favor of the Grand Designer alternative. If the point of the whole maneuver is the establishment of the existence of God, then the evolutionary option cannot be eliminated on theological grounds (on pain of obvious circularity). If the evolutionary option is to be eliminated, then it must be shown inadequate on independent grounds (perhaps it is ad hoc, sterile, and so on). It has not been so shown. So there is a known alternative sufficient ground.

2. Further, to establish the design hypothesis in any final way, we would have to eliminate some other alternatives, too—ones that we have not yet even conceived. The establishment of a sufficient-reason explanation involves enumerating all the options and eliminating all save one. Perhaps the world is the product of a design committee or a fugitive from Krypton. Perhaps it is but another projection from Dr. O's Braino machine. Nowhere near enough work has been done to conclude that the only viable sufficient source is some individual (and Divine) Maker.

3. Indeed, even if further labors did reveal that the only viable sufficient ground for the world-as-it-is is a single designer-maker, so that evolution and all other options could be convincingly eliminated, the question remains: "Is this designer-maker *God?*" All that a sufficient-reason argument can establish is a sufficient reason. If the whole gambit is legitimate, then the best that the occurrence of our world can establish is the prior occurrence of a designer-maker adequate to design and make our world. Such a designer and maker would, doubtless, put Tom Edison and Henry Ford to shame, but no "God" seems called for. A rudimentary Ba'al would do. Even if you seek a maker for the whole cosmos rather than our local world, there is still no necessity for all the innumerable characteristics that make the Central Figure of theism what It is—justice, mercy, wisdom, and so on.

4. Indeed, since the point of the argument is the "shape" of the world rather than the bare "occurrence" of the world, there is no reason to exclude the possibility that the designer is some portion (or the whole) of the world itself. The move to demand that the designer be separate is a move straight back to the cosmological argument and its attendant difficulties.

Consequently, we are obliged to conclude (on substantially the same grounds) that the teleological argument is no more effective than the cosmological one that we have already considered. If this is not enough, consider the two remaining special difficulties:

5. The teleological argument begins by calling attention to the fact that man has the ability to distinguish between that which is designed and that which is not. The conclusion of this argument, however, is that everything is designed. But if everything is designed, then there is no distinction to be drawn between that which is designed and that which is not. So the argument dissolves its own foundation.

6. If it is then argued that the ability-to-distinguish, on which the argument is built, is simply the ability to distinguish between what man has and has not made, and that the move to the universal design (that comes from another source) is by analogy, then we must have some basis for establishing the analogy between what man makes and what another source makes and between man's making and this source's making. But the ability to draw such an analogy presumes that man has at least some *direct* familiarity with both of the analogues.[25] But the point of the argument is to get us to God from our reflection on our experience of the world. But, unless God is part of the world, then the point of the argument makes it impossible that we have any direct familiarity with one of the analogues. But if we have no familiarity with one of the analogues, then we certainly do not have some familiarity with both of the analogues.

For all of its persuasiveness, consequently, I am obliged to conclude that the teleological argument for the existence of God is not at all adequate to establish God's existence. If this were the only evidence, then even if there is a God we would not know it. We *could* not know it, on this evidence, because it is now circular, now inconclusive, now irrelevant. Of course, one may still *believe* that there is a God; and, in terms of this argument, weave that belief into a complex explanation of the world's source and form. But believing is not knowing.

Value   The axiological argument for the existence of God is really two completely distinct arguments. Both, however, are special cases of the "sufficient-reasons" approach, and are heir to all that gambit's ills. The first is a variation on the teleological case.

When we look at the world, we do not find merely facts and events, blind and neutral forces. Rather, we find a world characterized throughout by the presence of value(s). Even as we must, in giving a sufficient

[25]The use of analogy in theological inference is crucial. A section is devoted to it, below. See p. 116ff.

explanation of the world, explain nuclear fusion, so, too, must we explain this appearance of value(s). Value is neither eliminable nor
self-explaining. Obviously, this calls for something more than some
primeval billiard ball bouncing the world-material into motion. What
is required is some kind of person, because the natural source of values
(intention, judgment, aspiration, and the like) is persons. So, in seeking the adequate ground of the world-as-it-occurs, we are driven to
something more specific than an uncaused cause, or even an undesigned
designer—we are driven, instead, to a source with all of the value-fund-
ing characteristics of a person who makes and designs. So, God again.[26]

But why not look at the world itself in personal terms if you are
obliged to make this kind of move? Why not make a Hegelian identification of the world-whole as a person, spirit, or mind, or any other
identification of the natural order and value—as humanists, naturalists,
and pantheists have always done? It is certainly an open option until
we are shown precisely what it is that forces the move to an external
sufficient reason.

For that matter, if an outside source is called for, no more than an
adequate outside source is required. The sufficient ground must be
adequate to provide what we have—not any more than what we have.
Even as in trying to provide an account for the "neutral" aspects of
the world, so in trying to provide an account for the "value" aspects
of the world: is there any need to move to the notions of infiniteness typically associated with the theistic solution? Could not some
very benevolent (but absolutely finite) person be adequate to the job?
The option of such a finite and benevolent source would have to be
excluded (for good reasons) before the theistic jump could be considered established.

Further, if we are going to argue from values to the occurrence of
some personal and evaluative first cause, let us remember that all values

---

[26]Notice the essential parallel to the other sufficient-reason arguments we have
already examined. If you press any of these arguments you fall immediately into
the three difficulties enumerated under the general heading and made explicit
for the cosmological and teleological forms examined above. They all begin with
the notion that an outside cause is required. They all then eliminate certain
options on what that outside cause might be. The teleological argument goes a
step further than the cosmological, specifying something about the character
of the Source (Designer as well as Maker). We have seen the difficulties attendant
thereon. The axiological argument goes another step, saying that Designing
Maker has further characteristics, lending a purposive, intentional, and evaluative
dimension. In each of these cases, the elaboration of the argument simply adds
some specificity to the basic maneuver. If the basic maneuver is flawed, therefore,
we should not expect the elaborations to stand.

must be taken into account. There must be argument to exclude the option of a primeval demon before we can settle on a primeval benefactor.

Further, and finally, do we in fact find values in the world? Is it not possible to cut under the axiological move completely by pointing out the possible option that all this "value" business is a case of reading into the natural order something that we might wish or hope was there, but which is (in fact) absent? Is not the presence of "value," itself, just as arguable as the presence of the "source" of it? (And if there is no value, then there is no need for a source of value.) This option, too, would have to be effectively eliminated (i.e., without begging all the questions) before the argument could be considered successful.

So, again, the argument does not consider all the options, does not eliminate the options it rejects, and moves to a more-than-sufficient ground for what it is trying to explain. This time, it may also read extraneous suppositions into what it is explaining,[27] while simply ignoring other parts of what it is explaining.[28] For all the usual reasons (and a few extra), then, it does not work.

The second argument from value takes a considerably more imaginative direction; but it is still sufficient reasons, all over again. In this (rather Kantian) case, sufficient reasons are given for a state of affairs which is itself hypothesized in order to come to terms with experience. This argument begins with the conviction that good and evil are both present in the world. It then adds the further premise that good is essentially superior to evil in every way. So, as a first conclusion, it is inferred that good must and will conquer evil sooner or later. However, an examination of the world will quickly show that good simply is not conquering evil here and now. Therefore, in order to satisfy the necessary triumph of good over evil, there must be a dimension to ultimate reality, time, and history that is beyond this apparent reality, time, and

---

[27] It is in this sense that the axiological argument is more an argument "to" value than "from" value. Exactly the same point is regularly made about the argument "from" design. Given a certain theistic stance, one may read value (and design) into the world. But it is frightfully difficult to take a value/purpose stance and infer God out of it. (This is not to say that one must be a theist in order to see value and/or purpose. Indeed, that there are other ways to see value and/or purpose is the whole point of asking the question "does this argument consider all the options?")

[28] The possible ignoring of the "source" of evil is, of course, no problem unless you are looking for sources. One who uses the sufficient-reason move, though, cannot consistently ignore any part of that for which sufficient reasons are sought. This is why so many have seen the "problem of evil" as crucial to standard theistic arguers. (On this, see below p. 90ff.)

history. In that dimension, the scales can be balanced, good may be brought to fruition, and evil can be finally put down. There must, then, once we assume the necessary victory of good, be a world "beyond" this one. At this point, all one need do is shift attention from this "apparent" world to that "ultimate" one, and connect all of the arguments from cause, and design, and occurrent value there. Having done so, one might come to the conclusion that there must be a causal, purposive, etc., figure who is responsible for governing and bringing everything to ultimate fruition in the ultimate world. That, of course, is God.

But, obviously, all of the arguments that work against the cosmological, teleological, and (first-form) axiological programs in the context of the apparent world, will work just as well against these programs when transplanted to an ultimate world. "Moving the game" should not alter the rules. Further, the notion of such an ultimate world is entirely suppositional, and is one to which we have not yet lent any clear meaning. Further, the notion that Good must triumph may very well be more wishful thinking than an accurate reading of the facts. Where is it written that good must win? What assurance do we have?[29] If we have no assurance, then on the basis of what fancy could we suggest that there has to be another world in which everything will be "made right" and that there must be a cause and designer and purposer within that world to make it happen?

There are, of course, many more arguments aimed at underwriting knowledge that a God exists. We cannot examine them all.[30] Some, indeed, are not worth examination.[31] There does remain, however, at least one more basic maneuver that the theist is likely to make with some effect.

Encounters   Many theists would say, "Of course none of these appeals

[29]You can argue this. Edwin Lewis has a very interesting argument on this topic in his *The Creator and the Adversary* (New York: Abingdon-Cokesbury 1948). It is a highly imaginative exercise in bringing good and evil to terms with a sort of theism, making good come out on top, etc. It even has an independent argument showing *why* good is inherently superior to evil (evil is parasitic and derivative). It is worth reading as an exercise in theological ingenuity; but it certainly is not demonstrative of how one can get from a neutral reading of the facts of experience to a concept of a standard God.

[30]An exceedingly thorough list of arguments is surveyed by Michael Scriven in his bristlingly skeptical chapter on God in *Primary Philosophy* (New York: McGraw-Hill, 1966), pp. 87–167.

[31]For example: "There must be a God because a lot of people believe there is and God would not let that many people believe in Him if it weren't so." In contrast to such "arguments," the ones we have examined don't look half bad.

to general experience, causation, design, and the like, will work; but that does not mean that we do not appeal to experience. It simply means that you have not located the correct experience to which we do appeal. What we do appeal to is the direct experience or encounter that occurs between the individual man and God. It is here that man, having met and confronted God, knows Him; not out of an experience of the world, but out of an experience of God." Such a thoroughly noninferential "direct encounter" stance is commonly advocated in evangelical Christendom. Indeed, in such circles, the notion of reaching theistic knowledge by means of inferences drawn from general experience would seem highly artificial. What is sought is not some discovery of the order of the universe from which a Designer, Maker, First Cause, or Final Arbiter may be distilled. Rather, the aim is for the individual to so structure his own life that "lightning may strike" and then wait for it to happen (i.e., encounter God, have the conversion experience, be made new, etc.).

A parallel may help. One can imagine a situation in which a freshman completed the academic year without meeting the president of the college. Does he know one exists? He might try all sorts of inferential arguments to try to settle the riddle. The college has a set of policies and parietal rules. Policies and rules must come from someone. It is unlikely, however, that such reflection would settle the issue firmly. Obviously, the thing for our freshman to do is to arrange to meet the president. Then he will know. But there is a problem here.[32] How do you know whom you are meeting when you meet someone? In ordinary circumstances, of course, we know "by authority." That is, we are introduced by someone who already knows. But behind introductions there are more basic identification procedures. Primarily, we identify people in terms of their roles and behavior. We see this man preside at faculty meetings. Then we see him leading the academic parade. Then putting the arm on a wealthy alumnus. Then expelling an unkempt sophomore. And so on. We would have been sure all along that we had met someone; but not until the network of actions and roles is fixed can we be sure just who the someone is.

Returning to the theist's identification procedures: just what is it that clinches the identification of the one encountered as God? It is difficult to say. Some suggest that later, after you die, you will have His identity retroactively confirmed. But it may not be any easier then than now. Assuming resurrection, which is, at least, arguable, someone

---

[32]Indeed, there are several possible problems. One can imagine it to be a Kafkaesque search in some schools. The problem that concerns us, though, is one that remains even when the "President" is found in the flesh.

may introduce you; but that is only shorthand for an appeal (sooner
or later) to what "He" does. But what could this Figure do that would
settle Who He is? Three points:

   1. Whatever we see Him do, our final identification will be based on
some substantial assortment of observed actions over a period of time.
The meeting itself is not self-guaranteeing.

   2. Our final identification of some individual as God (in terms of the
activities we observe) presupposes the prior specification of "what it
takes" to rate that classification. Encounter-classification is an interpretive move that requires a logically prior set of rules. No encounter
is self-interpreting.

   3. It takes a great deal to rate the classification "God." If we fall back
on the criteria used in the arguments we have already examined
(World Maker, First Cause, etc.), we run the substantial risk of over-
rating what is encountered. You cannot get from the data to a more-
than-sufficient cause. Nor can you get from an encounter to a more-
than-sufficient classification.

   The point of these three points is simply that while an encounter
may initiate human knowledge of Divine existence, it does not establish it. Having initiated it, it leaves us in the midst of all the problems
and difficulties of the arguments we have already considered. So we
have not advanced.

   Indeed, to the extent that the encounter in question has to be retroactively confirmed in "eschatalogical" experience, we have regressed.
This "eschatalogical" experience is just as suppositional as the argument
it is being used to reinforce. As such, it does not help much. If the encounters could be interpreted and classified in terms of our present
experience, then we might gain knowledge from them. But to achieve
that it would be necessary to stipulate that the activities and behaviors
that earn the title "God" fall comfortably within the range of standard
human perception. If that is allowed, then some evidence of the existence
of God would be possible (in exactly the same way that evidence of
the existence of the president of the college is possible). The question
would then really be open to empirical and rational settlement. However, this also opens the door to possible empirical and rational refutation. But theists are not commonly willing to stipulate that "the
activities and behaviors that earn the title 'God' fall comfortably within
the range of standard human perception." So the whole gambit is
broken-backed.

Transcendence and the A Posteriori Arguments   Again and again,
evidence offered against a posteriori existence arguments is met with
the bristling assertion of Divine Transcendence. I cannot postpone

examining this notion any longer; for if it is effective in *this* role, it is identically effective (and for the same reasons) in pulling the plug on any a posteriori God-talk whatever.

Clearly, the God that theists talk about is more than some vague "I know not what." He is, indeed, endowed in their discussions with a fairly explicit character. But this can generate problems if He is also deemed to "transcend." Because of this, some medieval writers who affirmed and emphasized the transcendence of God went on to say that we cannot say anything affirmative about His specific character— that, due to God's transcendence, the best we can do is to make negative references to what His character is not.[33]

Certainly, the supposition of transcendence militates against any a posteriori and/or empirical existence proof, if it does not bar it altogether. There are two surface problems:

1. Giving sense to the notion of passing with understanding from the idea that something "transcends" to the idea of what it is that "transcends."

2. Giving sense to the notion of discovering, *a fortiori* showing, that the designatum of the last line of some argument (say, the cosmological) is transcendent as well as characterized by the attributes exploited in the argument proper (say, unmoved-moverness). Both these cramps arise in trying to give sense to the notion that discernible, describable attributes and transcendence can consistently be attached to the same *X*.

To sort such matters out with any success, we must get clear on what "transcending" might amount to. I think that we can specify at least three different main notions of what it is to "transcend." I shall get at these by constructing a number of case-stories where one or another use of "transcends" or "transcendence" makes sense. Once such possibilities are spelled out, with examples, we should be able more clearly to see where the apparent difficulties in the notion of a transcendent-but-characterized *X* are only apparent, and where they are, in fact, uneliminable. Then we can make a reasonable judgment on whether appeals to transcendence hurt or help the notion of theistic cognition.

Let us begin by considering some different animals' systems of perception. Dogs can see only in shades of gray.[34] So we might say that

---

[33]And, perhaps, make some analogical claims while noting the incompleteness of the analogies. There are interesting problems here. See below, p. 116ff.

[34]I believe that this is, in fact, so. Even if it is not, we can assume it for the purposes of argument. The rods and cones are not present in the appropriate way. The dogs do not respond to tests in the way that they would if they could color-discriminate.

color "transcends" ("goes beyond" or "does not fall within") the dogs'
discriminatory and perceptual capacities. Generally: X transcends Y if X
is beyond the grasp or discernment of Y in some unremediable way. (In our
example, *colors* transcend *dogs*.) I shall call this the Transcendence of
Otherness or transcendence$_1$.

This situation, if genuine, is not one of which Y can likely speak. *We*
might say, "Behold the dog, whom color transcends!" But dogs are
blocked. Rin Tin Tin was never known to say, "Ah, all that I see is in
shades of gray; would God that I could see in color." Dogs not only do
not say that—I venture they cannot because they cannot think it. It is
doubtful that dogs are even aware *that* they are so transcended; and it
is certain that they do not know just *how* they are transcended.

Noting that colors transcend$_1$ dogs, we may go on to ask, "Is there
anything that transcends us the way colors transcend dogs?" But we
can do little more than wonder, on the account given so far. For, to
the extent that some X did transcend us in the way that colors transcend dogs (T_1), the character of that X would be quite inaccessible
to our experience and comment. To the extent that some X is accessible
to the experience and comment of some Y, the X just does not tran-
scend$_1$ Y.

Now imagine a society of dogs that have developed intelligence to a
sufficient level that they have a culture—have organized themselves,
are constructing artifacts, making tools, and the like. But they still
have no color vision. Further, imagine that their locale is also populated
by horses—no less intelligent, versatile, and cultured, and *with* color
vision. As the scales of the two societies develop, the dogs will become
aware that horses can do some things that they cannot. They would
discern that at times horses "talk" on topics or in terms they do not
grasp. At best, the dogs might give pragmatic content to the puzzle
conversations, to the extent that the horses perform some tasks more
effectively than dogs.[35] But, even at the point of suspecting that horses
are perceptually endowed in some special way, the dogs still would
not be able to spell out the nature of that endowment. What dogs cannot by their nature share, they may neither describe nor comprehend.
What is beyond is beyond.

So far: looking at an imaginary situation from the outside, I have
tied one working role to "transcends," dubbing it the Transcendence
of Otherness. One of the implications of this suggestion is that

[35]In fact, in order for the horses to genuinely convince the dogs that they
possess a range of perception that dogs lack, they would have to be able to
produce some such distinctive "output." Otherwise, the dogs would dismiss the
puzzle conversations as "mere talk."

"transcendent," so understood, would have only limited and nonsymmetric use "from the inside." The transcender can be far more explicit than the transcendee. The limited use available to the transcendee amounts generally to his admission "There are things going on around here that I do not understand." So used, the label is not an explanation, but an indicator that there is no explanation known. Even when used by the "superior" party, the label does not explain the character of whatever they possess and others lack. (Perhaps the "superiors" can explain it, but only to each other in language the "inferiors" cannot understand.)

The same sort of case can be made for situations in which some individual or group is itself indiscernible to some other individual or group. If ghosts observe men, but men cannot observe ghosts, terms like "transcendent" could abbreviate an explicit narrative for the ghosts; but it would only mark qualms of inexplicable limitation for the men. As, in the dog/horse case, the dogs may affirm (on the basis of performances) that horses have a capacity to discern something which transcends the perceptions of the dogs (but cannot affirm just what that something is), so men might here come to say: "there are agents at work in the world whose effects we discern but whose agency is beyond our ken; they transcend us and they transcend our grasp."

Grounded in the discovery of bona fide inexplicable states of affairs, or of observed performances the agency of which is unknown, a transcendee can talk about either agents or events being beyond him (even as the dogs wondered at and commented upon the horses' cleverness). The grounding is in the performance or output that demands the supposition of undiscerned agents or unshared capacities. But it entitles no license to say what these agents or events or capacities might be. So, while "transcendent$_1$" can have use with regard to a range of situations, its use is neither trouble-free nor transparent.

Further, it is not at all clear just which discerned performances or "outputs" really *demand* the supposition of new agents, etc., to be added to all the suppositions that we ordinarily make in order to string our experiences together. The ancient principle of metaphysical economy encourages caution here. Further still, we must remember that any distinction made between agents-so-supposed is not only based on, but *amounts to,* the distinction between the discernibles that elicit the move. The agent behind tipping tables is just that: the tipping-tables-agent. Finally, we must observe the gap between "undiscerned agent" and "indiscernible agent"—the difference, for example, between ghosts we do not observe and ghosts we cannot observe. Clearly, one can use transcendent$_1$ in either case; but, equally clearly, the notion is

full-fleshed only when it is *per principium*. Consequently, it will be useful to make a further distinction: I shall call those things that are only
circumstantially beyond one "transcendent$_2$," or say that they are
characterized by the Transcendence of Darkness, and reserve the label
T$_1$ for cases of necessity.

In any new case of ungrasped data, it is initially open whether T$_1$ or
T$_2$ is involved. Consider a situation where we might note (and remark)
the fact that some dimension of our surroundings transcends (in some
sense) our discrimination, discernment, and/or comprehension: Suppose
that you walk into the commons and find two men in heated debate.
Another observer tells you that they are arguing the correct interpretation of Onkwitz's general theory of ramified danglers. He says, further,
that the crucial issue is whether or not ergwhats dangle in W*. Suppose,
then, that the argument resumes—leaving you, if not any ergwhats,
dangling. Now it is not at all clear that the niceties of ramified danglers
would escape you of natural necessity. I have no reason to think that
ramified danglers *by their nature* are beyond your grasp *by your nature*.
There are many things we *do* not grasp that, given a virtuous expendi-
ture of labor, we *could* grasp.

In the case at hand, you certainly have reason to think that something is going on; and you may even have some suspicion of what. If
you can and do get clear, then we have a case of T$_2$ resolving into
understanding. But if you never get clear, then there is more ground
to suspect a case of T$_2$ resolving into T$_1$. Of course, even if the case
is strictly T$_1$, you may still grasp that there is something going on; but
to the extent that you do not grasp *what it is,* all you can say is,
"There is something going on that I don't understand." If you could
say any more than that, it just would not be "beyond" you (and, so,
not T$_1$).

I have used this example because it is sufficiently close to home to
be plausible. It is not, however, a close parallel to our dog and horse
story, for it does not deal with straight discrepancies, apparent or
genuine, in sensory capacity. Lest we be diverted by this, it should
be noted that other (and only slightly less plausible) stories can be constructed that do preserve it. For that matter, many real performances
have occurred that have brought men to affirm unshared capacities
and unknown (and even unknowable) agents. They run a gamut from
the Russian lady's putative elbow-reading, through Edgar Cayce's
diagnoses and predictions, and on as far as either credulity or test and
confirmation will carry us into a world of spirits, ghosts, demons,
angels, poltergeists, and (eventually) Gods, as agents behind tipping
tables, visions, transports, and (eventually) the world as all-that-is-so.

In all these cases, "transcendent" appears to play a role in the construction of explanations. But any such "explanation" is marked by several distinct liabilities.

First, it tends to terminate inquiry unjustifiably. It may be no great hardship that a neighbor takes "it has something in it" as an informative and terminal explanation of aspirin's easing pain, but we expect more of the pharmacologist. To terminate inquiry with such an "explanation" is an admission of ignorance and an exercise in sloth. This easily occurs in "transcendent power" explanations as we pass gently from "We don't know what is happening here" to "There is an Unknowable Agent at work here." Admitting ignorance keeps us humble, but making a virtue of ignorance, by shifting T_2 to T_1 unnecessarily, is pernicious.

Second, there seems to be an inbuilt tendency toward collapsing all explanations in terms of transcendent agents into one case of the Transcendent Agent. But not all who die of unknown causes die of the same cause. "The unknown cause" is not on the killer list with heart disease and cancer. It is admittedly difficult to differentiate one unknown agent from another.[36] But one can individuate agents in terms of *how* they do what they do, even if their own character is quite veiled. For this reason, we do not lump cases of crib-death syndrome and multiple sclerosis together, even though the final output is the same (death) and the ultimate agents indistinguishable (unknown).

Such difficulties occur in intensified form in theistic talk. Assuming that the closure of argument involved in the move from "unknown" to "unknowable" is justified, and assuming that we have good reason for narrowing the set to the one Unknowable Agent, how and why can we come to call It *God*? And how could we justify those two assumptions? There is yet another difficulty in attributing specific characteristics to that which is already affirmed "beyond our grasp." A difficulty of consistency. Yet, clearly, the Transcendent One whom the theist may affirm as wholly other (T_1, ineffable, other and beyond) is also said to keep watch in love over His own, and to create, sustain, and adjudicate the entire natural order. If not all this (and more), then surely not *God*; but if all this (and more), then how *transcendent*$_1$? Any attempt to construct arguments based in human experience and aimed at proving that a T_1 God exists is utterly futile unless the argu-

---

[36]It would be even more so in the case of unknowable agents. If they are, indeed, unknowable, it would seem that no characterization is possible; and, hence, any individuation is whimsical.

ment-maker is content to begin with inexplicables and end with some such statement as "There is something unknowable behind these inexplicables." But that is unlikely, for it is quite obscure what religious function might be performed by the reification of some "ineffable somewhat" behind each unexplained or unexplainable event.

In theistic settings, then, it appears that the notion of T_1 is especially problem-producing, over and above the general problems that adhere to transcendence-in-general. Should the religionist, then, limit the transcendence he attributes to God to T_2, perhaps? It is not entirely alien to the setting. Everyone knows the "now in a glass darkly, but then face to face" verse, and many have affirmed that we will "understand it better by and by." Perhaps the attribution of transcendence to God is merely the admission that *now* He escapes our grasp, discernment, perception, and understanding—but that *per accidens* and not forever. Does this lessen the strain?

1. If the opacity, which is now by assumption *per accidens* is clearable by effort on our part (as, say, the opacity of organic chemistry is clearable for me by me), there is one problem: what sense can I give to the notion that a once-opaque-but-now-cleared-by-my-effort X is *God*? How can a *mysterium tremendum* that is by my effort no longer *mysterium,* but only *tremendum,* be the holy object of my worshipful veneration?

2. If the opacity is clearable by Divine act, there are other problems. Either it clears by a change in God (bringing Himself within our grasp) or by a change in us (endowing us with capacities we now lack, to understand what is now beyond us). The former will not do, for it is not only a change in God, but also a lowering (a Divine Mark-down Sale). Further, the latter will not do, for now it is not man understanding God, but only some X that is historically related to man understanding God. Whether God brings Himself into our present grasp, or magnifies our grasp until it can encompass Him, in neither case do we have man *qua* man grasping God *qua* God. So in neither case can *man* rightly say of *God,* "He is transcendent and loving, creative, etc."

3. Perhaps, however, natural man has fallen from grace and can by grace return to a state in which he can "see" God (the scales having fallen away from his eyes). But then: in his back-in-grace state he could only say, "loving, creative, and once transcendent"; and out of the state he could only say, "There may be something going on I don't understand."

So, I conclude, T_2 poses equal problems of coherent predication to those of T_1; plus, I must add, a theological equivocation. Is the opacity of God to man merely contingent? Surely, if transcendence is a Divine

essential, it is as essential on the other side of Jordan as it is in this
present wicked world. And what accidental properties has a God? So
the Transcendence of Darkness will not do what needs to be done.

Can, perhaps, the strain be eased by filling in our alternative option
(T_1, the Transcendence of Otherness) in less-stark terms? Perhaps a
"partial" T_1 would carry the necessary freight and be less constraining
to theism-in-practice.

Consider the case of a man who is red-green colorblind. He can make
some color distinctions. Still, the dimensions of his color perceptions
are limited when compared to those of ordinary people. Ordinary perception includes, but surpasses, his.[37] The realm of color partially
transcends him.

A parallel notion can be worked out for entities that occasionally or
dimensionally escape our grasp or perception. One example would be
a specter that is discernible only when the temperature is right (who
"comes and goes" with the weather). Another would be a being that,
with regard to certain aspects of its nature, transcends$_1$ man, but which,
with regard to other aspects, is humanly accessible. Or, returning briefly to dogs and horses, we may note that colors are not only accessible
to the horses, they are also among the properties that the horses display. For this reason, not only do colors generally transcend$_1$ the perception of dogs, but also horses (who are colored) transcend$_1$ the
perception of dogs in one, but not all, of their aspects. So, while there
are some things about horses that dogs can directly know, there is at
least one thing about them that dogs cannot directly know. Similarly,
there is one thing about the poinsettia plant that our red-green colorblind man cannot directly know; viz., that the leaves vary in color from
the bracts. So the lowly poinsettia transcends$_1$ our sample man in one
of its aspects.

But, where there is partial transcendence, there is still a limit, even if
intermittent or isolated. Staying with the perception cases, even though
one was aware of the limit and aware of performance disabilities linked
to it, one still would not in any sense perceive beyond the limit, whatever it is. If our colorblind man could genuinely *perceive* the difference
between red and green, then he would not be red-green colorblind. It
is not the transcendence that is partial. Rather, part of the color realm
transcends his visual capacities, and part does not. The part that transcends simply transcends. *It* is not partial. The label "partial transcen-

---

[37]Such an individual can often coordinate the patterns of his own perception
with the color talk of ordinary men so that it takes sophisticated tests to determine that he is limited. Still, for all the coordination, the limit is there.

dence" only indicates that the gaps have limits. The gaps are still gaps.

So, if one wanted to say that God was partially transcendent$_1$ (i.e., transcendent in some aspects, but not in others), he could go on to talk about (or argue for) God in whatever aspects did not transcend. But in those areas (whatever they might be, and we could have no notion at all of what they might be) where the transcendence of God was maintained, the transcendee's silence would still be required for consistency's sake.

But, is it those aspects of God that transcend or those that do not, that make God *God*? If the former are necessary, then all that a posteriori proofs and experience could reach would be those aspects of God that do not settle His divinity. There would be no clear grounds for thinking that what they did reach were aspects of *God*. And, if only the latter were necessary, then traditional Christian theology at any rate is just mistaken in not treating the transcendence of God as incidental to His godhood. So partial transcendence hurls us back into the same difficulties encountered with transcendence unqualified.

Perhaps, even as certain aspects of a partially transcendent God are accessible through plain reason and experience, the remaining (transcendent) parts are also accessible, but now only by (say) "revelation." Then "transcendent" could be read as "not accessible by natural means." This re-poses some problems already seen, for again it appears to depend upon either the Divine Mark-down Sale or the Transformation of Man into Something Else. We still would not have a case of man *qua* man knowing and being able to say of God *qua* God, "transcendent *and* good, wise, etc." But, perhaps, that is not really too serious. Why should not it be that by the transforming power of grace man might be so refashioned as to know what was, in his natural state, "beyond him"? But there is still a rub; for is it not the case that God, if He transcends at all, transcends even transformed men (former men)? If so, then all the problems remain; and, if not, then how is God *God* to the transformed?

Another possibility is that men, alongside of those nontranscendent aspects of God they *do* perceive or grasp, "feel" the weight of "something more." Thus, perhaps, while we know of God that He is straightforwardly wise, good, etc., we also know (feel?) that "this is not all." And, furthermore, it is this feeling of *more* that brings us to say not just "wise," "good," etc., but also *God*. But this poses a problem of its own. First of all, the "more," as it stands, is contentless. It thus seems quite rash to label the nucleus of "*more* feelings" *God*. It also partakes of the collapsing of unknowns into one and personifying them as The Unknown. But could this not be remedied by filling in the "*more* feelings" by means of the experience of special men (saints, Apostles, etc.)? Not effectively, because (1) if the special men were yet truly men, they partook of the same problems of getting at the beyond that we do; and (2) if they were only quasi-men, so that what is beyond to us was not beyond to them, then there is no more reason to think that what they have to say will fill in our "*more* feelings" than to think that what horses have to say will fill in the dogs' "*more* feelings" on seeing a sunset. The appeal to saints, *et al.,* nicely transplants the problem into the recesses of the past, but transplanting a problem is not solving it.

Thus, I do not find that partial transcendence is any real improvement over transcendence unqualified. If the transcendence of God is the transcendence of otherness (T_1), then either all or part of what we keep trying to say in theism cannot be said. The Transcendence of Otherness, partial or unqualified, is too austere, even as the Transcendence of Darkness is demeaning.

Perhaps all that the theist really means when he says that God is transcendent-and-characterizable is just that He is *very* grand and impressive in all His characteristics. "Transcendent," then, slides into "transcendently . . .," a kind of adverb of magnification. Call this the Transcendence of Heft (T_3). We certainly use the word "transcendent" this way sometimes, and it need have *no* overtones of mystery. Perhaps we once saw the young Nureyev dance, and on leaving the theater murmured, "Wasn't that transcendent." If so, we certainly would not have meant that the performance was "wholly other" or beyond the grasp of humans; rather, that it was magnificent, marvelous, impressive, uplifting, better-than-we-ever-thought-possible. But quite immanent. We were there and we did see him dance. If the performance had not fallen within the dimensions of human perception, there would have been little point in paying ten dollars a seat and going. When I urged my friend to attend the next night, I surely did not urge upon him an evening of "watching indiscernibles."

T_3 operates as a kind of absolute magnifier, and could be applied to any quality, attribute, or thing. Certainly the serious theist does talk about certain characteristics that are said to be absolutely magnified in God: goodness, wisdom, and power, to name three. It is even said that "His goodness transcends our goodness," clearly indicating magnification. So this is at least part of what is said when theists say that God transcends.

If this were all that was meant, then the transcendence claim would be effectively clear of the problems that have heretofore occupied us. The trout would be out of the soup; we would no longer be taxed with trying to make sense of "God is good, wise, loving, and also utterly beyond the discernment of man—ineffable, inaccessible, other." But, of course, even if we do use "transcends" this way after concerts, and even if this is some part of its force when men speak of God, this is not the whole of it. For, even when we say that "God is transcendently good" means "God's goodness is maximal and absolute," we also always go on to say, "and, furthermore, His goodness is not like ours, for He is not like us, His ways are not our ways, He is the Holy One." And there we are again: caught between silence and predication, driven to characterize the uncharacterizable. To think that talk of God involves only the Transcendence of Heft is to exercise oneself in cheap and desperate anthropomorphism. What, then, shall we do?

We can, of course, bite the bullet. The Christian tradition, especially, is disposed to do just that. It affirms, explicitly, that God is entirely Both. No intermittent winking in and out, and no mere magnification. God is known *and* transcendent$_1$. And thus the paradox of saying the unsayable is affirmed along with the paradox of a "wholly other" who is "wise, good, and strong." Must this be the final stop? If so, it calls for a decision, sooner or later, on how we shall react to apparent inconsistencies in serious argument and inquiry. In all our ordinary, everyday situations, we worry at them—vigorously indicting ourselves for having failed to gather sufficient evidence or construct sufficiently viable theories to reconcile the apparent inconsistencies into some kind of intelligible order. We could react the same way here. On the other hand, we could take paradox in religious contexts as the mark of profoundness and successful insight. But, if we were to make them the signs of success in religion, we would need to work up some grounds and reasons for the move; and I, for one, cannot imagine what such grounds and reasons might be. I wouldn't deny that there might be some; but I would note early on that when "truth" is pursued in a cloud of unresolved paradox, the argument disappears. If you buy contradictions, you sell logic. Maybe that is the thing to do; but I suspect that silence is better.

But there are those who say that this is to chain God to the Moloch of Logic; that God is above all that; that God is *really* transcendent. Call this the Transcendence of Murk. It may well be that the grander and higher some idea is, the more difficult it is for us to understand it or to know that it is true. But devotees of the transcendence of murk seem to be going for the converse. But where is it written that the more difficult to understand some idea or claim, or to know that it is true, the higher and better it is?

I have distinguished three working notions of transcendence: Otherness, Darkness, and Heft. I have tried to show that the latter two are essentially inadequate in theism in that they essentially degrade God or trade upon an equivocation between the understanding of natural man and that of "man transformed." I have concluded, then, that the core use of "transcends" for theism must be in the Transcendence of Otherness. But I have noted that this blocks the use of any kind of empirical argument. It may be impossible, then, to maintain serious theism on an empirical base. But that suggests that it is irrelevant to ordinary human affairs. The notion(s) of transcendence, then, even while shielding the arguments from evidential refutation, undercuts the possibility of any relevant (much less coercive) a posteriori theistic proof or cognition.

Summary

We have examined many different arguments that have been used to try to show that men know that there is a God. First, we considered the a priori approach in several slightly different forms. But we found that the best that they could do was to show that whatever Gods there may be are uncontingent; and that does not determine whether there are any or not. Then we considered quite a variety of a posteriori arguments—from causes, from design, from value, etc. But we found that all of these are variations on one basic "sufficient-reasons" approach, and that this approach fails to prove enough. Even if they did establish an uncaused cause, a world maker, and a value arbiter, they leave us far short of the establishment of the sort of God that theism propounds. For that matter, we saw that they do not really establish such causes, makers, and arbiters, because they do not effectively eliminate alternative and equally sufficient explanations. Then, we considered the notion of divine encounters, and found enough trouble with their interpretation to discount the notion that they generate unambiguous beliefs, much less cognitions. Finally, we took a close look at the notion(s) of transcendence, and saw that even as it insulates a posteriori arguments from counterevidence, it equally insulates them from any use.

You should not get the impression that the point of all this is to show that no God exists. The verdict that we have reached so far is a Scottish verdict—not proved. What we have shown is simply that on the arguments examined, one may not claim to *know* there is a God. There could still be one without our knowing. Or there might not be one, and we might know that somehow. The next section covers that. The factual question of God's existence is still entirely open and is not even our question. Our question is about our *knowledge* of Divine existence. We are halfway to an answer.

KNOWLEDGE THAT NO GOD EXISTS

We have looked at all sorts of arguments intended to demonstrate that God does exist, thus underwriting affirmative theistic knowledge. Now it is time to turn the coin over and look at some arguments which purport to demonstrate that there is no God, thus underwriting negative theistic knowledge. The arguments, at least in principle, could be either a priori or a posteriori.

An A Priori Appeal and a Rejoinder

It has already been argued that a priori arguments about what does or does not exist are, in fact, arguments about the descriptive capacity of assertion-attempts. A successful affirmative one locates "those claims that are so vacuous that they fit any and all worlds whatever," and a successful negative one locates "claims that are so flawed for descriptive purposes that they are sterile." An "ontological" proof of the nonexistence of God, then, would be a demonstration that the term "God" has a sufficiently inconsistent definition that it can find no coherent application. The term "God," of course, is not here taken as a proper name, but as a title, the legitimate use of which is predicated on the satisfaction of some coherent list of qualifications.

Consider the title "generalissimo." It is suitably applied to one who can be described as "most supreme commander of a military or paramilitary force, typically that of a nation-state but sometimes an insurgent body." There are no inconsistencies in the qualifications, so "generalissimo" could be legitimately used if the occasion ever arises. (Whether that occasion ever arises, of course, is a matter of fact to be settled in experience.) But consider the definition of the title "zoltar": "male enuch from birth, mother of two sons, ambidextrous, limbless, and still-born." There are so many inconsistencies in the qualifications that "zoltar" cannot be coherently used. The qualifications cancel out. There might also be titles that are sufficiently vacuous to have universal application. Consider "bumblelope": "a member of either the class of all carbuncles or of the class of all noncarbuncles." Since the two classes are complementary, then the title can be used for anything whatever.

An a priori argument for the nonexistence of God would amount to a demonstration that the title "God" is the same sort of title as "zoltar." There is some basis for saying that it is. As the title is used, it purports to mark One Who is omnipotent, omniscient, totally benevolent, perfectly just, perfectly merciful, the creator of all that is or ever will be, the sustainer of the natural order, the final arbiter of value, infinite in all regards, totally "other," noncontingent, worthy of absolute worship, and so on. In specific contexts, He is also said to be: jealous, retributive, holy, open to supplication and entreaty, and the like. It could be argued that the inconsistencies are abundant. Consider the combination of "creator-sustainer" and "final arbiter" along with "perfectly just." There is a strain. There is even greater strain in the combination of total transcendence and moral relevance.

Thus one might conclude that we know there is no God, because we know that the title "God" has no consistent use. There are some possible rejoinders, however:

1. God is infinite and cannot be captured in or confined to the limits of logic. To attempt this is to place logic above God, which is blasphemous. The main thing wrong with this rejoinder is that it is viciously question-begging. It assumes the existence of God in order to dismiss objections to the assertion of that existence.[38]

2. The qualifications only appear to be contradictory; but, in fact, are perfectly consistent. Certainly, "totally just" and "final arbiter" and "creator of everything" do not display collective complementarity in the direct way that "carbuncular" and "noncarbuncular" do. Add "avenging," however, and the list is rather harder to reconcile. It is the whole set that makes the real problems. And if it is argued that the reconciliation cannot come clear now (but must wait for eschatalogical illumination), then one would be obliged to note that there is no way to use the title now, either.

3. The list of qualifications suggested is arbitrary and unjustified. It may be inconsistent; but it is not the right list. The right list would have no such defects. This may be so, but a correct list-that-nobody-has is not very helpful. Besides, we are trying to find out if the title is coherent *as it is used*. The fact that we might coherently use a homonym, on the basis of some qualification list not yet specified, is irrelevant.

4. God is transcendent. Consequently, none of the labels that we attach to earthly affairs describes Him univocally. The inconsistencies we find in the qualifications for the title are predicated upon an ordi-

[38]Further, given a legitimate use for the title, *is* God above logic? See below, pp. 132–134.

nary understanding of the expression of those qualifications. But this
is improper. These expressions do not apply to God like they do to
men, affairs, and things. We have no way of knowing what the necessary character of God might be, for He transcends our experience,
thought, and comprehension.

This, of course, is question-begging, the way the first rejoinder was.
Even dismissing that (after all, maybe circularity is all right in the
transcendent realm), if no one knows what the necessary character of
God might be, then no one knows whether there is a God or not.
Decide whether "quampliote" has legitimate use without settling its
conditions of application. You can't.

I reach two conclusions: First, if Divine Transcendence is maintained, then the theist has his defense against assertions of knowing
there is no God. This defense has a high price. By insisting on transcendence, the theist would appear to move the question of God's
existence outside the realm of possible knowledge either way. Second,
if Divine Transcendence is not maintained, then the theist must either
admit that qualifications for the title "God" are inconsistent (and yield
to the atheist), lay claim to some eschatological clarification and reconciliation (and yield to the skeptics' charge of irrelevance), or plead the
proper use of some alternative list (and change the subject). The very
best result the theist can obtain is that we do not know there is no
God—on the very same grounds that we do not know there is one. A
priori arguments against the existence of God may be met, then—yielding the same Scottish verdict we obtained on the affirmative side; but
meeting them opens the way to numerous and serious charges that God
(if one there be) has no relevant connection to the human situation.

A Posteriori Appeals and Rejoinders

The arguments are all basically *modus tollens*.[39] Consider: If that beast
is a Welsh corgi, then it is a mammal. But, in that it has scales, lays eggs,
is cold-blooded, has no mammary glands, and is limbless, that beast is
not a mammal. So it isn't a Welsh corgi, either. Consider another: If
there were free water vapor in the atmosphere of Saturn, then its photo-
spectrograph would show line pattern 42. But the only line pattern
you get is 57. So there is no free water vapor there. The argument form
is applied in the appraisal of theism by asking, first, "What would follow

[39]*P* implies Q, but Q is false. Therefore, *P* is false, too. This is a perfectly valid
argument form with countless substitution instances. Since the form is valid,
whether the conclusion in a given case is true will depend wholly on the truth
value of the premises.

if there were a God?" The implications of Divine existence spell out the "if P then Q" line of the argument. Then we would examine the world to see whether or not the implications are, in fact, true. If we find that they are not, and if our analysis of the implications of Divine existence is accurate, then we could conclude, "There is no God."[40]

The most likely question to be raised at this point is "How do you fill in that 'if P then Q' line of the argument?" One must, of course, avoid filling in the line improperly because then, in spite of the fact that the argument form is valid, he would have no assurance that the conclusion was true. If someone were to say, "If there were a God I would be King of the World; but I am not King of the World, so there is no God," the trouble would be in his first premise, not in his logic. But how does one determine what the implications of Divine existence would be?

At the very least we must table any private notions that we might have about the implications of Divine existence and turn, instead, to the concept of God as it occurs and is used in commonplace theistic discourse. We should expect disagreement to increase as a function of increasing detail. We might also expect a certain amount of hedging if and when some specified implications show themselves unfulfilled in actual fact. But if we confine ourselves to basics, some affirmative implications should come clear.

Since among theists the common notion is that anything worth calling God is at least (a) the creator of everything, (b) perfectly good, and (c) unlimited in both intelligence and skill, we are perfectly justified in asserting, "If there is a God, then there must be a beneficent design and order to the structure of the world." It is very difficult to sort this out in anything like satisfactory detail; nevertheless, it is regularly agreed that (whatever the details may be) if God is by definition perfectly wise, perfectly good, and perfectly powerful, then whatever He has made would have to be the best of its kind possible. Further, if God is deemed to be the Creator of everything that is, then everything must be the best of its kind possible. Specifically, the world must be the best of *its* kind: "If there is a God, then the world is the best of all

---

[40] Of course if he found that Q was true, nothing conclusive would have been proved. An argument of the form "if P then Q, Q, therefore P" is fallacious. It does not follow. You cannot say, "If this is a Welsh corgi, then it is a dog," look at it and discover that it is a dog, and then infer, "Therefore it is a Welsh corgi." The reason you cannot do this is that it might be a dog without being a Welsh corgi. It might be a Pomeranian, a Great Dane, or a Chihuahua. Negative results shoot down an hypothesis. Affirmative results may give it some support, but they do not establish it.

possible worlds." If there were some way in which the world could be better than it is, then surely a perfectly wise, perfectly good, and perfectly powerful Creator would have made it that way. Consequently, if the world is found to be less than the best of its kind, it cannot be of God's making. Either it was not made at all, or somebody else did it, neither of which is compatible with the existence of an all-wise, all-good, all-powerful Maker of everything. So, if the world has flaws, God (as defined) does not exist, (i.e., nothing that does exist deserves the title "God").

But, are there ways in which the world falls short of perfection of kind? Are there conceivable ways in which the world might be improved? Many people are convinced that there are many. They cite three main kinds of events: evils, natural disasters, and the occurrence of disorder and/or dysfunction. Any rejoinder is obliged to take the form of a denial that evils, natural disasters, and disorder and/or dysfunction occur, or else a denial that such affairs are incompatible with Divine existence.

The General Pattern of Argument and Rejoinder   Consider the case of the man who was plowing his cornfield one day in a long-established agricultural area of Mexico. (I read about this when I was in grammar school.) So far as anyone knows, he was an ordinary sort of fellow and was going about his work in a perfectly ordinary way, walking along behind his mule and thinking whatever is apt in such circumstances. Suddenly, a great chasm opened in the ground and a stream of lava burst forth from the earth—a gout of gas and flame.

To the best of my recollection, the farmer was in the other end of his cornfield, escaping with singed eyebrows and a good scare. It was a near call. Isn't this a case where the chain of events that make up the world is open to some improvement? But if it is open to any improvement at all, then either there is no God, or else the existence of God does not entail perfection-of-kind for the world He made and sustains.

Or, if near ones don't move you or suggest the possibility of improvement, consider the great earthquakes of the New Madrid, Missouri, valley in the nineteenth century, or in Lisbon long ago, or Chile or Alaska just lately. Do not these lethal orgies of geological violence suggest minimally that the world is "out of control" in spots, or never was "in control" to begin with? But neither suggestion seems compatible with the minimal implications of Divine existence.

Or consider the girl who lived in my neighborhood in the 1940's. She contracted spinal meningitis, but her parents (devotees of a particular religious sect) allowed no treatment. So another grim and unnecessary

death. Aren't there at least two things here that could be improved—
the occurrence of such vicious and pointless disease, and a political and
social organization in which mulish adults are allowed to sacrifice the
life of a child to carry out their religious beliefs willy-nilly?

Or, simply consider that, in our world, conflicts of rights (of the sort
just exemplified) occur. In the example, the conflict is between the
right to believe what you will and the right to be spared the deadly
consequences of other people's beliefs. The core of social morality has
to be working out a hierarchization of rights in conflict; but wouldn't
a world in which rights did not conflict be a better world? Is not this
fact, that we live in a world where the fulfillment of certain rights entails the sacrifice of others, just one more indication that this is not
the best of all possible worlds?

To nontheists, such events and situations pose no problem, for
there is no need for them to suppose that anything serves any end.
Events may just happen. But to the theist, they do pose problems, for
he is contending that the world has been designed down to the hairs of
our heads and the tiny sparrow's fall.

And so the *modus tollens* has its bite. If the theist is correct about
the existence of God, and if the notion that nothing less than the all-
creating, all-wise, all-powerful, and all-good One could possibly qualify
for the Divine office is correct, then everything that happens is in order,
is functional, is perfect-of-kind, and cannot be improved in any way.
But this simply does not fit the facts. The world is a blood-stained,
pain-filled arena of chaos from the piranha-filled basins of the Amazon
to the gas ovens of Dachau. So we know, wherever the world came
from, that God (as defined) does not exist.

Rejoinders are many in number and varying in quality. Let us examine them rapidly and dialectically to see which, if any, are cogent enough
to demand close scrutiny:

1. Natural disasters are apparently dysfunctional, but actually they
serve to keep man alert and "on his toes." If it were not for the occasional upheaval, people would not pay sufficient attention to their environment. They would grow lax, and "gamboling on the slopes of
Vesuvius" would run the risk of annihilation. These events, like symp-
tomatic pain, enable us to avoid greater suffering. So they are functional.

But: while we may grant that those who build houses on Vesuvius
(or in southern California) invite catastrophe, it is still in order to ask
the theists: First, "If the natural disasters that do occur work as object
lessons for those who escape, what is their function for those who do
not? Isn't it a bit gratuitous to claim that the thousands who died re-

cently in Chile did so to encourage the rest of us to stay away from major fault lines?" And second, "Isn't there something bizarre about rationalizing some disasters as a means of avoiding greater ones? Isn't the whole point to ask why there are any such things at all? Can the best of all possible worlds be one in which a few fry to save the rest, or would it be a world in which the threats were removed altogether?" This line of argument does not answer the riddle. It just conceals it in a bigger one.

2. The atheist claims that certain features of the world are bad or dysfunctional . We can grant that this appears to be so. In fact, however, the atheist is simply not giving the features of the world the close attention they deserve. He is confused. There is, in fact, no evil at all—only the nonbeliever's own error in judgment. Everything is good.

But: this encounters practical difficulties. It is extremely difficult to look at a newborn calf that has been attacked by screwworms and is being devoured alive in mindless terror and pain, and say, "This may look bad, but it is really good." It is equally difficult to examine the machinations of Hitler, Stalin, Batista, Duvalier, and their ilk, and be overwhelmed with the aura of goodness. If you claim that all events in history are good, you simply do not understand the language as it is used. If you claim that they are simply neutral, neither good nor bad, you are on better ground, but problems remain. While a nontheist could read value descriptions of ordinary events as a plain case of anthropomorphic overinterpretation, theists cannot. If you have begun with the notion that all events are functional products of the Divine Person, you must either find their function or retire, before a charge of groundless wish-fulfillment.

3. This takes a terribly short and narrow view of things. We perfectly well know that in a musical composition a crossing harmony that is taken out of context may grate upon the ear; but we equally well know that in context it enriches the texture and effect of the composition. We know that if we sit three feet from the contrabassoon we will get a distorted grasp of the symphony. What we must do is move back and get a proper perspective. *Sub specie aeternitas,* all of this "evil" and "dysfunction" will be reconciled They are but grace notes on the Divine Symphony. It is highly improper to blame the Creator for our limited view.

But: (a) why not blame the Creator for our limited view? If a man bought tickets to the Kennedy Center and found himself three feet from the contrabassoon, he would certainly blame somebody. In that case, probably the ticket seller. But in the case of the world "symphony," this Creator is (by definition) Composer, Maestro, Arranger, Building

Architect, Acoustical Engineer, Ticket Seller, *et al.* If the view is limited, whom should the man blame except the One who made him, gave him all his capacities, and flung him into a place of His choosing in a world of His design? He is either a poor Designer, or there was no designer at all. In either case, the use of the divinity title is unjustified. Besides, (b) what is all this "grace notes" business? We are not talking about harmonic theory. We are talking about pain and death and fear and terror and bereavement and children with bone cancer. Tell the man with Hodgkin's disease that he is a "grace note." This kind of romanticism just does not face the facts. And, (c) maybe this *sub specie aeternitas* business would be helpful if it was, in fact, available; but who can look at the world that way? We are trying to discuss this world, here and now. If, from some other perspective, it could look good, then there is at least one thing totally wrong with it; namely, that beneficent perspective is not available to men. The same thing is wrong in the preceding argument, too. If everything that is apparently "bad" is just error and faulty perspective, then error and faulty perspective are themselves the very paradigm of dysfunction. If another perspective would erase the pain, then the fact that we occupy the perspective we do is itself gratuitous.

4. But all these assertions that the world is bad and dysfunctional lose sight of one basic fact. Since there is a God and He made the world and is perfect, then all of these things are good by definition, however they may appear.

But: this is simply and violently question-begging. You cannot test the hypothesis of Divine existence in terms of its entailments and, at the same time, interpret the events of history in terms of the very hypothesis that is in question.

5. Well, we may grant that there are some things wrong with the world—though not nearly as many as there seem; but it is a serious mistake to blame them on God or to deny the existence of God because of them. These bad things are man's own doing. God, in fact, is man's best ally in trying to remedy these defects.

But: this is also question-begging. Nevertheless, assume that there *is* a creator of some sort; then, since man is not his own author and source, he can be, at most, mediately responsible. The final charge-ticket goes elsewhere. What can man do except he possess the capacity? But if man is "made" so as to be mediately responsible for evil and dysfunction, and his "maker" is ultimately responsible for evil and dysfunction, then his "maker" cannot be God.

6. No, the ultimate source of evil and dysfunction is the Evil One (Satan). Man is responsible because he has chosen to follow Satan's

direction. It cannot be laid to God, for it was the Serpent who tempted and it was Man who fell. God's virtue remains intact.

But: either Satan (if such there be) is also Divinely made, or else he is not. If the former, then "God" is still finally responsible and the suitability of His title is highly doubtful. If the latter, then "God" is not the creator of everything and the suitability of his title is utterly lost. Satan theories and related rejoinders are completely ineffective in defending theism from attack. They are effective only in replacing theism with an alternative and distinctly different position. Dualism may have some merits, but that is not our issue. Buy dualism and you have given theism away.

7. Well, certainly, if there is a God, then God made everything. So, if there is a Satan, then God made him, too. Indeed, as Job saw, Satan fills a thoroughly functional role in the Divine government, that of putting man to the test. The whole point, though, is that it is man who chooses. Evil and dysfunction arise because man chooses, and the very ability to make such choices is one of the necessary conditions of a "best world." Some events in the world may be less than ideal in the short run, but all these events work together to achieve the best in the long run. Even as you need the sorrow of parting so that you can gain the joy of reunion, you must have the possibility of choice to achieve the value of freedom. The trouble with the atheist's view is that he is focusing on means and ignoring their ends and consequences. The end is human freedom and autonomy. How could there be a "best world" without freedom and autonomy? How could there be freedom and autonomy without having real choice and all the attendant grit of human interaction? Thus, in God's wisdom, there occurs the possibility of error. He is responsible for that; but the actualizing of evil and dysfunction comes down to the choices men make, and these choices are *their own* doing, not God's.

But: while this has possibilities, it certainly will not carry the issue. Perhaps the beneficent necessity of human freedom will take care of a whole set of malodorous events in history; but will it take care of them all? This is worth a closer look, for what it does cover, but even if certain events in the world can be reconciled as the cost of human freedom, there remain gratuitous dysfunctions sufficient that we know no God could be their source. But since God is the source of everything, by hypothesis, then we know that there is no God.

8. These "gratuitous" dysfunctions are, in fact, easily explained. Since God is virtuous and sin is man's own doing, then there must be Divine retribution. A God of Justice could not let evil deeds go un-

punished. Thus there comes into the world all the hardships of existence—Divine wrath for human folly!

But: in the first place, there is no known correlation between "sin" and "retribution." In the second place, a vast portion of the dysfunction under consideration is not in the area of human affairs. Whose sin is requited in the torment of the hyena's prey? Still, we must look closely at this move, too.

9. All these arguments are but the struggling of finite and puny human minds to grasp the plans and intent of the infinite and transcendent mind of God. God's ways are not our ways. He will make it all come right in the end. We will understand it better by and by (when the morning comes). We cannot capture the Divine mind in the net of human argument. God is beyond, ineffable, the *Mysterium Tremendum*, the Transcendent Other. Do not kick against the goads!

But: while we must grant that we do not know whether there is an Ineffable One or not, is that a victory for theistic cognition or a wholesale abandonment of it? We now need to examine a number of core arguments.

Action and Choice   Part of the given, with which an account of the world must begin, is the existence of man. But man is not merely a sentient organism. He is a reflective and active organism. He can think and he can do, render judgment and make choices. Whether "ideal" or not, this is part of the way the world is. If, in the context of these observations about the world, we assume that there is a God Who has created the world and ordered it, and that this God is a designing, purposive being (so that nothing happens in the world through misadventure or accident), then it may be argued that "evil" in certain of its aspects is the logically necessary price that has to be paid for man to possess this autonomy. If, then, "freedom" is seen as an essential good in a "best possible" world, those evils which are necessary to its achievement are "justified."

Consider a very homely example: Suppose that a parent tells his child, "This Saturday is going to be 'Freedom Day.' You will get to make all kinds of independent and autonomous choices and decisions. I will arrange it." In order to do this, he surely must arrange Saturday to provide the child with some genuine options. He cannot put the child in a situation in which his only "choice" is between mowing the lawn and cutting the grass. That would be no choice at all, and "Freedom Day" would be a cruel hoax. There must be at least one set of real options if a choice is to be possible—say, between mowing the grass

and going fishing, or between going to the library to read Plato and
going to the dime store to buy an *Incredible Hulk* funny book. Otherwise, the child just is not free. Back to the larger case: Man must have
some such range of real choices or else he cannot be free, that is, be a
person rather than, say, an automaton.

Now, if "freedom" and "personhood" are essential for this world to
be "best possible of its kind," any proper God would surely recognize
the derivative necessity of choice options. So, He might well have made
a world in which choice is really and fully open to man—indeed, a
world in which the range of options is virtually without limit. A man
might, then, choose disastrously and have to reap the consequences.
Even so, perhaps even in the process of his own annihilation, he could
look back and say, "How good to have been free! No mere automaton,
I was a man for a brief and glorious moment, even if I blew it." There is
an essential assumption here: that, like Camelot momentary and
fragmented, freedom excels even the indubitable and external "security" that would attend a providentially guaranteed, but depersonalized
and bound, existence.

There is a host of interesting implications in such a notion, even independent of its theological applications.[41] The relative merits of
"freedom" and "security" have been the topic of much recent and
nearly recent political and literary comment. You recall the novel
Brave New World. From one point of view the life situation in that
world would not be bad at all—at least everyone there is *happy*. Even
the Epsilons laughed and made jokes as they crouched in the mines at
their work. Individuality and autonomy may be missing, but not happiness. To say that this is not the good life is to say that it would be
better to live in a rude old world where there is choice, even with occasional attendant grief, than to live in a brave new world where there is
ceaseless joy without choice. This poses a good question for our time:
Which is more important in the development of the good life—independence and all its attendant risks of disaster, suffering, and death, or
a somewhat Skinnerian universal bliss? It also poses a very basic question for our theoretical ethical reflections: Can value questions be set-

---

[41]Is it possible that being "real persons" (i.e., free, with a range of real choices
open) is a morally crucial thing? If so, it would seem that many things we do in
society and in the academy are aimed at the erosion, rather than the increase,
of value. Consider core curricula, parietal rules, curfew, etc. Perhaps God in His
wisdom, then, is doing considerably better in His role than most parents, college
administrators, and government officials are in theirs. At any rate, He better
fits contemporary liberal bias.

tled solely in terms of consequences, or must we take the means of achieving those consequences into account?[42]

In any case, the theists' point is a straightforward string of conditions: without the possibility of error there is no choice, without choice there is no freedom, without freedom there are no moral agents, and unless there are moral agents we are not men and there is no value in our existence. But there is value in human existence, predicated on freedom and its attendant risks. A "best possible" world could not be a world without value, nor could it be a world predicated on a cruel hoax. Further, God not doing anything by misadventure, that we be free is clearly part of His purpose. Therefore, working within the limits of logical possibility, in order to achieve a logically consistent creation, God had to provide choice and the attendant evils of possible error and its consequences. This was logically inevitable: given the purpose of creating moral agents (a necessity in a "best possible" world), there is no logical possibility other than presenting man with the ability to choose and, hence, the occasion and possibility of error.[43]

This is, of course, open to question. Must a "best possible" world include moral agents? Is there greater value in moral agency than in

[42]Indeed, these are but practical and theoretical formulations of the same question. The adoption of a thoroughly utilitarian or consequentialist position in ethical theory seems to ignore the possibility that there are values directly attached to styles of behavior, independent of their results. Thus, if one adopts the view that the good life consists of maximum distribution of happiness (and if one is at all bright), one quickly sees that there are two routes open: raising the common level of achievement, and lowering the common level of demand. Every benevolent despot should read his Pavlov. If demands can be lowered enough, then happiness can be universal at a low unit cost (or more universal at the same net). Perhaps it is an insight attendant upon power. Who gives the children white meat? ("Who wants the jolly drumstick?") Consequentialists, of course, have a reply: you must consider all options, including universal satisfaction of high-level demands. It is worth reflection in a welfare state.

[43]This (i.e., the logical limitation of God) is a theological move which everybody who is interested in making coherent theological moves has to make sooner or later. Such labels as "omnipotent," "omniscient," etc., have to be given some kind of intelligible content, even for the theist. Recognition that, for example, "omnipotence" cannot mean more than "able to do that which can be consistently done" is a very crucial recognition. It immediately takes out all of those medieval puzzles ("Can God make a rock so heavy He cannot pick it up?" etc.) that are predicated on the notion that omnipotence entails being able to perform contradictions (i.e., to do and not do the same thing in the same regard at the same time). A coherent God can do everything that can be done, know everything that can be known, etc. One cannot ask for "more" consistently.

simple happiness?[44] Isn't the whole formulation of the rejoinder question-begging at two levels: first, in the insistence that this is a "best world" when at this point that needs to be shown; and, second, in the repeated importation of God and His intent into the argument when, in fact, the existence of God (*a fortiori* His intent) is what is ultimately at stake?

But we must give credit where it is due. Recall that the point of the present argument is not whether someone knows that God exists, it is whether someone knows that God does not exist. Consequently, the only duty incumbent upon the rejoinder is to show the affirmative's possibility of error. The alternative rationale that is given may not be sufficient to convince us of its truth, but it does seem enough to convince us that the atheists' claim to know is not adequately supported. The notion of freedom as a necessary condition of a "best world" is neither obviously true nor obviously false; but it is obviously plausible enough to keep the gate open. So, even as we concluded some time ago that we do not know that there is a God, we may add that at this point we do not know that there is not one either. The "Scottish verdict" *still* stands.

However, the atheists' argument for God's nonexistence was not limited to dysfunctions that can be so plausibly explained in terms of human error. Perhaps we may know that there is no God without considering human affairs at all.

Cosmic Fall and Retribution   After you have explained as much evil as you can, in terms of human freedom and its necessary cost, there still appears to be plenty left over. These leftovers are what are now at stake. If they cannot be taken into account, then the world is not the "best possible," and the atheists' claim to know that there is no God is still intact.

1. There is a widely held view among various evangelicals that *all* of the evil in the world is the direct product of human acts—that when man "fell," the world "fell" with him. Having explained the occurrence of obviously act-connected evil as the necessary price of human autonomy and freedom, this argument goes on to claim that all so-called natural evil is simply the impact or effect of human actions on the natural environment. In an era much taken with ecology, such a view

[44]This is another formulation of the issue(s) noted above. We cannot settle it here; but note that the pattern of theistic rejoinder we are examining is not open without appropriate adjustment to your general value theory. But how long can one tamper with outside affairs for theological purposes without earning the label "ad hoc" for his maneuvering?

cannot be lightly dismissed. We are all familiar with the devastating effect that human action can have on the environment—from the pollution of air and water to the extermination of species and the production of super-pests.[45]

Many dysfunctional situations which appear to have no connection with human conduct might be traced back and explained in these terms with a little effort. But to make the argument effective, one must assume that they can all be so traced, given world enough and time. Is this a reasonable assumption? Can we explain, for example, the decimation of the Central American Indians from "Spanish Fever" on this pattern and without casuistry?[46] Is there much hope for tidal waves and earthquakes? Is there any reason at all, other than ad hoc desperation, for such theories as the aboriginal vegetable diet of all animals? (And why did tigers give it up and sheep "keep the faith"?) No. For, while even a brief look will show that man has had many adverse effects on his world (along with a beneficial one or two, surely), the primary pattern was there long before man appeared. The "law of the jungle" antedates man and it is not the best law. Perhaps a versatile supply of natural horrors was needed, however, to provide ready retribution against man when the need arose.

2. Can we not bind all evils together in a single rationale of consequence and retribution? Suppose that there were a definite correlation between the badness of deeds and the extent of the disasters that surrounded them. That is, suppose (*contra* Job and common sense) that the rain did not fall on the good and bad alike. In this suppositional world, fury would swoop upon the evildoer; and, even if the good man gained no affirmative rewards, he would be spared the furies. In a world like that, disasters could be explained as retribution, and the rampant bloodletting of the lower orders could be explained as Divine Preparedness. But this is extremely peculiar if we have already justified human evil as a necessary condition of freedom. It is difficult to call instant-retaliation-upon-fulfillment-of-programmed-potential "retribution." If we have been preprogrammed to have the options, then, surely, the responsibility goes back to the Programmer. Consequently,

[45]I read of a new breed of California mosquito that is impervious to all known chemical pesticides; and I am glad of the High Sierras.
[46]This was explained to me as a boy as the cost of their "unseemly conduct." Apparently it was not unseemly until the Spanish soldiers arrived with bacilli to which they were resistant through previous "misconduct." Did it take longer for the cosmos to fall so far from Eden? Or maybe the Indians just didn't break the seventh commandment until the Spaniards taught them how. There's a thought!

it would seem that a retributivist account of "natural" evil (in such a context) would demand that at least part (and probably all) of the retaliation be directed upon the Programmer Himself. He built the system. He programmed the actors in the arena. He provided the range of options within which they act. There may be no way for Him to assist us in avoiding the direct consequences of our acts themselves. (Those who leap from mountains are dashed to pieces in the valleys.) But can He wheel in the big guns of retribution—plague, earthquake, shingles, hailstorms—in good conscience? It would be even odder if you accepted a kind of traditional religious notion of foreordination.[47] A Divinity Who had set up a world in which people were foreordained to be bad, and Who was going to mete out retribution for all bad things, would have to give Himself the major part (if not all) of the retribution He meted out. He is the One who "made" it, after all. So: even if one says "bad things only happen to bad people" (whether in terms of pre-destinarian view of events or not) in order to explain natural dysfunctions as the price of bad action (which is explained as the price of freedom), the retribution would wind up being aimed at the Divinity *unless the Divinity Himself is fundamentally unfair.* This is not a move that the theistic community is prone to make. Nor should they; anything "unfair" hardly deserves the title "God."

For that matter, of course, the natural evils that we are talking about do not happen exclusively and without fail to people who have done bad things. They happen indiscriminately. This being so, the notion that natural evil occurs as retribution just does not fit the facts unless "God" is careless and inaccurate (as well as unfair). People who read the funnies and drink beer on Sunday mornings are not struck with the heartbreak of psoriasis. People who systematically exploit the lives and resources of American blacks vacation in Nice and send their children to Harvard. Fill in your own definition of "sin"; it does not correlate. The rain falls whither it will.[48]

---

[47]The point here is not to bring up a theological issue in order to argue it; but simply to note that the very common hard-determinist variety of theism really makes problems with the concept of evil because it lays responsibility squarely on the Maker. In which case, for fairness' sake, retributive evil must descend just as squarely on the Maker. The conceptual problems of theism are not confined to questions of existence.

[48]A few years ago, I was introduced to a philosopher at a professional meeting. He, in turn, introduced me to Lola: "This is Lola, she comes to meetings with me." Lola's contributions to the meeting were in the "Gosh, Mr. Busby, that'd be swell" genre, but she had her compensations. Has "Spanish Fever" struck? Of course not. Is the philosopher consumed by anxiety and inner chaos over his perfidy? Not to an extent that Lola cannot remedy. No thunder, no lightning,

It would appear, then, that either the retribution theory is bankrupt, God is inattentive, or some people will have "hell to pay" later on. This last, of course, is the obvious next move. There is retribution, but it comes on "later." That might explain why the evil prosper; but it does nothing for the righteous who are beset by nature's wrath. But the point of the whole discussion was to offer a rationale for evil here. All the "hells" you can imagine do not contribute to that end, so this move is essentially irrelevant to the question at stake.

The possibility remains that the righteous who suffer here will have it all made good "in Heaven." So-called "pie in the sky when you die by and by" has consoled good people who have despaired in trying to right the world's wrongs in a lifetime. It has also been said to keep aspirations down and the masses in their place. It will be nice if it happens, but why should there need to be such recompense? The question is why there is such evil in the world now. Why must a child be born a cretin at all, even if he will have goldy curls and play a harp "some sweet day?"

Suppose that all of the following were true: all of the sufferings of the righteous will be "made good" in the end;[49] all of those who have sinned will get horrible punishment in the end;[50] and everybody in the world is now in a position to know these things.[51] Natural evil still surrounds and devours both the good and the bad in the world *now*. It cannot function as retribution here. But it is here anyway. It is superfluous and irrational here, even if the above suppositions are true, and even if the direct evil that men do is handled as the cost of freedom.

Without these suppositions there is no reason to think that there is any such thing as "retribution." With them there may be retribution,

---

no tidal waves, no plague, no degenerative diseases, no poverty, no starvation— just a good post, a high salary, frequent travel, and good companionship on the road. In short, a rich and happy life, not the least blessing of which is Lola herself.

[49]How does joy tomorrow make up for pain today? In the best of all possible worlds there would be joy today *and* tomorrow. How many days' bliss for one kidney stone? How many decades for being lynched in Mississippi? How many centuries for being born in Calcutta?

[50]How do you reconcile the notion of "punishment" (not therapy) with the notion of Divine Perfection, anyway? Where does the final bill go, after all?

[51]The claim to know such things is a consolation to many. There have been books written on the special joy of beholding the final payout. It is said that the chosen will sit at long tables along a parapet that juts out from Heaven and overlooks the pit where the rest are consigned, and that their initial entertainment as they feast in the Alabaster City will be the screams of the damned coming up from the pit, and sublime happiness as they reflect on the justness of such an arrangement.

but the suppositions are based on the very realization that the world in which we live is not "right," that evil is here inexplicable. (If it were explicable, no such suppositions would be required.) Either way, we are left with evil in the world that is gratuitous and unexplained. So this world is a dysfunctional world. No God could have made it. No God could be in charge of it. No God could let it be made. No God could let it run unchecked. So we know that there is no God.

3. At this point there is usually a rehearsal of one or another sort of dualism. Of course if the evil did not come from God, or if He is not aware of it, or if He cannot control it, then He can hardly be blamed. Of course. If there is no God, then there is no need for this world to be "best possible"; and if "God" suffers any of the three limitations enumerated, then He hardly deserves the title. He wouldn't be God. But that is hardly a useful argument to refute the atheist. "You are wrong in saying you know there is no God, because when we talk about God we do not really mean God. We are talking about a Super-being locked in cosmic struggle with Satanic Forces. There certainly is one of those!" To which the atheist may reply, "There may well be. Maybe we can talk about that sometime. We were discussing the existence of God, however. We are glad to see that you have seen the light and joined us. We affirm there is no God. You admit the same. Done!" There is no help here.

4. Another possible move is to suggest that the occurrence of evil in the world is a kind of logical necessity, similar to that necessity which secures act-evil as the price of freedom. It goes this way: There is no way for something to happen that is good except in the context of, and in contrast to, something that is bad. So you see, if God wants to do things for man that are good and beneficial, He has to do things for man that are bad and detrimental. If there were not any bad occurrences, then there could not be any good occurrences. So God sees to it that the minimal amount of necessary evil occurs in order that the good may be given substance; and, thus, He has made and maintains the best of all possible worlds. That is the way the argument runs, but it is guilty of a very serious confusion of the necessities of something's occurring and the necessities of our commenting upon those events that do occur.

You certainly could argue *this* way: If there were no bad things at all, then you would not be able to talk about the goodness of the things that did occur. If there were no value distinctions between the things that occur, then we would have to discuss them simply as the things that occur.[52] This is a very important point. Let us grant for

[52]The point is not that the occurrence of value language makes necessary the

purposes of argument that evil is a parasitic notion that can only be defined by contrast to good; or, if you like, the reverse. We are granting that they are polar notions. This is what is behind the argument "There must be evil in order for there to be good." But that is actually a comment about definition and language meaning.

Imagine an extremely limited world comprising only four inherently appraisable things, two good and two bad: human affection, aesthetic beauty, ugliness, and spite. Suppose, further, that we were able to subtract ugliness and spite from that world, leaving only human affection and aesthetic beauty. Then we would not have any occasions to use words for the purposes to which we now put "good," "bad," and the like. Such words would no longer have any working role (meaning), because there would not be any contrasts to lend them use. But we would still have human affection and aesthetic beauty, even if they had no evaluative name at all; and the world would be, although we would not be in a position to say (or need to say) so, a better world by the removal of spite and ugliness. The point is that the parasitic status is one of definition and language; so, while we can perfectly well grant that we could not meaningfully say "good" except in contrast to "bad," this does not entail the impossibility of anything beneficial happening save in the context of other things that hurt. We might not be able to say, "It is beneficial," because we would not have any use for the words, there being no contrast to draw; but it would still be beneficial. Indeed, we could, without logical troubles, have a world in which everything was good; and even though in such a world we would have no occasion or inclination to comment on that fact, the world would be none the worse for it. But we don't have such a world; and how shall we explain *that* and be theists?

The Transcendent Nature of God   The maneuvers we have considered so far are mostly attempts to redefine the notion of "good," or to show that what is apparently "bad" is actually, or in the long run, good. Another whole avenue is open, however, which consists essentially of attempted redefinitions of "God." But "God" already has a basic common meaning in theistic discourse. Our question has been whether *that* is compatible with the way the world is; and no crude redefini-

---

existence of objective values in the world. I am simply observing that value language does occur and it has some meaning. You may define that meaning any way you like (human desire and aversion, the common good and detriment, as you will). The point is that the terms are used to draw a contrast; so unless there is at least a perceived contrast, the terms have no use. Hence there is no way for one term to have a use unless the other term has a use too. If we didn't like some things and dislike others, we could not talk about liking things.

tion will help answer that question.[53] Nevertheless, a more subtle route
is open through the emphasis on and exploitation of certain notions
that do "belong" in the basic common definition of "God," especially
the emphasis and exploitation of the notion of Divine Transcendence:
"Since God is, by definition, wholly other, it must follow that you do
not settle issues about God on the basis of things that are immanent,
apparent, or experiencable. Indeed, to try to make any accommodation
to some "argument from evil" (or any other empirically derived athe-
istic argument) would undercut and destroy the very character of the
Divine Figure we revere, namely, His otherness. Anytime someone
attacks our reverence and Divine knowledge on *empirical* grounds, they
simply miss all that is central and crucial. The core of our knowledge is
immune to any refutation from apparent 'facts.'"

Of course, if you go back in time a little,[54] the religious community
comfortably and commonly made straight affirmations of "fact"—
"this is the way things are" claims, directly supportable (or refutable)
in human experience as it occurred: God made the world in seven days;
when Joshua did his thing, the sun stood still; and so on. Claims about
past, present, and future were all flatly asserted. But in making such
claims in the twentieth century, the religious community has often
found them counterexampled by the evidence piled up by scientific
research. (For example, there is a severe discontinuity between the
notion of the sun standing still and what has been discovered through
geophysics and astronomy about the behavior of the solar system.)
The frequent theological response has been both interesting and curi-
ous: abandoning the field and shifting to new ground. Thus, when the
Darwin business finally came home to rank-and-file religionists, many
said, "We will stand and fight; evolution is a lie!" But the more theological response was instant capitulation: "Whether man evolved or was
created ex nihilo isn't really crucial to anything important; we can
all be evolutionists without changing anything basic in our views." This
is almost a history-in-capsule of much recent Protestant liberalism—

[53]As, for example, through the sharp limitation of one or more of the "omni-
traits." But reconciling events with, say, an all-benevolent, all-knowing, rather
powerful being does not reconcile them with God. What theist would make such
a move? Many have been tempted. How else did God "die?"

[54]For the laity, back to when our grandmothers were young; but for the theologians, one needs to press back a bit more. But in fundamentalist and dispensa-
tionalist circles, one need not go back at all. Sometime read C.N. Kraus's excellent
Dispensationalism in America (Richmond: John Knox Press, 1950) or W.H.
Branson's gothic piece *Drama of the Ages* (Washington: Review and Herald,
1953) if you feel isolated from such bold assertion. Read *The Plain Truth*
or listen to *The World Tomorrow*.

the abandonment of one claim after another as "not crucial" until we finally suspect that no empirical claim is crucial.

In a battle, when an army abandons one outpost and retreats to another, *seriatim*, there comes a point at which the troops either (1) stand and are annihilated, (2) stand and win, or (3) abandoning the last redoubt, surrender. But it appears that in conflicts over the empirical support or refutation of religious claims, theologians have found a fourth option: retreating at length from redoubt to redoubt, but never admitting significant defeat. (They admit all the defeats; but none of them are "significant.") "Any attempt to describe God or to support or refute theism on empirical grounds entails some kind of finiteness, thus depriving God of a part of His Ineffable Nature." Of course, this gets the theist off the hook of "arguments from evil" and the like, by denying that evil, and the like, are in any sense problems. But if, then, there is no possible means of putting a theological claim to any experiential test, if the existence of a God is experientially indiscernible, insupportable and unattackable, then what difference could it make to humans whether One exists or not?

Carnap once said that the religious community is left with a hard choice between admitting that their claims are substantially erroneous or affirming that they are systematically irrelevant—between categorizing their utterances as only myths, or admitting that they are nonsense.[55] One might think that religionists would all prefer myth; and, perhaps, once they did. The tendency today, however, seems to be to retreat into ritual noise rather than to risk error. For, if the nature of God is beyond the dimensions of any human experience, then experiential knowledge of the existence of God is impossible. So: if this is what the theist does mean by "God," then no one knows a posteriori whether there is a God or not. Completely cut off, in principle, from such inquiry and knowledge, the issue is wholly irrelevant to human affairs and conditions. This is the perfect out. If this is what "God" means, then nobody knows anything nonanalytic on the topic, and there is nothing more to say. This certainly buys security—at a price.

Summary

"Free will" may cover human depredations, but the only ploy that gets theism off the hook of natural dysfunction is the claim that God is utterly beyond the realm of actual or possible experiential knowledge.

[55]Rudolph Carnap, "The Elimination of Metaphysics Through Logical Analysis of Language," in A.J. Ayer, ed., *Logical Positivism* (Glencoe, Ill.: Free Press, 1959), p. 66.

In the absence of a priori knowledge, this claim admits (or affirms), quite inevitably, that there is no theistic knowing at all. Given a transcendental notion of God, we must agree that there is no a posteriori knowledge of Divine existence—affirmative or negative. A posteriori transcendentalism is either incoherent or agnostic. The Scottish verdict is secure.

3

AGNOSTICISM
AND
DIVINE EXISTENCE

The word "agnostic" means "nonknower" and properly that is all it means.[1] An agnostic is a person who claims, vis-à-vis some state of affairs, that he does not know. Agnosticism[2] is one of the very few basic alternatives on the issue of Divine existence. We have examined the affirmative claim to know and the negative claim to know, and we have found that in the case of a transcendent God (which is the direction in which the argument pushes theism), neither is possible. So we must examine the claim to *not* know. It is the third main option. (To keep the issues straight in our examination, I will distinguish between traditional, de facto agnosticism, and new-style, necessary agnosticism.)

Being an agnostic certainly does not entail an inimical attitude toward what one claims (admits) ignorance about.[3] If agnosticism

---

[1]The word "gnostic" is the same one that shows up in the heresy of the same name. Its root, "gnosis," is also the word from which the English "know" is derived.

[2]Hereafter, by "agnostic" I mean religious agnostic unless specified otherwise.

[3]I am uncomfortable with "ignorance" here because it brings in a judgmental tone—the suggestion that one should know and, hence, that not knowing is a fault. It suggests that there are facts available of which the individual has not availed himself. But, if such facts are *not* available, such a presumption of fault is not justified; and the whole contention of agnostics (old and new) is that such facts are not available. "Ignorance" prejudices the issue.

entails any kind of value attitude, it would be one of value neutrality. As people are popularly categorized by the religious community, the religious agnostic is often automatically placed with the "enemy." But his claim (admission) of "ignorance" is, in fact, quite impartial to theism and atheism alike.

The traditional agnostic takes the position that we just do not have enough data about the existence of God to make a strong case either way, and, consequently, that to assert or deny that there is a God, on the evidence at hand, is rash. Under our present conditions, he feels that a sane and conservative man (the Virginian in the street) will adopt a wait-and-see position. He believes that we should wait until there is more evidence available, collected, and made intelligible. Those who are interested will, no doubt, collect whatever evidence is available; and they may eventually settle the issue one way or the other. Then we will be in a position to say. After the issue is well settled, people who still say that they do not know may be accused of ignorance (and those who claim the opposite of what is evidentially shown may be accused of willful obtuseness); but, in the meantime, since there is not enough evidence now at hand, we are justified in suspending judgment. We may, of course, believe (or be inclined) one way or the other, while we wait upon evidence sufficient to support knowledge.

How would we settle the question whether there are slaves today in Watusiland? We would probably go to Watusiland and see. How would we settle the issue whether there is a caliph of Yqem, whose word is law and whose will is arbitrary? Although it might involve great risks, we could go to Yqem and find out. But how might we find out if there is or is not a God? That is a little more difficult to fill in. What evidence is relevant? Because of this difficulty, new-style agnosticism has sprung up—an agnosticism that denies not only the actuality of knowledge of Divine existence, but also the very possibility of such knowledge.[4] Neo-agnosticism goes beyond claiming that we have no cognitions on Divine existence to claim that the issue is not even cognitive—to claim that in this area it is not even possible for men to know. The traditional agnostics' disclaimers were circumstantial or de facto; but the neo-agnostics' are *per principium*.

In this chapter we shall look at both kinds of agnosticism to see how

---

[4]This is the move that A. J. Ayer made when, having to his own satisfaction demolished the sorts of things that claimants to theistic cognitions are prone to say, he added, "His assertions cannot possibly be valid, but they cannot be invalid either. as he says nothing at all about the world, he cannot justly be accused of saying anything false." See *Language, Truth, and Logic* (New York: Dover, 1952), p. 116.

they work. We shall ask what kinds of replies the theist can run against them, and how effective these replies can be—how much impact they have on the agnostics' posture and how much residual feedback they have on theism itself. We shall examine traditional agnosticism first,[5] along with assorted theistic maneuvers that are attempted in that context.

THAT WE DO NOT KNOW, BUT MAY BELIEVE
(DE FACTO AGNOSTICISM)

The Knowledge/Belief Conflict

The theist may say, "Of course we do not know. In fact, we do not want to know. If we did know, it would be a bad thing, for such knowing would destroy the very possibility of faith, and religion wouldn't really be religion unless you had to exercise faith. If God had done what Bertrand Russell shook his fist at Him for not doing (i.e., given us more evidence), it would have undercut the venture that is essential to the religious quest. Man would not be able, then, to relate to God by act of will and affirmation; he would be coerced by the very weight of evidence to go along, and that would destroy the whole point. So, the agnostic is right; and that is a good thing for genuine theism."

But people have always shown a remarkable ability to avoid being coerced by evidence. Even if the evidence were there, it seems probable that people would still have plenty of opportunity (willful as they are) to run against it if they liked. Besides, the idea that this notion of "faith" (i.e., as something that cannot occur in the context of supporting evidence) is the notion that is essential to theism is quite wrongheaded.[6]

---

[5]You might think that if neo-agnosticism is well founded, then there is no reason to look at the traditional variety at all. In a sense that is true. Further, I am firmly convinced that neo-agnosticism is on firm ground. That, indeed, was implicit in Chapter 2, above. Neo-agnosticism on Divine existence is unassailable unless we radically reinterpret "God exists." But there is still good ground for talking about traditional agnosticism: it has long been the focal point of public controversy, it is the kind of agnosticism with which the religious community is familiar, and it is where most of the argument with and within the religious community is still going on. A few theologians have, in recent years, begun to recognize and voice a tentative kind of response to neo-agnosticism, but most of them have missed the point of the issue completely. We will examine it with care, but we should get the groundwork down first.

Nevertheless, this is one response that the theist can make to traditional agnosticism—join it and make a virtue of it—thus converting the asserted lack of evidence into one of the supposedly praiseworthy attributes of his enterprise. But there is something fishy about this move.

When there is nothing that we can do about the adverse circumstances in which we find ourselves, it is not uncommon to try to make a virtue of them. For example, in national foreign policy, we have nickeled and dimed our way into a catastrophic world situation. No one ever selected that as a specific national goal, but it has happened anyway. So one morning we woke up to realize that we were fighting simultaneous wars in Vietnam, Cambodia, Laos, and Thailand, were on the brink in India, Pakistan, North Africa, and Panama, and that things looked bad in Haiti and northern Ireland. How did this happen? No one is sure. What can we do about it? Not much. But our "national prestige" is on the line. We have lost fifty thousand men, but we "dare not allow their deaths to have been in vain," so we shovel in fifty thousand more. We are overextended, but our "credibility" and "honor" are at stake so we make a virtue of the situation with torrid prose about delaying the Yellow Peril and saving whoever survives from the terrors of a collectivist economy. None of this is very convincing, but it salves the national ego where the facts bind. Another example: A wife discovers, after fifteen years of marriage, that her husband is "cheating." There is little she can do about it, for she depends completely on him for her support, care, and well-being, and he is an unreasonable, selfish, and volatile man. If she makes any fuss about it, he will "fling the baggage out." So she makes a virtue of his vice and says to herself, "Everyone ought to have some variety. Lothar's affair with Lola may even make him a better husband and father." Or, a final example: Lorenzo is expelled from the university for pushing smack at a nearby grammar school. But he says to himself, "I never really wanted to go to that crummy college anyway. Staying in school is just copping out. There is more to life than this establishment robot factory." Moves like these are common enough; but in most of them are we not inclined to think that the move is an exercise in self-deception? Is there any special reason why what constitutes self-deceit in politics, foreign policy, family relations, and the like should not be seen the same way in religion?

[6]There is a notion of "faith" that is crucial to the religious (and especially the Christian) enterprise; but what that has to do with the acceptance of propositions in an evidential vacuum is not at all clear. I shall examine several notions of "faith" below. See p. 126 ff.

The admission of the theist that he has no knowledge but really never wanted any anyway is especially parallel to the Lorenzo case above, and rather reminiscent of Aesop's fox. "So Darwin has given good grounds for saying that the world is not teleologically ordered? That is all right; we never needed teleological order anyway. So geological evidence has given us solid ground for the claim that the world is many millions of years old? That is all right; we never needed the Mosaic account as history anyway." And after many steps: "So a careful assessment of the evidence shows that we do not know anything about the existence of a Divinity at all? That is all right; we never needed to know anything about the existence of a Divinity, indeed we do not want to."

But this is a very dangerous game. How far can one play the game, giving away this item and that and making a virtue of their loss, before a look in the bag will show that it is empty? What is the difference between an odorless, weightless, invisible, nontactile, tasteless, and silent gardener and no gardener at all? But, of course, the reply is forthcoming: "While we may not know whether such an ineffable gardener tends the flowers, we are still free to believe that one does. Maybe it is not entirely ingenuous to claim that the lack of knowledge is a boon to faith,[7] but we can believe in spite of it (if not because of it), and we do."

But when the theists affirm that they do not know, and offer their beliefs (either because or in spite of their knowledge-lack) in lieu of knowledge, it is appropriate to ask, "What is (can be) the basis of the knowledge surrogate offered?" Several such bases can be advanced. The residual, though noncoercive, force of the arguments dealt with above, special "encounters," and a kind of insight that is purported to come through analogical inference are important among them. We

---

[7] If faith is lost upon the occurrence of knowledge, and if only faith will save, then I suppose that as soon as you find out any facts you go straight to Hell. That would seem to follow. Given such a notion, some elements of the religious community have good pragmatic grounds for their long-standing record of opposition to education in any form. When I was a boy in Washington, it fell my lot to guide a family friend on tour. She balked at entering the Museum of Natural History and flatly refused to visit the archaeology collection, explaining that a young friend in West Texas had examined a mummy or two and had "lost his religion." She wanted no part of it. In a sense, she showed good judgment. If you are committed to creation in 4004 B.C., then there is not much point in examining artifacts older than that. The obvious fear here is not of knowledge confirming what was once faith (and so undercutting salvation). It is, rather, of knowledge refuting what faith once affirmed. But the latter has, no doubt, made some contribution to religious anti-education forces alongside the fideists' fear that we might come to know that there is a God and thus be unable to believe it anymore.

must examine these moves, along with some of the assorted replies that a skeptical agnostic can make to such expressions of fideistic agnosticism.[8] Then we shall turn our attention to the new agnosticism, which affirms that one cannot believe, and see what happens there.

Possible Bases of Belief as a Knowledge Surrogate

The Residual Force of the Arguments   Insofar as the arguments work at all (i.e., insofar as the Divine falls within the even limited purview of human reason and evidence-gathering), one could claim that there are some grounds for theistic belief even though the matter cannot presently be established. Perhaps the ontological argument does not conclusively demonstrate that a necessary being occurs in fact, but it makes a lot of sense. Encouraged by the admittedly less-than-coercive force of the argument, we may believe its conclusion until we are in a position to confirm it. Perhaps the other arguments do not conclusively demonstrate that there is a first cause, designer, intender, etc., but again encouraged, we may believe. The only trouble with all this is that it systematically ignores the force of the negative arguments from evil and dysfunction. For, as we have seen, the "God" that escapes the force of those arguments is only that "God" which equally escapes the net of reason and evidence. If we confine ourselves to what we can reason out and experience in the world, and would make a move toward belief on such straightforward grounds, the weight of the evidence is chillingly negative. For such reasons, fideistic agnostics turn to other grounds.

Encounter   Again, we are considering the occurrence of distinct religious encounters as a basis for making theistic claims, only in this case claims to believe rather than claims to know.[9] We have already seen that such encounters are not adequate as a basis for knowledge because they are ambiguous, unless they are subjected to question-begging restrictions on their interpretation. Many people would claim, however, that such encounters do engender legitimate belief—that they are a sufficient basis for the affirmation that a God does, in fact, exist.

[8]Obviously, the religious position here, despite its affirmations of belief, is agnostic. As soon as one says, "Okay, we do not have a sufficient basis for knowing, but we do believe" (by whatever means), he is essentially saying, "Okay, we are agnostics, but . . ."

[9]Not experience of the world from which a theistic conclusion is inferred; rather, direct and unique experiences of some sort of "divine" phenomena themselves. See above, p. 72 ff.

1. An evangelist once claimed in my hearing to have had more than one direct conversation with God. The culmination of one of his stories ran this way: "When I saw the terrible effects that the fire had had on little Sammy [when a blowtorch exploded in his face and covered forty-five percent of his body with third-degree burns], I ran from the emergency room, ran to my house and up the stairs, fell down on my knees by my bedside, and prayed, 'Oh God! Dear God! If that's what fire will do to human flesh, then please God, dear God, don't let Hell be literal fire!' But God reached down and put His hand on my shoulder, and said, 'I'm sorry, Max, but that's the way it is.'" As we have already seen, there is very little basis on which Max could claim to know that his communicant was God; there are several alternative adequate explanations, none of which have been eliminated; this particular explanation is question-begging unless and until some adequate ground rules for God-identification have been spelled out, and so on. But the same difficulties that block knowledge based on such encounters also block any adequate basis there for belief. Had the setting been appropriate, it would have been instructive to ask Max, "What made you believe that it was God? How did you eliminate the possibility that it was (a) a temporary or passing delusion in your mind; (b) an extra-terrestrial being that is invisible though audible (Glassman, maybe); or (c) the product of some very deep kink in your psyche, produced by a harsh upbringing and a steady diet of hellfire sermons when you were a child?" Even as an expression of belief, a statement like "I have had an encounter with God" stands in need of so much support itself that it is an unlikely candidate for the job of propping up the theological enterprise. If we are trying to decide whether to subscribe to theism or not, certainly the question of who it was that Max talked to must remain open.

If Max says, "I believe that there is a God because I talked to Him last night," I would not dispute that he had some experiences then, even some experiences that he calls "talking to God." But is this interpretation of his experiences the most fruitful, consistent, intelligible, productive, theoretically economical, non–ad hoc, and fertile interpretation that can be put on them? If it is not, then all we have are opinions—casual beliefs that are not responsive to argument and evidence. Unless and until grounds can be specified for evaluating the interpretation, and unless and until the interpretation is deemed satisfactory on those grounds, then the belief that it was God is quite unjustified. We know that we have experiences of different kinds; but until we can structure those experiences in some defensible way, we cannot claim to have a reasonable belief that they are of God. So, at best, what we wind up with here is the possibility of weak belief waiting upon more evidence, and (even more important) waiting upon the development of some viable criteria for the interpretive rubric in use.

2. Some have suggested that the shaky status of such beliefs can be shored up by linking them to hoped-for future, more direct, and more explicit encounters. Such an increasingly explicit and reconfirmed faith might be, eventually, so thoroughly confirmed that we will, then, know. This is the notion of eschatalogical confirmation, discussed before and found inadequate to underwrite present theistic knowledge, now advanced as providing eventual confirmation for present faith.[10]

Project yourself again into a fantasy situation: Suppose that we have lived out our allotted time in this world, arguing along the way over whether the theistic assertions are true, and eventually agreeing that there is no sufficient evidence available here and now to know either way. Then we all die and are transmogrified. We look up into the sky and see in the east an alabaster city descending from the heavens. A mountain splits before our eyes, and the city comes down and settles into it just so. So we all go over to look, and then on into the city, hoping finally to settle the lifetime argument. But what will achieve that end? Shall I walk up to the Proprietor and say, "My name is Hall, who are you?" or does He walk up to me and say, "I am God and I know everything, so there is no need for you to talk"? Or does the Figure that confronts us carry calling cards, suitably engraved "El Shaddi" or "Ahura Mazda" or (just for convenient ambiguity's sake) "God"? Suppose that he does. Further, suppose even that he is surrounded by bolts of lightning and feathered harpists. Still, how do you know that this is God?[11] But if you do not know then, how does that encounter reinforce and support the belief now? The same problems that block knowledge now also block knowledge then; and, in blocking knowledge then, negate belief now.

Of course I have put this very crudely and in physicalistic terms. It need not be put that way. If you prefer: "What do you do when the base vibrations of your finite nous come into a cosmic encounter with the transcendent vibrations of the Super Nous? How do you tell what key it is in?" Put it in any argot you like, the problem is the same problem: when you encounter something (even eschatalogically) what do you make of its character and ultimate identity? You would have the same problem "over there" that you have over here.

[10]Cf. John Hick, *Philosophy of Religion* Englewood Cliffs, N.J.: Prentice-Hall, 1963), p. 100 ff.
[11]See above, p. 73 ff.

Perhaps the final encounter occurs in such a way that the Divine Mind's output crashes through all the finite barriers of our human understanding, and we are suddenly "opened up" and "made new," so that we directly "know" His status. But, even if that could happen, it would be predicated on a change in the character of our own organism, of sufficient scope and impact that we would no longer be men who merely know there is a God. We would have been changed into some kind of new creature who, using new abilities, has knowledge which is inaccessible to men. So this line of argument does not actually open up a way in which men can believe in anticipation of eschatalogical knowing. Rather, at best, it is a way in which men can hope that they may be historically connected with another kind of being which, because of its differences from themselves, might know what they cannot. But this is no basis for human belief of any kind, *a fortiori* for secure belief. So final encounters are no more helpful in providing a knowledge surrogate than the ones we have here.

3. But if the theologians' contentions about the transcendence of God are correct, then we are not ever going to know anything about God (even at a later date), no matter how many "encounters" of whatever sort we might have. At the very point that the evidence was sufficient that we might know, the claim of transcendence would be false. To the extent that the Divinity is transcendent (and remains so), there cannot be any evidence to seek. Even if man were genetically connected to some different kind of being (man-made-new) which could have some knowledge, while God would be immanent to that being, He would remain transcendent to man, and man would remain in the dark. Exactly so long as God transcends man, then, man never knows whether there is a God or not—by "encounter" or otherwise. (Besides, it is contradictory to talk about "encounters" with something that is transcendent, anyway.) But if man is blocked from ever knowing anything about Divine existence, because of God's transcendence, then confirmation of theistic belief is utterly impossible.

But some possibility of confirmation is necessary. Genuine-belief utterances are not mere noises. If they do express genuine beliefs, then those utterances must carry some assertive freight (even if their force is not yet confirmed, they must be confirmable). This is simply to remind ourselves that genuine-belief utterances must be cognitive, even when they are not expressions of cognitions. An utterance that is not even open to the possibility of confirmation is not cognitive— it has no assertive force, whatever other functions it may perform.[12]

To carry this on through: a "belief" that is inconfirmable in principle

---

[12] See above, p. 16–18.

is not a genuine belief (tentative cognition). It follows that where there is no assertive force at all, even belief collapses. On this analysis, men may not even believe that a transcendent God exists (or doesn't). This, of course, is the new agnosticism to which we have referred. We shall return to it and examine it with care later in this chapter.

4. So: I do not think that the encounter route will help us to understand theistic belief. At the very best, it gives us some inchoate hopes, waiting upon some kind of later verification within the consciousness of a being that is somehow related to us, but is not us. But, then, that ultimate result (should it occur) is not our knowledge. Therefore, it cannot be the target of our tentative cognitions. Even the hope is totally formal in a transcendentalist context. What does one hope to encounter under the label "ineffable"?

Analogy   It is often claimed that we may gain insight into the nature of God by appeal to analogy or analogical inference, thus underwriting belief in areas where we do not quite know. This is rather persuasive because we use analogical inference, in just this way, on many occasions and for many purposes. However, it is misleading in this case. While we should not be afraid to reason analogically, we do not want to fool ourselves into thinking that the method will achieve miracles of insight.

Analogical inference is not coercive, of course, but few kinds of argument are coercive. Most of the discourse and argument that goes on in everyday affairs is only probability-yielding—persuasive, influential, but not certain. Analogical inference is just this kind of probability-yielding inference—one of several kinds of induction.[13] It is not to be despised, but it does have its limitations. To see precisely what its strengths and weaknesses are, we must spell out its procedures with some care.

What makes a probabilistic argument specifically "analogical"? An analogical argument is one based upon observed similarities or analogies which are then used as the basis for the projection or inference of further, unobserved similarities between two or more groups or individuals. For example, one might contend that since an honor system works at Hopkins, a system essentially like it ought to work at some

[13]An argument whose premises, if well formed, furnish coercive grounds for its conclusion is called "deductive." One whose premises, even if well formed, furnish only probabilistic grounds for its conclusion is called "inductive." This is a more useful employment of these labels than the old general-particular/ particular-general distinction, for it includes that and covers a lot of other forms of argument as well.

other institution essentially like Hopkins. He would be suggesting that there are some relevant analogies between the two institutions, and inferring conclusions about one that are based on observations of the other. This is an analogical inference because it draws a conclusion about an X on the basis of some observed similarities between X and some Y, when we know that the same conclusion can safely be drawn about the Y.

Analogies can be weak or they can be strong. The strength of an analogy depends largely upon the number of points of known similarity between the analogues. Thus, if one argued that an honor system would work at Q.B. College analogous to the way it has worked at Hopkins, and also argued that one would work at St. Andrews analogous to the way it has worked at Hopkins, the inference would probably be much stronger in the latter case than in the former. The reason is that the points of known similarity between St. Andrews and Hopkins are far more numerous than those between Q.B. and Hopkins. But the strength of the analogy also depends upon the relevance of whatever points of similarity are known to occur. Sheer numerousness of similarities is not enough. After all, Q.B. and Hopkins have many similarities—both are located in Maryland, most buildings on both campuses are of red brick, most students on both campuses are male, and so on. You could list, perhaps, thousands of parallels; but sooner or later you would have to decide which of them make a difference, which of them are relevant to what it is you are trying to establish. Is it relevant, when trying to decide whether an honor system will work at one as it does at the other, to note that the architecture of both is Georgian Revival? One is inclined to say no. Deciding what is relevant and what is not is easier to do than to explain,[14] but somehow the decision must be made.

In the example at hand, we might say, "The fact that St. Andrews and Hopkins are both strongly oriented toward individual development and emphasize independence and self-motivation is an honor system–significant similarity. That Q.B. and Hopkins diverge widely on goals and curricular structure is an honor system–significant dissimilarity. That the buildings at both Q.B. and Hopkins are mostly of red brick is honor system–insignificant." We would go through such a procedure at length and step by step. Only then could we, noting in one case a large number of relevant similarities, claim the probability of

---

[14]I will admit darkly that it is not entirely clear just why one feature is relevant and another is not. What makes the difference is, of course, causal connections; but they are best explained in terms of relevant statistical correlations, which is elliptical if not outright circular.

further (predicted) similarities obtaining. (It should go without saying that the point of such analogical inference is always to make some probability statement about something that is not directly perceived. If it were directly perceived, you would not need to use analogical arguments.) So, on the basis of an extensive number of significant similarities observed, we reach some conclusion about some further similarity between an observed characteristic of one analogue and a not-yet-observed characteristic of the other. Perhaps we look at Hopkins and St. Andrews, note 172 significant similarities—curriculum, goals, type of students (region of recruitment, maturity, intelligence, socioeconomic background, mildly compulsive puritan culture-heritage), and finally note some specific characteristic of the best known of the two analogues (for example, the fact that the honor system works at Hopkins), and conclude: "We have discovered 172 significant similarities, therefore one additional similarity will probably hold, namely, that an honor system will work at St. Andrews as we have observed it to work at Hopkins."

Of course, what we immediately do, then, is institute it and see whether it works or not. Analogical inference is always a tentative and temporary move. We weigh things by analogical examination before we make the leap (institute the policy) to find out whether the leap is advisable; but as soon as we make the leap, we will find out in a much more direct way whether it was advisable in fact (whether the analogical inference was legitimate or not). Analogical inferences can be, and often are, mistaken. I can sit down and say, "Here is *A* and here is *B*, and *B* and *A* have 101 discernible characteristics in common; and since I have catalogued twenty additional characteristics of *A*, and enjoy making bets with myself, I will wager that *B* also has most of those twenty properties." And then I can examine *B* and discover that it doesn't. That happens. I suppose all of us have, perhaps without knowing that this is what it amounted to, made faulty inferences of this kind more than once. We try to anticipate the behavior of a person whom we do not know very well, on the basis of analogies that we draw between what we do know about her and the known character of other individuals we know very well indeed. Witness Agatha Christie's Miss Marple and her inferences from the characters of the villagers in St. Mary Mead.[15] Miss Marple is very successful in solving mysteries on this basis. I would, however, be leery of it in

---

[15] Her technique, if you are not familiar with vintage Christie: she infers by analogy the characteristics of the suspects based on innumerable years of experience with village life, and on the conviction that human nature is pretty much the same wherever you go (it only comes in so many standard models).

real life. Disasters would probably ensue, and quickly, I should think. The flaw is not in the use of analogical inference as such. Rather, it is in the extreme diversity of human character and in limited exposure or too narrow selectivity of parallels. Hasty analogies are as bad as hasty generalizations, while neither analogy nor generalization is bad *eo ipso*.

But, while we are all familiar with our own attempts to reach conclusions about incompletely known situations, based on what we know about other, somewhat parallel, situations we know better, and while we are well aware of the disastrous errors that can ensue, we are equally well aware that sometimes this is the best handle we have and that we have to use it. In this way, hedging and subject to continued check, we proceed to underwrite belief while we wait for knowledge.

Note, however, that the essential basis of every such inference is that we know something about both analogues. We cannot reason by analogy to some conclusions about an *X* of which we have no direct knowledge. The function of analogical inference is to decrease the discrepancy in our amount of knowledge about two analogous states of affairs. We know a lot about one and only a little about the other. By analogical inference and subsequent testing we increase our knowledge about the latter. But if we do not know anything at all about the latter, then there is no basis for drawing an analogy in the first place. If I know that the Rotary Club and the Kiwanis Club are both businessmen's luncheon clubs (and an additional assorted list of similar facts about both—the same sorts of people belong, etc.), and if I know, further, that the Kiwanis Club has a philanthropic "cause," then I may reasonably believe (based on analogical inference) that the Rotary Club probably has one too. (I can believe it until I check it out. Then I know that it does or know that it does not.) But if I know a lot about the Knights of Columbus and nothing at all about the Nights of Scheherazade, I would be on very precarious ground in trying to say something about the latter by analogy to the former. I must know something about both analogues—a successful analogical inference has got to be "two-legged." It has to have a foot firmly planted in direct knowledge on both sides. One-legged analogies are about as much good as one-armed paperhangers. Not much. But this makes trouble for those who would reach beliefs about God "by analogy."

If we knew a great deal about the world and knew a little bit about

---

She is convinced that as soon as you lock into a few significant aspects of a persons's behavior, you know what type of person he is. Then you can go back to everything you know about Simon the greengrocer's son and what he did, and aptly predict your suspect's conduct.

God, and if what we knew about the world bore some relevant known similarity to what we knew about God, then we might fund further beliefs about God with analogical inferences drawn on our knowledge of the world. But this all presumes (a) that there is a God at all and (b) that we know something about the God there is. Theism, because of the transcendence business, negates (b); and, in any case, (a) is the issue at stake and can hardly be assumed.

That is the problem with using analogical inference in trying to underwrite the theists' existential affirmation that "God is." Given that whatever Gods there be are transcendent, wholly Other, etc., on what known analogy can an inference-to-belief be based? The whole enterprise is, in very essence, one-legged.

To summarize: An analogy is a connection between two different sets of data. It must connect both ways (be two-legged). An analogy, so-called, that is to inform those of us in field X about events in field Y, but has connections only to field X, will be sadly uninformative about Y. Another analogy, so-called, that is to inform those of us in field X about events in field Y, but is connected only to Y, might inform someone richly about Y, provided he could get at it; but, unless it is connected in some way to X, he cannot get at it, since X is where he is. An analogy is a two-place connector. It is double-bonded, if you like. Those that only connect once are bound to fail. Those that purport to underwrite theistic belief are only connected once. In the context of transcendental religion, "analogies" are inevitably one-legged and, hence, inevitably uninformative. In the context of immanent religion, analogies could be well formed; but immanent religion thrusts the argument back into straightforward evidence-weighing, and we have seen what happens there. So, while it has been said, "Although we cannot, because of transcendence, have knowledge of God, we can avail ourselves of certain analogical inferences that yield a knowledge surrogate, a kind of insight, a belief," we must conclude that transcendence blocks belief-by-analogy just as it blocks knowledge-by-evidence. Just as? Because.

THAT WE DO NOT KNOW AND CANNOT BELIEVE (NECESSARY AGNOSTICISM)

In the previous section we have been talking about agnosticism "old-style," the point of which is that we happen not to know, but that our ignorance is due to immediate circumstances. Given some changes in these circumstances, the notion is that we very well *might* know. The new style of agnosticism says explicitly what I have already tried to show is implicit in the old; namely, that in any area beyond reason and evidence (like the transcendent, into which theism so often withdraws), we not only do not know, we cannot know. It further implies that, in such areas of necessarily absent knowledge, there is a resultant and equally inescapable absence of significant belief. Many writers have affirmed what they take to be the necessary absence of knowledge. The corresponding necessary absence of intelligible belief is not as commonly made clear.

The New Agnosticism

In running an argument about religion that essentially parallels an argument that they had previously run about metaphysics in general, A. J. Ayer and Rudolf Carnap[16] (and other philosophers as well) assert that when we move into an area that is, by hypothesis, beyond the scope of human experience (and is not a matter of logic), so that our topic is evidentially inaccessible, we have moved into an area in which it is not meaningful to make assertive utterances. Other sorts of utterances might, of course, be quite acceptable; but in such a domain there is no possible assertive content in any utterance one might make. Emotive force, imperative force, ceremonial role, ritual enactment, intention reinforcement through conditioned speech/behavior associations—all these matters and others may be present (the Logical Empiricists gave them but little attention),[17] but when one says, "There is a wholly transcendent Other, beyond all human grasp and experience, who has properties *X, Y,* and *Z,*" or when one says, "I know that there does exist an ineffable Other," then noises are being made that bear no cognitive freight at all. Similarly, the one who says, "I know that there is no ineffable Other," or the like, engages in the same mistaken enterprise—claiming to know, and appearing to assert, in an area that is assertively proscribed by hypothesis and, hence, sterile of cognitions.

People like Ayer and Carnap are perfectly willing to allow that

---

[16]See Carnap's "The Elimination of Metaphysics Through Logical Analysis of Language," in *Logical Positivism,* edited by A. J. Ayer (Glencoe, Ill.: Free Press, 1959), p. 60 ff. and Ayer's *Language, Truth, and Logic,* p. 116. Carnap was a member of the Vienna Circle. Ayer made Logical Empiricism (neé Logical Positivism) accessible to English readers. Logical Empiricism is not, as such, a tenable position. It has an entirely too-narrow restriction placed on the range of linguistic phenomena it examines, confining itself almost entirely to the language of description and assertion. The points that it made regarding description and assertion, however, can be ignored only with great peril. This will be examined with care in Part Two.

[17]A pity, perhaps, but not to their everlasting shame. Sorting out assertion is task enough for one group I should think.

there may be innumerable things (and sorts of things) that we do not know about. Perhaps one of the things we do not know anything about is some sort of "God" Who is, by His nature, inaccessible to us. But once we stipulate such inaccessibility (and would something accessible conceivably deserve the label "God"?), it is suggested that we abjure any move that would claim any knowledge, pro or con, about Him. There is, then, a perplexing dilemma thrown up before us here. To the extent that one could know at all, the object of one's knowledge must fall within the domain of what is accessible to his thought and experience. But to the extent that God is deemed transcendent, He falls beyond the scope of human thought and experience. So, to the extent that he transcends, we have no knowledge of Him, and to the extent that we have knowledge of Him, He does not transcend. Consistency will not allow it both ways. If, then, you argue that God is by nature transcendent and wholly Other (as theologians have long argued), then the extent to which you have knowledge of some X is precisely the extent to which that X cannot be God, and the extent to which some X is God is precisely the extent to which you cannot have knowledge of It.

What range of responses is possible to the claim that theological agnosticism is thus necessary? One pattern involves plain denial—affirming that religious utterances are straightforward assertions, subject to test, thus maintaining that the theological enterprise is cognitive. It is, of course, necessary to abandon all notions of transcendence if one would make this move consistently. (It is also necessary to anticipate that some of the claims will fail some of the tests.) The evangelical wing of Christendom has tried to do this, although, even there, one can perceive a tendency to hedge into transcendence when the tests get negative results. But, if one is willing to handle religious claims on this level, then all one need do is to lay the claims up against events, weigh the evidence for himself, and follow it where it leads. Few theologians have been willing to do this.

Another pattern, and a much more interesting one, has been to accept the charge that the new agnostics have laid down, and fall back to paradox and mystery—not as a roundabout way of getting at cognition, but as an alternative to cognition. This response—accepting the indictment that has been made and trying to live with it—involves a retreat of startling scope, however. As before, it may not be too disturbing if, in the face of Darwinism, one affirms, "Okay, we can give up special creation, we don't need that," or if, in the face of geological evidence, one affirms, "Okay, we can give up 4004 B.C., the flood, and all of that." But, when this continues to the point of affirming that we must abandon cognition altogether, one begins to feel uneasy. Where the theologian falls back on "mystery," there is nothing left to test, nothing to fail or succeed, nothing to know, nothing (even) to believe! There is where the added bind comes. For, when it is not that you don't know, but (rather) that you cannot know (because there is no content to know), then there is no choice of believing. Believing a vacuity is no easier than knowing one.[18]

Further, what is the conceivable factual relevance of what is said by one who has affirmed that his utterances are necessarily devoid of all evidence-connected freight? When the retreat has gone so far as to abandon all possible knowledge and (hence) belief, and the informatively contentless utterances are uttered, one is virtually obliged to ask, "What has that to do with me?"

The theist has at least two answers that he can offer: mystical faith and paradox in lieu of knowledge and belief. Before examining these offerings, however, let me underscore the fact that I am not suggesting that an utterance which lacks informative or cognitive freight has no bearing at all on the human situation. That is a mistake, predicated on the false assumption that human nature is an entirely cognitive bundle. But human nature is not entirely cognitive. There are the emotions, the will, the intentions, the ritual involvements, the conditioned behaviors, and on and on. All of these aspects of human character are of tremendous importance. Yet, while I am not suggesting that this kind of move would make noncognitive utterances irrelevant to the human condition in all its aspects (a pardon is not an assertion—is neither true nor

---

[18]For example, suppose someone asserts that "the absolute enters into, but does not undergo, transformation and change," but we find that in the argument the term "absolute" is set up in such a way that no claim about its supposed denotation is testable in any way. This, of course, prevents us from knowing whether the absolute undergoes transformation; for, under these conditions, we are unable to give any definitive meaning to "the absolute" and, hence, similarly, unable to give any meaning to the sentence in which it occurs. We cannot grasp what it would be for the absolute either to enter or fail to enter into transformation since we have no inkling whatever of what "absolute" means. But, if we cannot even grasp what it would be for the absolute to enter or fail to enter transformation and change, how can we believe that it does or that it does not? What, precisely, would we be believing? Lewis Carroll's Queen once urged Alice to believe something that Alice suggested was impossible. You will remember that the Queen went on to affirm the ease of believing impossible thoughts, especially before breakfast, through strenuous exertion. Carroll was (as usual) making a point and not just telling a tale. At least part of that point was that we can no more believe impossibilities and absurdities than we can know them. My point is parallel. We can no more believe vacuities than we can know them.

false—but we often need one), do we want to make a move that would make such theological talk (since, by stipulation, noncognitive) irrelevant to human *thought?* to human *reflection?* to *evidence?* to *argument?* I think that it would be a very costly move. You must make your own judgment; but when we come to the point of repudiating argument, of saying that what is going on in theism does not have anything to do with thought, reason, weighing alternatives, or making judgments on evidence, then I think that things have come to a very grim situation indeed. Is there *any* judgment that can be brought to bear on individual things that the theist has to say? If there is, and if all he has to say is cognitively vacuous (so that "true" and "false" are barred), it will take some searching to dig it out.

Part Two is devoted largely to that task of digging. First, though, we must examine two patterns of response the theist may offer in lieu of knowledge and belief; and then I must try to summarize what I see as the central issue that has come out of our inquiry thus far: specifically the cramp, the bind, between the notion of transcendence on the one hand and the notion that knowledge is evidence-bound on the other.

Possible Alternatives to Belief as a Knowledge-Surrogate

Mystical Faith   If knowledge and belief-moving-toward-knowledge (ordinary belief) are barred, something like mystical faith may be suggested to take their place. We must note what is involved in making this move, the submoves that have to be made, and the attendant costs. Clearly, the move to mystical faith admits or affirms that the theistic enterprise is not merely lacking in cognitions but is quite thoroughly noncognitive. (The grounds for this statement have been worked out in our discussion of knowledge and belief, above.) But that involves allowing or admitting that evidence is entirely irrelevant to the taking of a theistic position; and that, in turn, would seem to involve the consequence that the theistic positions one might take are factually irrelevant to any conceivable state of affairs that might occur within the range of human access (i.e., in the world). It seems to me, then, that the move to mystical faith disassociates theism from the human condition sufficiently to be alarming. Since it makes the theistic enterprise into one that is strangely disconnected from people where they are, I am quite convinced that this is a thoroughly self-defeating move for the theist, in terms of my understanding of the purported ends or purposes of religion. This may be no more than to say that I disagree, but I think that I disagree on some grounds. You will have to judge whether the grounds are secure.

Mysticism   A thoroughgoing mystical theist may very well accept, without any hesitation, the chain of implications that I have suggested and reply, "Of course, theism is not about the things that occur within the context of human experience—its connections run in a different direction altogether—otherwise, why call it 'mystery'?" But this admission does not make theism any less dysfunctional and self-defeating. If theism is thus disassociated from any state of affairs or sequence of affairs that might occur (i.e., if events are evidentially irrelevant to it) and it is (hence) factually irrelevant to events, then what conceivable reason could there be for any man in the world to involve himself in it? If nothing can happen in the world that will count for theism or against it, then what difference can it make in the world, and what difference can involvement in it make in the world?

It might make this kind of difference: an individual who "subscribes" to the mystery (i.e., an individual involved in the accustomed ritual and regularly voicing the accustomed expressions) might well be conditioned into a fixed pattern of attitudes and behaviors, regarding everyday affairs, that distinguish him from the ordinary citizen. He well might have a different set of appraisals and style of action from those that nonsubscribers have. But these attitudes and behaviors could be in no inherent way tied to the particular mystical subscription he displays. One could, by appropriate conditioning, associate attitudes and behavior of the same kind with any ritual style that people display, or with none. This is because unless and until the ritual style is given some kind of cognitive content, the truth or falsity of which could make some difference, it is no more or less amenable to one set of attitudes than to any other, and vice versa. It may well be that in association with mystic utterances involving such terms as "trinity" and "grace" I display an altruistic concern for my fellowman; but my concern could just as easily be associated with a mystical utterance like "There is transcendent identity tween the ergwhat and the whither," unless the terms like "trinity" have content and force that can be connected intelligibly to the attitudes in question. The connections that come along between attitudes and behaviors on the one hand and particular mysteries on the other are accidental and conditioned connections only, unless there is some relationship of implication or evidential basis between the attitude and the mystery. But if the mystery is a *mystery,* such a relationship is blocked in principle.

I am not, however, suggesting that once one becomes a mystic everything he says and does is "irrelevant." Mystics can (and do) do all sorts of things that are interesting and important and even vital; but they do not have any rationale for the important things they do in mystic settings, for the mystical (by their own hypothesis) is factually disassociated from any and every aspect of the world. The mystical and their own (even distinctive) behaviors are, then, only accidentally connected. But it would seem to me that few, if any, theists would tolerate the suggestion that their actions, behaviors, attitudes, feelings, and so on, have only accidental connection to the core of their theism. Rather, they would affirm some real and binding connection. Consistency, however, prevents it. If there were a real and binding connection, then the core of their theism would have to stand the test of events. In that setting, the core might be found true or found false, and certain styles of behavior and thought could be intelligibly affirmed or avoided for reasons. Outside that setting, the core has no freight to be tested for truth; and, if there are reasons for affirming or avoiding certain behaviors and thoughts, they must be quite independent of that core. It seems to me, then, that the move toward mysticism is a kind of intellectual and behavioral retreat of a most complete sort. It gives the mystic security rather like that of the radical skeptic; that is, his position is unassailable because it is disassociated from any and every test and is, thus, impossible to test. But in becoming unassailable in this fashion, the mysticism removes itself from the arena of argument altogether and enters into the impregnable citadel of factual irrelevance. When the mystic says that all of his mystic utterances fall outside the arena of tests and evidence, knowledge and belief, he protects himself totally from attack. We may never again win any of his marbles. But this is not because he is so good at the game. It is because he has quit the game. Maybe he is playing a different game.

Faith In evangelical Protestantism, of course, the notion of "faith," rather than mysticism as such, has been heavily emphasized. Thus, it is often said, in these circles, that religion is not a matter of knowing but a matter of faithing. It seems to me, however, that when this move is made, it is essentially parallel to the mystic's withdrawal discussed above. In fact, two things are wrong here: first, if "faith" simply equals belief, then the content of faith is subject to evidential test and all that that entails; and second, if "faith" is not simply belief, then the irrelevance of untestability ensues with the same results we have just seen with regard to the mystic. Religionists divide over whether or not faith is simply belief. The fundamentalist tends to equate the two, preferring to fight his battles over evidence and its interpretation. The transcendentalist cannot equate them, of course, for that which is in principle unknowable (outside the arena of evidence and test) is, by the same token, outside the arena of belief as well. So, if faith (or mystery) is claimed to be operative here, yielding insight, it cannot be belief. Faith, like mysticism, abandons belief with knowledge, and yields ritual utterance contingently associated with a lifestyle. That could be *called* "insight" if (like Carroll's Humpty-Dumpty) we think that anything at all can be called anything whatever. (Many apparently emulate Humpty-Dumpty: students who call papers they have bought "my own work," politicians who call tyrannical dictatorships "democracies," trustees who call indoctrination centers "universities.") But calling a rose a violet does not make a rose a violet.

Another Notion of "Faith"   Christian theism is often predicated on something that is called faith; but this "faith" does not amount to the ritual acceptance of unintelligible utterances, nor to straightforward belief in the occurrence of certain states of affairs in spite of evidence to the contrary. While some would affirm faith as ritual utterance of the mystic, and others would affirm faith as the assertion of claims that run counter to all available evidence, there remains another option. I am no theologian, but from what I can perceive, the faith that came into the early discussions of Christian thought, and was mentioned in such claims as "By faith ye are saved," has less to do with mystery and the rejection of patent evidence than it does with the affirmation of a lifestyle and set of values based upon the presumed character of a specific personal interaction. All of us have substantial faith in some of those persons with whom we are involved, a faith amounting neither to mystical ritual nor to counterevidenced assertions. It amounts to trust, to having an attitude toward a person as trustworthy and fundamentally reliable in the give-and-take of our interactions. I think that the religious writers are getting at something like this when they are at all astute.

It is, of course, predicated on the existence of the person with whom one interacts and in whom one has faith. This poses no problem when the focus is one's sister. It does pose problems when the focus is claimed to be God. You would have to fill this in and support the claim that a faith of this kind is possible in some sort of human/"Divine" interaction. This, of course, would bring us back into the questions we have already run: whether the whole notion of a divine Counterpart (with Whom to interact) is even intelligible, much less true. It would not be intelligible, of course, unless it were brought within the dimensions of evidence and test. If it is placed beyond those dimensions, then it is undercut, as are all other notions so placed. I mention this here, not to claim that this notion of faith is without problems; rather, only to indicate that not every reference to "faith" in theism necessarily amounts to either mystery or (directly) belief. Taking faith out as trust-ing-a-person leaves innumerable problems about whether there is a Person-to-trust; but I do believe that it is a truer account of how Christendom's "faith" should be understood than the more theological notions of mystery and the more reactionary notions of affirming patently false descriptions of the world.

Conclusion   The move to mysticism or the nonbelief kind of "faith," in lieu of cognition-oriented, evidence-connected belief, makes the religious enterprise factually irrelevant and evidentially disconnected from all possible human affairs, and makes the utterances of the re-ligionist, in that they cannot carry cognitive freight, of only ritual and accidental import. Such maneuvers do not commend themselves to me as means of funding and underwriting theism. The fundamentalists' equation of faith with simple belief (usually of things we know are not so) founders on its own ground. Faith as trust-in-a-person may have merit but cannot be used to support the basic theistic move because that basic move is the affirmation of the claim that there is a person (God) to have trust in. The main alternatives seem to be the mysticism and nonbelief faithing first dealt with. But a person who takes this kind of posture is cutting himself off from the family of human com-munication and interaction. He is saying things and purporting to talk about things that by his own hypothesis are quite unconnected with the circumstances of men and the world around us. I cannot argue that his utterances are false for I do not know what they mean. He cannot argue that his utterances are true for he does not know what they mean. This is a travesty of religion, bought with mystic faith for fear of tests and evidence. Like the transcendentalist in general, the mystic can say, "I feel that what we perceive is not everything—something more is going on," thus recognizing (properly) that there are limits on our understanding. Beyond that, there is really nothing that he can, and consequently nothing that he should, say—on pain of self-contradiction. The otherness and mystery that he imported to quiet his oppositon require his own silence for once and for all.

Paradox   Some, of course, find refuge in paradox and the "absurd." Tertullian is famous, among other reasons, for his assertion that he believed "because it is absurd." A goodly number of devotees of Ter-tullian seem to be on the scene today. There are, of course, several senses in which the word "absurd" could be used. We might mean, simply, that some claimed state of affairs is astounding, incredible, or unprecedented, or we might mean that it is inconceivable or impossible—that its description is inconsistent.

No special difficulty would attend upon believing a claim that is unlikely, improbable, or unprecedented. We don't ordinarily, of course, believe a claim *because* it is unlikely, improbable, or unprecedented (it would seem rather idiosyncratic to do so). But improbability and nonprecedence do not in any sense interfere with the possibility of belief (belief in a perfectly straightforward sense). On the other hand, if the state of affairs that has been "affirmed" appears impossible (not consistently describable), then "belief" that it has occurred is problematic indeed. For, as we have indicated previously, there is even question about the possibility of there being any net content in a contradictory utterance to be believed.[19] Consequently, if someone were to speak of believing this sort of absurdity because it is absurd, we would be very perplexed.

In recent days there has not been a great deal of talk about belief because of absurdity, but many religious writers have focused on what they call "the paradoxes of the faith" and have claimed to find in the very paradoxicalness a special sign of profundity, importance, and significance. This should remind us of Tertullian, and should make us cautious. Even as there are several senses of "absurd," so are there several uses to which the term "paradox" may be put. If we can locate an intelligible use with reasonable care, we can then formulate some appraisal of the intelligibility and probity of "believing paradox," *a fortiori* believing paradox because it is paradox.

It seems to me that the most useful way to define "paradox" is "a state of affairs (or a set of states of affairs) that seems to be describable only in inconsistent, contradictory terms."[20] A paradox is a puzzle, something we don't know quite how to describe. It threatens our

---

[19]See above, pp. 26, 58-9, 84.

[20]Note that I do not suggest that the term "paradox" be used to label a state of affairs that must be described in inconsistent, contradictory terms. Note also that I am defining "paradox" as a kind of state of affairs. The word "paradox" is also used as a label for a set of claims or descriptions about such a state of affairs; and it is in this latter sense that one may speak of believing or not believing a paradox—it is the story or the claim that is believed or not believed, not the state of affairs itself. One does not, after all, believe or assert states of affairs. One believes and asserts claims, and believes and asserts thereby that some state of affairs obtains. We may also, of course, speak of "paradoxical" beliefs—i.e., some set of beliefs which distributively do not seem to mesh in good order, or seem to harbor inconsistency within themselves.

well-ordered description and explanation of our surroundings because it appears to present intractable inconsistency.

It may be helpful to enumerate, on a mundane level, a few "paradoxes" so that we may have concrete examples in mind before turning our attention to religion. In one of Hercule Poirot's noted cases, he was perplexed to discover that the villain who had been observed in London by a half-dozen respectable and unimpeachable witnesses, had also been observed at that very time in Paris by another half-dozen respectable, unimpeachable witnesses. But one man cannot be in London and in Paris simultaneously! Yet the two sets of witnesses swore to their depositions and a paradox was propounded. Or again: In my elementary studies of biology in high school, I recall having described to me a living creature, the freshwater hydra, that ambulates about the bottom of its pool, feeds itself by grasping morsels of food in its tentacles and thrusting them into its mouth, has a rudimentary nervous system, and is (then) clearly animal; but which also, being possessed of chlorophyll in its cells, carries out photosynthesis (thus producing its own foodstuff in part by natural process), and is (then) clearly botanical. But "something cannot be both an animal and a plant," I thought, and found myself greatly perplexed by the paradox my instructor propounded. Or again: The Baptist denomination is noted for its lack of any episcopal hierarchy, and takes great public pride in "the priesthood of all believers," the "autonomy of the local church," and what would appear to be a thoroughgoing grassroots ecclesiastical democracy. The Methodist denomination, on the other hand, is noted for its subscription to an episcopal hierarchy, the vesting of considerable authority in its bishops and councils, and a rather tightly structured ecclesiastical oligarchy. However, among the Baptists we find, through peer-pressure and institutional inertia, a dominant force for conformity (called "cooperation") bordering on the compulsive. Among the Methodists, on the other hand, we find a frequent openness of debate, progressiveness of policy, and regional variety of practice that yields a sometimes startling diversity. Thus, the Baptists, less organized, are more rigidly uniform and the Methodists, more organized, are less rigidly uniform. This "paradox" has been the source of amazement to many a young divine.

These few "paradoxes" are the merest sampling of the gamut that could be run, but they are sufficient, perhaps, to indicate something of the texture of the phenomenon. They, of course, have their solutions. Poirot discovers, in the last chapter, that his villain has a twin. I discovered, upon careful examination, that "animal" and "plant" are not complimentary sets and need not be considered in mutually exclusive terms at all. Even rudimentary sociological inquiry leads us to discover that there is a distinct difference between professed social structures and real ones, and that it is only rarely that we can find or make accurate predictions of the conduct of a group solely on the basis of its constitutional or documentary organization. The "paradoxes" thus resolve upon examination: what appeared to be only describable in contradictions are discovered to be perfectly consistently describable; the puzzles come clear.

Our common attitude, upon the discovery of a paradoxical state of affairs, is perplexity at first, but then a redoubling of our efforts to discover additional facts and relationships so as to achieve resolution. In ordinary affairs, the discovery of a paradox is never seen as the terminal point of an inquiry, but rather as *prima facie* evidence that inquiry cannot yet be terminated. The discovery of a paradox is a stimulus to the inquiry, not an indication that inquiry is complete. It is such a stimulus because of the overriding and fundamental assumption on which almost all of our inquiry is based: that apparent inconsistency in our accounts of the world must be resolved, that contradictions cannot be harbored in our world view. This presumption is made, of course, because we realize (perhaps without articulating it or knowing precisely why) that the incorporation of inconsistency or contradiction into our world view shatters the possibility of utilizing that world view as a means of increasing the range of our perception and grasp of what is going on. It is not just that we have a psychological aversion to any attempts to incorporate P and non-P into our world view (although that aversion is certainly regularly present). It is also because we realize that once P and non-P have been incorporated into our world view, it is then possible to infer any and all conclusions whatever, without exclusion, from the premise-set so affirmed. Once we have accepted inconsistency into our principles, we salvage no technique for distinguishing the true and the false in terms of those principles. Given our desire to distinguish the true and the false as we attempt to understand, describe, predict, and control events, we usually cry "Hold!" upon the discovery of paradox and redouble our efforts, striving as vigorously as we can to reconcile or dissolve the puzzle and set our inquiry back in good order.

There are those, however, who do not share this antipathy for paradox—who, indeed, cry "Eureka!" rather than "Hold!" upon the discovery of such puzzles. In fact, it has been suggested that the classification of paradox as a kind of puzzle, an occasion of inquiry demanding resolution, is a grossly narrow and fallacious way of taking our world. Black and white thinking! Antipathy toward unresolved paradox is seen by some as typifying a narrowness predicated on a slavish devotion

to two-valued logic and excluding from our grasp the rich variety
and texture of our universe. Everyone knows what folly it would be
to insist that a rose that is not white must be black. Roses are also red,
and yellow, and magenta, and pink, and piebald. To try to exclude
the paradoxes that abound in our world as states of affairs that are
misleadingly described and need to be resolved, is to try to force the
pattern of human thought into a strait jacket that would deny such
obvious facts as the multitudinous hues of the rose! To which the reply,
of course, is "nonsense!"

Anyone would be a fool who claimed that any rose that isn't white
is black; but one would not be a fool to claim that any rose that isn't
white is nonwhite. Black is not the complement of white. Black is but
one small part, one narrow subset, within that vast complementary
class of colors "nonwhite." Even if we went to a three-valued logic,
such that the value of a proposition might be 1, 2, or 3, the rule of
exclusion would continue. A sentence that was not classified as 1
would be classified as non-1 (and could then, of course, be further
classified into either of the subsets of non-1, namely, 2 or 3). The
class 1 still has its explicit complement (non-1), and that complement
has its own internal structure. This should not need to be belabored,
but it is an important point often ignored. Those that reject the incorporation of unresolved paradoxes into their world view are not
binding the pattern of our thought to some overnarrow and provincial
logic. They are, rather, keeping things sorted out in a simple and
straightforward way which, for all of the ease with which it can be
misunderstood, can with equal ease be grasped if we can be bothered
to take the time to think it through.

When we turn our attention to the occurrence of paradox in theological discussion, we will soon note not only the recent extolling of
the virtue of paradox as a sign of portent and depth, but also the
suggestion that the exclusion of paradox (or the insistence upon its
reconciliation) is confined and strait-jacketed thinking. (And also the
claim that any attempt to bring our religious thought under the aegis
of consistency and good logical order is an insidious kind of idolatry
that places logic above God and thus makes a God of logic.) Paradox
has come to be seen as profound in recent times, I think, largely
because antitheistic argument has pressed again and again to the
conclusion that theism can be maintained only by flying in the face of
evidence or by withdrawing into mystic transcendentalism, which
makes consistent theistic affirmation impossible. It may be claimed,
then, that accounts and descriptions of the Wholly Other do constitute a paradox in the face of that Wholly Otherness, but that this is

all right; that the claim that God is both transcendent and immanent is inconsistent, but that this is all right; that the claim that we know God by way of analogy (although we know nothing of God on which to predicate an analogy) is inconsistent, but that this is all right; that the claim that God "loves us as a father" but that His ways are not our ways and that these words have, then, only symbolic meaning, is self-canceling, but that this is all right. For, after all, to insist upon consistency would be to place God in the strait jacket of our patterns of finite thought, to place the Moloch of logic above the Ground of Being, and thus condemn ourselves to fruitless (and damnable) idolatry. Thus, if we would seek truth, we should seek paradox. If we would seek insight, we should search for contradictions. Not as occasions for inquiry and reconciliation, but as occasions for their incorporation into our belief-set, indicating simultaneously the inadequacy of human belief and the unfathomable depths of Divine Truth. This, of course, would make Tertullian very happy indeed.

Should we subscribe to such a position, we would at one thrust have solved most, if not all, of the problems that have been posed in the preceding pages about the possibility of theistic knowledge or straightforward theistic belief. The burden of much of the argument thus far has been that theistic knowledge is impossible, and straightforward theistic belief impossible, because of the retreat into transcendence and mystery that has transpired, as a result of continued defeats, when theism is placed in the arena of ordinary evidence. But if the retreat into transcendence and mystery, embellished with paradox and decorated with contradiction, is a retreat into profundity and insight, a retreat into that which is better than knowledge and better than ordinary belief, then the retreat is not a retreat at all. It is the ultimate and final vindication of the theists' stance. Can it reasonably be so taken?

A short answer is no, by the very definition of "reasonable." But the theist could well reply that this begs the question, since (after all) his claim is that reason and reasonableness are strait-jacketing confiners of our insight and grasp of truth; and, thence, that the inability to maintain his posture "reasonably" is not a flaw but a virtue. Again, we are dealing with a position much like that of the radical skeptic. Unassailable, but unassailable not by virtue of the cogency of its argument, rather by virtue of its withdrawal from any cogent and structured argumentative enterprise whatever. If the theist, on withdrawing into transcendence and mystery, surrounds himself with paradox and absurdity, and avows its significance, there is little (perhaps nothing) that the ordinary man can do to convince him that he is mistaken. The very notion of mistakenness is predicated on the notions of evidence, consistency, and argument. The theist is secure, but again at great cost—the cost of disassociating himself altogether from the fabric and the interaction of human commerce. Those of us who reject the withdrawal into paradox and absurdity may comfort one another with reminders of the price that the paradoxical theist has paid; we may even try to show him, during his ordinary hours, the pragmatic cost of confusion and dysfunction that is attendant upon parallel withdrawals in other areas of human inquiry (science, history, and so on); but we can in no way demonstrate to him, by argument, the incorrectness of his view. For: "demonstrate" and "argument" and "incorrectness" are terms the standard definition of which he has rejected for his purposes, and which, consequently, by his lights, have no bearing on the endeavor in which he is engaged. Thus, in paradox even as in mystery, his marbles can be preserved, for he has again left the game. The cost of his leaving, however, is great. For it leaves him with a body of affirmations which, by his own admission, furnish no coherent ground from which inferences may be drawn, and which, consequently, offer no evidential ground on which they may be preferred to any other body of affirmations that anyone might offer. A rational theist could argue against the wiles of the atheist or the agnostic. The paradoxical theist cannot, and in that inability must abandon all attempt at convincing his hearers. Then, either in silence, or in the fervor of spirit independent of all rules, coherence, and tests, hope and wish that the world might come to share his abandonment of reason. Thus paradox and absurdity are a "final solution" to the problems that rational and empirical men pose, as they weigh and deliberate the sense and grounds of theism. Like other "final solutions," it commends itself to me but little. Surely something has gone awry when those who talk the language of Zion, repudiating the confines of all rules of sense, seize security through self-contradiction and impact through obscurity.

4

THE
KNOWLEDGE/
TRANSCENDENCE
CRAMP

The notion of a philosophical or conceptual "cramp" is, perhaps, not elegantly expressed, but it gets the idea across very nicely indeed. A conceptual cramp is what happens when you are trying to maintain a set of notions that are indigestibly incompatible—a kind of philosophical "stitch in the side." Many think that the primary responsibility of philosophical inquiry is locating these cramps and, because they interfere with and debilitate our thought, trying to work them out. Working them out amounts essentially to making them go away by analyzing the component concepts that produce the strain, and in some way reconciling them, or modifying them, or discovering an interpretation of them that will ease the pain.

In Chapters 2 and 3, I have tried to show that there is a very substantial conceptual cramp in ordinary theistic religion. I have done this by locating some of the basic ideas and concepts that are used in theism and trying to bring them out in the open for careful and attentive examination. Rather than addressing attention to theological questions themselves, I have explored the concepts in use in order to locate the philosophically prior questions of meaning and use.[1] In our examination, it has quickly become apparent that the assumption that

---

[1] Perhaps you are familiar with the distinction that can be drawn between "baselevel" and "metalevel" inquiry. Baselevel inquiry is inquiry about some

the enterprise is cognitive (knowledge-directed) and that its claims are often knowledge claims or at least claims of belief (i.e., claims which become knowledge claims upon the garnering of sufficient evidence) is commonly and uncritically operative. But, at the same time, we also discover the regular (if not universal) uncritical assumption (made, perhaps, for purposes of worship originally) that the focal point of theistic reflection (God) is in some sense radically transcendent, wholly other, quite inaccessible to human minds, entirely beyond the dimensions of human experience. But it is fairly clear that these two notions simply do not mesh as they stand. Abandon one and theism can be maintained in awesome silence. Abandon the other and the arguments in theism can be pursued fiercely to some demonstrable conclusion (or at least probability). But maintain both and the resulting "stitch" is crippling.

We have not yet arrived at the point of proposing a solution to this cramp. To be sure, we have gone through many of the tentative moves that advocates of theism have proposed and that opponents of theism have proposed; but what we have distilled so far, it seems to me, is only the problem and not its answer. (I have not suggested, nor am I suggesting now, that the theists' cramp has no solution or therapy. Even though it may be untreatable in the terms in which we have so far been able to state it, there still remains the possibility that the cramp may be eased by restating the issues in ways that will preempt its very occurrence. More on that presently.) If we could settle the problem, relieve the strain, then the theists and their adversaries would be in far better shape to pursue, adjudicate, and settle their disputes. For instance, the arguments from and about evil could be carried to straightforward conclusions if and when some clarity was achieved on the question "How and on what grounds may we dispute the correctness of claims about a purported God and His interactions with the world around us?" But until some clarity is achieved there, just so long as the theist hedges on knowledge and waffles with the ineffable,

---

set of facts or data in the world of a straightforward descriptive sort (empirical or otherwise). Metalevel inquiry, however, is not about some set of data in the world; rather, it is an inquiry into the apparatus with which the baselevel inquiry is conducted—into the concepts and ideas and patterns of thought that are involved when baselevel inquiry is carried on. So you may have, e.g., straight scientific inquiry (baselevel), and you may also have investigation into the concepts, thought apparatus, etc., of science (metalevel, philosophy of science). Such metalevel questions are always "prior" to any issues that are posed in the concepts which are the objects of the metainquiry. Thus, clarification of such notions as knowledge and transcendence is prior to any conclusion on whether or not we know x, y, or z about some transcendent G.

then any attempt to drive the "evil" arguments to their conclusions is foreordained to failure. There is no way to get at it. Knowledge, belief, and transcendence must be clarified before the majority of properly theological inquiries can be made.

We have seen a number of different ways of trying to get around this, but I do not think that any of them work. Moving to analogies, appealing to "faith" and mysticism, retreating to paradox—none of these modify or ease the cramp at all because the ordinary Western theist still wants to say that we do have religious knowledge and that we have it of One who is "wholly other," and obscurantism in none of its forms will make that inconsistency go away. Some better therapy must be found, or else the cramp must be accepted as incurable.

One of the themes that I have been repeating in the discussions so far is that the theistic community has been to a considerable extent pushed into these confining straits by the expansion and reinforcement of our general knowledge of the world. This is to say that while there was very likely a notion of transcendence built into theism to begin with, the religious community has increased and undergirded it by abandoning, one after another, descriptive claims as being germane to the settlement of the basic theistic issue. Thus the theists do not wind up in a strong transcendentalist position accidentally. They have frequently chosen it as a preferable alternative to trying to maintain a straight testable set of assertions in the face of disorder, grief, the argument from evil, Darwinism, geological history, and so on. By claiming transcendence and inaccessibility, and the indiscernibility of Divine ways, they have gotten themselves out of the bind of advancing claims that seem clearly counter to ready evidence by saying, "Evidence is irrelevant," "Evidence is not germane," "Argument does not count here." But this leaves us in the extremely strange position of taking an area of common human concern, one that has been of great importance in history, and substantially withdrawing it from the arena of human affairs. For, as I have tried to show, the claim that evidence (what is going on in the world) is not relevant to the theists' posture has the alarming corollary that this religious posture, in turn, has no relevance to what is going on in the world. But this is passing strange, for the religious community, at least from time to time, has quite obviously been trying to make a whole set of proposals about the proper pattern and structure of human life and social interaction—clearly affirming that religion is not only relevant to the condition of men, but crucial to it. So, the cramp that we have noted is not a merely academic one. It poses a threat to the whole enterprise of theism as a viable perspective on man and his affairs. The

withdrawal from evidence, then, while reasonably intended, entails a
cost that is surely unacceptable to the religious community—the choice
of irrelevance in the face of apparently demonstrable errors of fact.

You could, of course, have a religion that involves intermittent
revelation coupled with Divine concealment. That would not entail
the cramp we have seen in transcendental theism. There would be no
insurmountable problem with a God who keeps some secrets. Everybody keeps some secrets. Richard Nixon keeps some secrets, but I do
not think that he is beyond human ken. He falls within the range of
human experience, and the things that he says fall (at times) within
the scope of human understanding. Nevertheless, there are a lot of
things about him and his possible thoughts and intentions that we do
not, in fact, know. Perhaps it is this sort of thing that many conservative theists have in mind when they say that we have not plumbed the
depths of the Divine mind. But this is not what the transcendentalists
are usually saying. They are saying that God is of such a qualitatively
different kind from man that He is inaccessible in principle. It is not
that we have not explored far enough or that we do not have enough
facts in hand; rather, it is that there is no such thing as enough facts.
God is wholly other. Nothing said of Him is true. (And, since both
P and Not-*P* are said of Him, it follows that nothing said of Him is
false, either. It makes one think of Tillich.)

I think that the typical evangelical theist thinks of God as in principle accessible—within the dimensions of human knowledge—though
awesome, and goes on to make many theological claims that he takes
to be testable and is convinced (perhaps mistakenly) are true. He
makes a whole string of straightforward claims about what has happened in the world, and what is going to happen in and to the world,
and what will become of you and me by and by. He is ready to have
these claims put to test. Of course, if Carnap is right, then most of these
claims are false. (There are certainly grounds to think that many are
doubtful at best.) But they are maintained, even when in the face of
or in ignorance of the facts, in a coherent and intelligible way. Perhaps
this is why, when such religious conservatives encounter facts, they
tend to go secular.

This is, however, a very different sort of thing from what goes on in
the neo-mystic wing of theism. Strongly influenced by Hegelian specu-
lations, and containing a definite element of the East, the cramp is
plainly put. Nothing can be predicated of the Ground of Being; but
then the nothing is predicated at great length. The conflict is clearly
apparent in this joint denial of predication and affirmation of innumerable predicates, which utterly fails to take into account the necessity

of making consistent choices if one would have his talk intelligible. It may well be true that as things become more and more profound, they fall less and less into the grasp of the human intellect; but the converse, that as things fall less and less into the grasp of human intellect, they grow more and more profound, is pernicious. Since we cannot know anything at all about an altogether-transcendent God, believing anything about One is completely footless. Trying to conceal that in the mystery of paradox is an obscurantist cop-out.

So, we must try to find an alternative path. If we cannot accept the notion that inconsistency is profoundly true, and if, on the other hand, we cannot ignore the evidence that is all around us in order to preserve unlikely myths, then (still being convinced that something of importance is going on in theism) we must find a new and different analysis. In Part Two, I shall be trying to find just that, so that we can rehabilitate an intelligible way of taking the theists' enterprise. That enterprise, after all, is going on—whatever its rationale—with vast numbers of people involved, with tremendous impact upon the lifestyle, the nature and character of society, and on the quality of individual lives. Surely the theist is doing something besides prevaricating and fantasying, weaving something besides fantastic equivocations and impressively phrased nonsense. I shall try to locate and spell out what else is going on. In the process, we shall see whether this knowledge/transcendence cramp cannot be assuaged.[2] In order to do this, it will be necessary to look closely at the language of theism; and, just as in the case of knowledge, it will be necessary to look at some basics about language in general as well as considering the language of religion as such.

[2] I do not think that the notion of knowledge and the notion of transcendence can be reconciled. One cannot know what transcends—whatever transcends one does not know, whatever one knows does not transcend. I am not going to propose any way to make that clear truth go away; but I will propose a way in which we may see religious thought as viable, intelligible moves that do not violate the knowledge/transcendence gap in the first place.

PART TWO

❧

THE
LANGUAGE
OF
THEISM

5

THEISM
AND ITS DISCOURSE:
ALTERNATIVE
INTERPRETATIONS

So far we have been talking about the problems that surround the
notion of religious knowledge, especially where the idea of transcendence occurs. I have suggested that a severe cramp attends the joint
assertion that a God is transcendent and is either known or (straightforwardly) believed to exist. But people have frequently suggested
that theistic claims perform some other task than straight assertion.
That would ease the pain. So we want to consider what sort of functions could be going on when such utterances are made (i.e., any
utterance in which there is at least some apparent reference to a transcendent Being—a Divinity in the traditional Western style).[1]

In order to survey some options on the nature, function, and status
of religious talk, we need to locate such talk first. Just what talk counts
as religious? It is a tremendously variegated package. Surely the Shema
counts—"Hear, O Israel, the Lord our God, the Lord is One," and
surely "In the beginning was the Word, and the Word was with God
and the Word was God" is a sample of religious talk, too. It is equally
certain that "I had baked beans for supper" is not an example (except,

---

[1] I will not plague you with a long defense of the thesis that looking at language
is philosophically useful. Suffice it to say: (a) we are trying to get some understanding of the basic building blocks and structure of theistic thought; and (b)
the language used in expressing thought offers the most obvious and direct access

perhaps, for Pythagoreans). But there are other locutions that are somewhat more problematic.

We cannot answer the question simply on the occurrence of certain words. That would be nice and simple, were it possible. Maybe: "Every utterance in which the word "God" or some cognate occurs is religious." But then: "Goddammit, I said the monkey wrench, not the pliers" is religious talk! I think not; but if we decided whether talk was religious on the basis of the words in it, it would be.

Once, in jest, Hilary Putnam told an audience, "Philosophy is what philosophers do, and a philosopher is anybody who draws a paycheck from a philosophy department." You could do religion that way: "A religious utterance is the sort of utterance that religious people are inclined to make, and religious people are the ones who go to church a lot." The trouble with this is that it is much too loose. On such an account, Plato's talk and behavior was philosophical talk and behavior. But Plato ate three times a day, scolded his wife, and brushed his teeth from time to time. So you don't want to say that philosophy is what philosophers do, nor do you want to say that religious utterances are what religious people utter, without some restrictions.

Almost any utterance could be deemed religious if we made the definition of "religion" inclusive enough. So, if we would exclude any claims at all, some kind of functional definition of religion is going to have to come into play and, eventually, some specification of the forces necessary to qualify an utterance as properly religious.

Traditionally, religion has been understood as an organized enterprise (i.e., structured, but not necessarily social) that influences the pattern of human life, that ordinarily manifests itself in cultural institutions, and that is predicated on the notion that man recognizes some objective X outside himself against which his aspirations, desires, and values must needs be measured and to which he is in some sense responsible. This X is frequently (not always) called God.[2] It may be identified with the State, the World Soul, the Continuity of the Race—there are all kinds of possibilities—but the X is, in any case, outside the

---

to the goal of any such inquiry. If we find some other means of access, fine. I do not suggest that the examination of religious language is the only way to get at this; but it is one way, and it is clear and fairly straightforward. If phenomenologically inclined, we could try for the preconceptual raw feeling of religious experience, and analyze there. Having no notion of how that is done (and some suspicion that it is not possible anyway), I will focus our attention on the language as a means of getting at what is going on when religious things are said—a very paradigm of philosophical inquiry, as I see it.

[2]Cf. Geddes MacGregor, *Introduction to Religious Philosophy* (Boston: Houghton Mifflin, 1959), p. 2.

individual himself. If this definition is at all adequate for religion, then religious language would be the sort of language used when people are engaged in enterprises of that kind. Accordingly, religious language not only admits such theistic statements as the Shema, "I believe in God the Father Almighty, Maker of Heaven and Earth," "Hail Mary, full of Grace," and "There is no god but God," but it will also include, as functionally "religious," many of the credal and ideological statements we find expressed in the context of other systems—cannibalism as a way of life, modern political, economic, and ideological creeds, and so on. But the traditional kind of religion, the kind we have been talking about so far, is theistic. It involves not just "the recognition of some *X* outside oneself," but a God notion. That is, this *X* outside oneself is not deemed to be culturally produced or an event in history, but rather, an outside agency against which one's aspirations, indeed all human affairs, designs and aspirations, will and must be measured. From that standpoint, religious utterances would be the kind in which a narrower and "God-involving" enterprise is carried out. Thus it would be limited to utterances in which a specific sort of defined religious function occurs.

Looseness remains; but, pragmatically and practically, we can focus on a few utterances that are clearly religious in this fashion, and we can extrapolate from them to a general rule. When we do, it is apparent that there are at least two levels of language use going on in the religious context. First, there are utterances that I will call religious primitives (i.e., claims or particular kinds of claims that function as primitives in the religious enterprise). It is fairly clear that "God exists" is a primitive in theistic religious activity. On the other hand, "And God divided the waters that are in the heavens and the waters that are under the heavens into the firmament and the earth, and divided the earth into the seas and the dry land, and saw that it was good" is not a primitive, but rather, a locution in which the primitives are assumed and used.

Most religious discourse, it seems obvious to me, turns out to be nonprimitive. Indeed, only a few primitive moves are needed. The bulk of religious discourse turns out to be claims and descriptions and explanations and evaluations of ordinary affairs that are structured in terms of (or organized under the structure of) these primitives: for example, "Oh God, I have sinned and do most humbly and contritely confess my sins." All the business about wrongdoing, contriteness, humility, and confession consists of perfectly straightforward notions that could easily have nonreligious contexts; but here these ordinary kinds of events are brought under a specific rubric, structured in a certain way, and used to a religious end. The locution has been shot through with

the notions, not just of contriteness and confession, but of contriteness and confession in a God-ordered structure. Consequently, if we
could understand the meaning and status of the religious primitives,
we could, by expending the required effort, go ahead and extrapolate
them so as to understand run-of-the-mine religiously structured claims
as well. We already understand the ordinary part of those claims. We
know what confession is; we know what wrongdoing is; we know what
promising is; and so on. The unusual notion, the notion brought in
here that requires special attention, is the notion brought in by the
special primitives—in this case, "God."

So it seems to me that the religious locutions to which we are obliged
to turn our attention, if we want to get leverage on the whole affair,
must be some one or two of these primitives that structure and organize
all the others. If we thus focus our attention on an explicit utterance
("God exists"), it is not to say that it is the only religious utterance,
but rather, that in the context of theistic religion it is primitive to the
enterprise. What is going on when this primitive is uttered? What is
being done? This is the point on which our analysis will focus.

Not every analysis of the force and function of religious expression
begins here, however. Many attempt an exploration in the reverse order,
seeking the character of the full spectrum of religious talk ("derivative"
as well as "primitive"). Surveying a few such broader-gauge alternatives
may be helpful in bringing our own reflection into tighter focus. With
some grasp of them, we can then go on to ask whether, in our considered judgment, any one of them will begin to carry the freight. Then
we can do more detailed work in whatever direction(s) offer promise.
Among the many different analyses available, I shall briefly consider
a few mythic, psychological, emotive, moral, and perspectival alternatives.

MYTHIC

Auguste Comte, the nineteenth-century French classical positivist,
shared the not-uncommon view that the development of inquiry can
be divided into phases or epochs, each "better" than its predecessors.
The chief epochs he saw were "theological," "metaphysical," and
"scientific."[3] Each of these epochs is said to be distinguished by its

[3]Auguste Comte, *Positive Philosophy,* translated by H. Martineau (London:
George Bell, 1896) Vol. I. However, if we divided the world-record into such
epochs, two caveats would seem to be in order: (a) use a lot more eras—the

own approach to the facts and events of the world, "theology" and "metaphysics" being attempts at different levels of "explanation," while "science" is satisfied simply to "describe."

The epoch of theology is essentially one of mythic explanation, and the distinctive character of "myth" may be seen in man's inability (or unwillingness) to attempt any rational description or explanation of the world in terms of itself. Rather, he attempts to project upon, or read into, the workings of the world something like his own willful and rather capricious power, to see the events of nature in an animistic and volitional pattern. Man in an era of myth (theology) interprets the world in personal terms.

In the subsequent era (the metaphysical), the system of thought becomes more complicated. Man attempts more and more to rationalize explanations and hang them together systematically, but he still fails to come to grips with the observable facts on their own turf. Metaphysics, like the theology-myth preceding it, seems less a means of coming to terms with apparent facts than a mechanism for avoiding that end. Theology and metaphysics are distinct, however, in their positions on the testability of their explanations. In the epoch of theology, when primitive man said, "The Incredible Mogoo swims in the bottom of Lalakuli Volcano and devours maidens alive when we throw them in each spring," his claim was straightforward.[4] There was no trouble with transcendentalism or nonconcreteness, as in the "metaphysical" epoch to follow. Just mistaken myths.

Religio-theological myths and their constituent claims have additional and crucially important functions that are separable from the explanatory enterprise at which they fail. They also have ceremonial functions. They also have the function of furnishing a focal point around which the society can be bound and given continuity. So, we would have to admit that these claims, even while they fail in the enterprise of truly describing, may very well succeed in the other enterprises for which they are used (i.e., social cohesion, tribal continuity, and even individual peace of mind). But there is no necessity that they

---

epoch of theology alone wants dividing into ages of animism, dynamistic magic, spiritism, etc.; and (b) take note that however illuminating this may be in broad terms, it is certainly not true in specifics. So you would want more stages, noting that they are not uniform or synchronous.

[4]If you had appropriate diving systems, so that you could probe the volcano without getting fried alive, you ought to be able to find the Incredible Mogoo; and, if you went on the right day, you should find Him devouring maidens. Of course, in our contemporary wisdom, we know that the claim is false. But it is no less an assertion for all of that.

succeed. Indeed, well-intentioned falsehoods seem to go awry more often than not. They are usually dysfunctional in the long run because they are not at all likely to produce the intended consequences. They may furnish some social cohesion and some temporary escape from adversity; but, in providing an escape from reality and thus preventing us from coming to grips with the facts in a reasonable and accurate way, they jeopardize, rather than reinforce, our ultimate well-being in the world. If the intent of religious discourse is to describe the world so as to furnish social cohesion and reassurance to the individual devotee, but the actual consequences prevent him from getting the comprehension of the world that he needs, and (thus) prevent him from living at the level of success at which he could live and (thus) disrupt his (and his society's) well-being, then there would be good reason to move on to another era. Too bad that "metaphysics" comes next, and we have to wait for "science."

So goes one analysis of religion's talk: as mistaken and dysfunctional escapist "explanation."

PSYCHOLOGICAL

Religion can be seen as a kind of neurotic adaptation. You sometimes see a psychoanalytic case history of the development of monotheism, tying it back to oedipal rivalry and linking it into a more or less Freudian theory of human development.[5] From such a perspective, religion is eventually dysfunctional for the individual, even as it was dysfunctional for the group from the previous viewpoint; even though, in stress situations of certain kinds, it may be the best and most practicable available adjustment mechanism that one can use to cope with his own idiosyncrasies and surroundings.

The neurotic, and the psychotic to a much larger extent, engages in the construction of routines and delusions to protect himself and find a niche for himself in living conditions he finds adverse. As the constructions become more and more systematic, the articulations of them begin to assume the form of a very complex structure of beliefs and behaviors with a (perhaps absurd and discontinuous) logical order of its own. Religion can so be seen.

Unable to cope with our environment (not so much our physical

---

[5]Cf. Sigmund Freud, *The Future of an Illusion* (New York: Doubleday, 1951); *Moses and Monotheism* (New York: Vintage, 1958); and *Totem and Taboo* (New York: Norton, n.d.).

environment here as our mental and emotional environment), perhaps especially unable to cope successfully with the father-son conflict that is so common, we project it into a constructed system of God and His creatures along with a ritual apparatus of reconciliation and atonement. Then we have a way to work out the anxieties and stresses that are produced (say) out of our feelings of rivalry with our fathers for the affection of our mothers.[6] The whole cycle of self-sacrifice, resurrection, redemption and atonement, and all the rest of it, thus works out into a kind of rationale to help us come to terms with our emotional distresses. Unfortunately, however, it does this by diverting our conscious attention away from the real root of our distresses. What we need to do is go through a course of psychoanalysis and realize this diversion, so that we can reintegrate the personality in a functional pattern.

From this perspective, then, the function of religious language is the invention, articulation, and expression of a fantasy mechanism aimed, primarily, at the establishment or achievement of emotive stability in the face of psychic conflict. It is not descriptive. It is constructive. It is not exactly true; but that is "beside the point." The only question that is strictly appropriate about this kind of discourse is not "Is it true?" but "Is it efficacious for its psychological purpose?" or "Does it yield the kind of therapeutic balance or equilibrium for which it is calculated?" The usual answer is no.

SOCIAL

Religion is often seen as a fundamentally social force, and the product of conscious invention. It does not come out of the turmoil of the subconscious. Rather, it is produced by the established strata of the social structure, calculated to keep that social structure static and to furnish those who are exploited by the system with a kind of imaginary redress for all its shortcomings.[7] It is an invention in terms of which those in charge can indoctrinate the exploited masses into the notion of pie in the sky when they die by and by. The idea is that if

[6] If one does not recall any particular rivalry with his father for the affection of his mother, maybe that is just because he has repressed it all (and, no doubt, compensated for it by getting involved in religion). You must be careful with a theory, though, which converts lack of evidence into proof.

[7] Cf. V. I. Lenin, "Socialism and Religion," *Selected Works,* Vol. XI, Pt. 3. Reprinted in J. B. Hartman's *Philosophy of Recent Times* (New York: McGraw-Hill, 1967), Vol. II, p. 123 ff.

one can sufficiently indoctrinate the masses with this notion, then they will not be nearly so upset over the fact that there is, for them, no pie now. It is a way of diverting the attention of the common man from his proper and immediate concerns, by substituting for them fictitious concerns for a fraudulent "world to come." The function and status of religious discourse then becomes, for the established, the function and status of an intentional lie—socially and culturally beneficial to those in charge, exploitative and destructive to the rest.

METAPHYSICAL

Rudolf Carnap had a view of religion and its discourse that is similar (as one might expect) to that of Comte.[8] He, too, talks about "myth." He does not go into the routine of sorting out the history of the world into eras; but he does pick up the rubric of Comte's division of things into myth, metaphysics, and science in terms of which he presents an explicit analysis of what is going on when theological discourse occurs.[9]

Carnap divides religious talk itself into aspects of myth, metaphysics, and theology. By myth he means assertions that are structurally well formed and that function in the role of description and assertion, but which purport to assert a variety of fantastic states of affairs the likelihood of which is extremely minute. So seen, some religious discourse is descriptive in structure and force, but blanketly mistaken. Most of religious discourse used to have that force, but the "metaphysical" has crept in more and more. Metaphysical discourse does not amount to well-formed statements asserting unlikely states of affairs. Rather, in its metaphysical function, religious talk comes down to statements which look like, or seem to be, ordinary assertions but which, in fact, are not assertions at all. This is because they are syntactically ill-formed, or because they involve referring terms that fail to refer, or because they are not empirically underwritten; because, in a word, they do not have "truth conditions" and are, hence, untestable.[10]

A claim like "Bacchus spends his April afternoons cavorting on

---

[8]Even as Comte was the central figure of the classical positivist movement, Carnap was one of the central figures of the more recent, twentieth-century (logical) positivist movement.

[9]Rudolf Carnap, "The Elimination of Metaphysics Through Logical Analysis of Language," in *Logical Posivitism,* edited by A. J. Ayer (Glencoe, Ill.: Free Press, 1959), p. 60 ff.

[10]"Truth conditions" and related notions are important. They are discussed in some detail, starting on p. 164.

Mount Mitchell" is perfectly testable. It would fall in the "myth" slot. If you want to check it out, go to Mount Mitchell on an April afternoon and look around. See if you find anyone who has the body of a goat and the trunk of a man, drinking lots of wine and playing the pipes. If you do, then you have confirmation. If you don't, then you have grounds for doubt (but not proof—he might have gone to Blowing Rock for the day). But: when you come to some claim like "The Transcendental Beyond invades the now with the immanent and ineluctable force of Becoming," there is no way to get a handle on it. There is no way to put it to any kind of test. It isn't true, and it isn't even false—it's "metaphysics." Now, metaphysics may serve a number of useful functions—keeping people off the streets and out of trouble, perhaps—but it is not informative. It carries no assertion-freight. It is cognitively empty.

The "theological" variety of utterance is a mixed variety—part myth and part metaphysics. It requires sorting out. A statement like "Jesus Christ, the Son of God, turned water into wine at Cana" is, so seen, a strong mixture of myth and metaphysics. All the business about the water and wine is myth. The business about Jesus being the Son of God is metaphysics. (How would you differentiate between someone who was the Son of God and someone who was not? How would you differentiate between something that was God and something that was not? How would you give the phrase or the word testable content?) So the thing to do is to separate the myth and the metaphysics. Then you forget the metaphysical part for cognitive purposes, and reserve judgment on the remainder until you have put it to the test. It would seem, however, that from this view what makes a claim distinctly theological is the metaphysical inclusion. Hence the distinctive function of such discourse would seem to be to appear to assert without actually doing so. Its effective freight would have to be of some nonassertive kind, probably emotive.

EMOTIVE

Some advance the notion that an utterance like "God exists" functions as a kind of self-directed reassurance ritual, essentially analogous to whistling in the dark; it enables the individual to postulate for himself the notion that the universe is somehow (appearances to the contrary) friendly. It is a ritual maneuver in terms of which we reinforce and elevate our life-morale.

You are aware that in the navy, particularly on board ship, a morale officer is assigned to each detachment of men. It is his task to provide a little smoothage from day to day, to see that the latest films are available and shown on schedule, that liberties are equitably distributed, and that if one of the men gets a "Dear John" letter, someone is available to cheer him up. (I am not mocking the morale officer's job. It is of crucial importance to the well-being and fighting efficiency of the team.) From this fifth point of view, his role is about the same as the one held by the clergyman vis-à-vis his flock. Religion boosts life-morale, and the minister is the officer-in-charge.[11]

Of course, that kind of analysis of what is going on in religion and its discourse forceably ignores what the theologians would call the "prophetic motif" in religious history. It is a little bit difficult to see Jeremiah as morale officer. Indeed, this kind of "There is a God, that is, we live in a friendly universe" equation which, in turn, equates religion with the cultivation of life-morale, omits a number of significant historical aspects of the religious enterprise. It is like equating marriage with playing slap-and-tickle, making a part into the whole. The life-morale business does occur in religion; but judgment, indictment, and woe also occur. Much of the talk sounds more like "This is an unfriendly universe—how can we get out of it?"

Many men look upon the environment as antagonistic. This is because so much of what happens is adverse to their interests and well-being. Some things reinforce human efforts; but many things counteract them. Thus, in primitive religion at any rate, much of religion is about adversaries who need placating. Indeed, even today, more events appear to run against our efforts than "help us along." It seems to me, then, that in confronting events, people see them more often than not

---

[11]The analogy is not entirely off the mark. I used to get distressed, some years ago in high school, when I would go to certain religious meetings. They were rather like pep rallies: songs, shouts, even cheerleaders. Or consider the message of Norman Vincent Peale, predicated on about the same level, striving after an affirmative attitude toward life and the universe, and strangely Victorian. Or:

The year's at the spring
And day's at the morn;
Morning's at seven;
The hillside's dew-pearled;
The lark's on the wing;
The snail's on the thorn:
God's in his heaven—
All's right with the world.

Or, with Coué: "Every day, in every way, I'm getting better and better." It is rather distressing.

as adverse, and that much of religion has to do with anthropomor-
phizing adversity. You could still take the life-morale business, coupling
it with this perceived adversity, and see much of religion as man's fabri-
cation of escape techniques; but this view still leaves out the "prophets,"
those who use religion to indict rather than to reassure. So it will not
do. Religion has traditionally incorporated into its own claims the woes,
the fears, and the adversities, and has viewed God not just as the One
who is going to provide the escape hatch, but as the One who is going
to bring judgment.

MORAL

R.B. Braithwaite has argued for locating the function of religious language in the arena of morals.[12] Religion, as he sees it, boils down to
an apparatus of "stories" that surround, support, and reinforce one or
another style of moral life. To subscribe to a religion, then, is to affirm
the desirability of a certain lifestyle, and to voice or express one's commitment to practice it.

Religious discourse, in such a setting, could be divided into three
families: (a) narrative, fictionlike, utterances, in which one reiterates
(or, on occasion, creates) stories that illustrate the lifestyle and the
virtue of following it; (b) certain ceremonial, somewhat performative[13]
utterances, in which one affirms, subscribes to, or endorses the lifestyle; and (c) judgmentals, in which one actually brings judgment to
bear upon human behavior in his own or other actual styles of life,
in terms of whether the behavior coincides or fails to coincide with
the model he espouses.

From this general perspective, the core of religious books (the
Bible, the Koran, etc.), as well as most of the religious talk of devotees, consists of the "stories." When uttered (self-consciously by an
astute person who has some idea of what he is doing), the stories are
not presented as assertions. They are offered as parables. Most of us
who have come up through a Judeo-Christian background are familiar
with the notion of a parable because they explicitly occur in scripture.
Braithwaite extends the notion considerably by suggesting that the
whole apparatus is a network of parables. All of it is narrative reinforcement of a lifestyle that has been modeled on the one expressed

---

[12]R. B. Braithwaite, *An Empiricist's View of the Nature of Religious Belief*
(Cambridge: Cambridge University Press, 1955).
[13]On the notion of a performative, see p. 168 ff.

in the tales. Curiously, he insists that we do not need to believe the
"stories."

Some parts of Braithwaite's formulation are, I think, extremely
astute. I believe he is correct in saying that religion is (usually, though
not always) tied into the notion of a style of life to which someone
adheres and which he espouses. As a matter of psychology, it is certainly true that morals and maxims are more effectively transmitted
in the context of "stories" than in lists. Stories illuminate and illustrate the application of the maxims, and bind the whole affair more
closely and persuasively to the context of our own lives.[14] It is hardly
remarkable, then, that religion involves such "stories." For, while
an occasional theologian may insist that the moral code is really an
independent matter—that what is really crucial is a package of items-
to-be-believed—when we come to religion as it is understood and
engaged in by the man in the pew, it is very much involved with the
moral enterprise at every level. So, it seems to me that there is considerable wisdom in the suggestion that a primary function of religion is
to serve as a supportive apparatus for moral commitment,[15] a kind of
"booster unit" to keep commitment strong and moral perception in
focus.[16]

[14]Even in nonmoral situations, telling tales is an effective pedagogical device.
Since people may remember the tale and not the point, some caution is, of course,
required. But preaching seems to be far more effective when it gets down to
cases. Or, consider reading a text in abnormal psychology. The level of interest
increases considerably when you get to Suzy Z., who had an inhibited rivalry
with her mother, and slides to vanishing when the text enumerates Frondlick-
Schmidlap's eleven varieties of neurotic adaptive behavior. Aesop learned this
lesson early, and Braithwaite would discourage the clergy from losing it.
[15]Giving credence to the idea that this is one of the primary functions of
religion does not negate the possibility that Bertrand Russell was correct in
saying that the primary effect of religion on society and on the quality of human
life has been essentially dysfunctional and morally destructive. To tie these two
ideas together, add only the notion that most of the moral codes supported by
religion have, in some grievous sense, been wrong. That is arguable in its own
right and is worth your exploring. See Bertrand Russell, "Has Religion Made
Useful Contributions to Civilization?" in *Why I am Not a Christian* (New York:
Simon and Schuster, 1957), pp. 24–47.
[16]By granting that one of the frequent (even primary) functions of religion is
the reinforcement of moral codes, I do not want to give the impression that I
am accepting the notion that a morality can only be predicated on some religion.
There are all kinds of serious things wrong with that idea, not the least of which
is the total dilution of the force of "religion." It is somewhat stylish to insist
that the real content of religion is exclusively moral, and that it is impossible to
achieve any significant or meaningful morality without religious encounter and
commitment. That is as wrong as can be. One can perfectly well pursue, be in-

There is, however, one serious difficulty with Braithwaite's position. Considering the man in the street, and not the self-conscious theologian, it would seem that some measure of straight belief in the stories is a very important (maybe even necessary) condition for the success of the apparatus in supporting the moral endeavor. Go to any number of "churchgoing" people. Ask them what the practical effect would be if the stories that surround their commitments were demonstrably fraudulent. What if it could be demonstrated (say) that Jesus was a con man who duped the people of his time—that, instead of "ascending," he packed up the seventeen bags of gold he had collected from widows and orphans, and took off by fast clipper to the South Seas? I am convinced that ordinary men would, at that point, reject the lifestyle and commitments that had been bound up in the stories for them: up to then they believed; now they don't anymore. A very significant number of ordinary people really do believe the stories or at least think they do; and they are the ones for whom the apparatus is supportively effective. To be sure, many other people have moved away from such belief. Finding people who really believe (as per H. L. Mencken) that "Jonah swallowed the whale" is difficult in some circles (it is especially difficult among theologians). But I find it difficult to think that the now no-longer-believed tales still carry any genuine moral freight for them. In any case, the broad-gauge backbone of Christendom is comprised of people for whom the lifestyle is important, and for whom the stories are important, and for whom the importance of the stories in supporting the lifestyle is clearly based on the belief that the stories are true.

I reject Braithwaite's account of religion to this extent: Braithwaite offers his analysis as an account of how religious claims do in fact work; he suggests that the "stories" are efficacious whether believed or not—that belief is finally irrelevant to the enterprise of religion—and that simply looks false to me. I suspect that if the bulk of people were disabused of their affirmative belief in the stories, there would be a radical change in the style of life to which they have subscribed. When you don't believe in Santa Claus anymore, you don't try to "be good the last ten days before Christmas" anymore either.

Now, if most people need to believe the stories in order for them to work, and if you argue that for the equilibrium and well-being of

---

volved in, be committed to, and live a life of moral involvement without any religious foundation at all. Unless you want to so bend the definition of religion that by virtue of the fact that a person is concerned to do the right thing he is *thereby* religious. But then the circularity is obvious.

society it is essential that they work, then what follows is: "Take steps to see that people believe them, whether they are true or not." A lot of people argue this way: "We have a primary social responsibility to guarantee the survival of institutional religion (and, consequently, affirmative belief in the stories that are packed into it) in order to maintain the social order; superior and learned creatures may know that it is all malarky, but we also know that it keeps the wheels of commerce rolling and the masses in their place; therefore, unless we want chaos and anarchy, we ought to be (say) teaching Sunday school—keeping people's false-but-useful beliefs secure." That makes me feel uncomfortable. One of my basic commitments is that one ought to believe what is true and positively disbelieve what is false. If that is proper, and if subscription to false beliefs is necessary for the welfare of society, then I am in the bind of believing that there is virtue in letting the welfare of society go by the boards. But are false beliefs necessary for social welfare? Surely not.

Braithwaite's notion is interesting. It may have more merit than demerit. If there is error in it, I think it resides in the assumption that such a religious/moral enterprise can work on the basis of stories without belief, and further, I think that any such religion/morality-linking view leads close to a precipitous cliff at the foot of which lies the notion that moral schemes can be predicated solely on religious bases. With these two caveats, I urge you to pursue the notion he offers, at length and with care, for yourself.

PERSPECTIVAL

In a public lecture, frequently delivered, Professor John Wisdom suggests that subscribing to religion amounts basically to "another way of seeing things."[17] The view for which he is arguing here is not entirely unlike that expressed by R. M. Hare, in which the holder of religious belief is seen as operating under a controlling interpretation or binding perspective on the world (which Hare calls a *blik*).[18] What both of these views suggest, at bottom, is that to become involved in religion is to take a certain vantage point on the world, to adopt a

[17]John Wisdom, "Another Way of Seeing Things," public address (Richmond: Virginia Commonwealth University, 1971).

[18]R. M. Hare, et al., "Theology and Falsification" (The University Discussion), reprinted in Steven Cahn's *Philosophy of Religion* (New York: Harper & Row, 1970), p. 116.

particular perspective on the events that occur around us, prior to and independent of any and all evidential check or test.

Hare amplifies the notion of a blik in a parable, now famous, of a demented student who is possessed by the notion that all the professors at the university are engaged in a nefarious conspiracy against him. It would be possible, of course, to hold such a view on entirely reasonable grounds, for there could, in fact, be such a cabal. (Not every "conspiracy" is a paranoid projection of the Justice Department. Only some.) What makes the demented outlook of the student demented and not reasonable, however, is that his outlook is not responsive to the particular character of the events that are occurring. That is, his outlook is not modified (or modifiable) by any change in the sequence of occurrent facts, but furnishes the framework within which each and every occurrent event is interpreted and seen. Are the professors gentle and kindly toward him in their behavior? That is their deviousness. Are they harsh and demanding? That is their cruelty. Do they ignore him, attack him, flatter him, cajole him, ridicule him, or even say (when asked) that they have never heard of him? Whatever they do is simply more proof of the lengths to which they will go to set him up for the kill. His conspiracy-outlook is, then, prior to all particular events. It is not subject to revision. Indeed, it is the fundamental conceptual apparatus within which and in terms of which everything that happens is structured and understood. The facts must bend to fit the blik. That, of course, is what makes it a blik and not just another working interpretation of the facts.

Now, Hare goes on to make it quite clear that, as he sees it, all of us are operating under one blik or another. That is, while the vantage point from which each of us views events (which obviates revision in terms of events) may vary from individual to individual, some such fixed stance surrounds and shapes the thinking of every one of us.

From this point of view, then, to engage seriously in religion is to bring to bear upon the events that constitute the world a filtration and sorting apparatus, subject neither to check nor revision, according to which each event that occurs is seen in a special light.

Professor Wisdom also presents the nucleus of his view in a parable, another that has become widely known and is the object of much discussion among philosophers and theologians: the familiar story of the garden in the wilderness.[19] In this tale, two travelers come upon

[19]John Wisdom, "Gods," reprinted in Antony Flew's *Logic and Language* (New York: Doubleday, 1965), pp. 194–214.

what is, to all appearances, a cultivated plot of ground, a garden, in the midst of wild land. But the two travelers do not share the same point of view, or way of seeing, with which to interpret and understand what they have discovered. One man is sure that there is a gardener who carefully tends, cultivates, and preserves this plot of ground; the other is equally certain that there is no gardener and that the "garden" is only a simple and nonpurposive natural event.

We can imagine such a situation occurring. Further, under ordinary circumstances, we could easily figure out how to settle the issue between them. We know what to look for in order to decide whether there has or has not been a gardener at work. But, Wisdom suggests, this dispute need not be a dispute about the facts. It may occur at a much more fundamental level, for the two men may genuinely be possessed by two "different ways" of seeing things. We would become convinced that the latter is true if we discovered that no amount of checking and inquiry and no amount of additional data, however detailed, are able to sway the views to which the two subscribe. If, after careful tests (with infrared cameras, bloodhounds, and whatever other devices you may imagine), and after appeal to all the standard canons of evidence, one of them still says, "I know there is a gardener," and the other says, "I know that there is not," we may be sure that they are not disputing the facts. They are, rather, looking at the "garden" in different ways—ways that are not evidence-based, ways which, rather, force an interpretation on whatever evidence occurs.

Now, to operate under a blik, or to see the world in a certain way, prior to evidence, is not to issue a set of assertions about the facts-in-the-world. It is, rather, to impose upon the world a structure in terms of which specific assertions of fact might, in turn, be made. But, while rival bliks or rival ways of seeing do not constitute rival families of truth-testable assertions, they nevertheless have distinctive output in their effects upon the dimensions and kind and quality of life that is engaged in by those who probe and work the world in terms of them. Our demented student is, we say, demented. His movements are furtive. The bulk of his time is spent in worry. His lifestyle is anxiety. His brow is furrowed with care. Our weary traveler, who is so certain that a gardener has been at work, probably looks on the whole world as purposive, organized under a telic structure, as a product of a plan. And, while looking at the world in this way is not subscription to a set of truth-conditioned assertions, it *is* to look at the world in a way which models and shapes the dimensions of your feelings, the content of your attitudes, and the whole style of your life.

It is because of this that both Hare and Wisdom insist that it is some-

how important and necessary to have the right blik, to "see" in the
right way, even though they hasten to add again that ways of seeing
and ways of bliking are not in any way subject to evidential test. This
poses a problem.

If a blik (or a way of seeing) is a firmly fixed way of taking the data,
one that is not subject to review in terms of the data, a fixed frame to
which all of the data is bent, then how does one judge that one blik
is "right" and another "wrong"? What kind of criteria might there be
for a stance that so strongly appears to be defined as criteria-free? Hare
and Wisdom do not fill this in; but I think that the most likely option
is some kind of pragmatic examination of the frame's output.

Now, if such a pragmatic examination is at all possible, it will most
likely occur from the outside. I don't think it is at all likely that an
individual can be practically concerned over whether he has the right
blik, for there is no effective way for him to get at that judgment. If he
is concerned over whether his stance is correct, then his stance is not
effectively operating as his blik. It is operating as some kind of hypothesis or theory, subject to review. But even when it does fully operate
as his blik and is not, consequently, subject to review by him, it is still
important for his own life's success that it be functional. Deliberation
over whether it is functional can be brought to bear from the outside,
however. Indeed, this is precisely what we do when we come to the
sorrowful conclusion that an individual has delusions, is insane, has
"lost his grip on reality."

If Hare is correct in his notion that every man operates under some
blik, it is of extreme social importance that the alternative bliks be
weighed for output and effect. I think that he is correct, for to say
that every man operates under some blik is only to say that any examination of facts must be conducted under the framework of some
perspective or conceptual vantage point. So it is important that men
operate with a productive one. I would, myself, avoid words like "right"
or "correct" here, because it does not seem to me that rightness or
correctness can be very intelligibly discussed at this level. The blik
or way of seeing with which you work determines the dimensions of
"right" for the work you do. But I do think that we can use words
like "productive," "functional," and "useful," with an eye on the welfare of individuals and their communities, to see that the bliks they
work under are not counterproductive, self-defeating, and destructive
to the very ones who occupy them.

Again, the fact that a blik to which you hold is destructive and
counterproductive is not likely to impress itself on you in such a way
as to get you to change. This judgment almost has come from outside

But we can look at the fixations with which people operate (consider the one of the student, that events are conspiratorially contrived), and fairly quickly discover whether they are usefully fertile or dysfunctional.

There is still no effective way to label a blik "true" or "false" because to speak of its being one or the other would subject it to the test of truth conditions and assertive evidence, and evidence must, itself, be interpreted in terms of one or another blik. Truth and falseness carry their freight inside the way of seeing, not outside it. But talk of productivity and counterproductivity is perfectly germane. Indeed, it is perfectly common. Here is a man who interprets the events of history in terms of a diabolical-contrivance blik. We discover that he, like others who work in this frame, becomes increasingly distrustful of all the events and persons that occur around him, increasingly withdrawn and unwilling to negotiate and talk and examine issues with other persons, and, finally, because of his way of looking, completely isolated and cut off from human interaction. And that is counterproductive, both for him and for the community. It works against both. In this sense, it is very important that a person have the "right" blik, and the whole purpose of mental health programs is to encourage him so to do.

We still cannot say, though, given what a blik is, that a person has some obligation to seek a "right" one. Because the moment that we recognize the possibility of error in a point of view and consider trying to correct it, that point of view is no longer operating as a blik for us. Rather, it is operating as some contingent belief within whatever other fixed way of seeing (other blik) has now assumed the role of functioning limit on our inquiry.

Religion, seen this way, is prior to all our describing and asserting. It is a frame imposed upon the whole enterprise of cognitive inquiry. It will show in our conduct and show in the dimensions of what we say. It may even show in particular ritual utterances that we voice, and thus mark us out as those who subscribe. But it isn't believing, *a fortiori* it isn't knowing. It is a way of bliking, or taking the world.

SUMMARY

The function, force, and role of religion and its discourse have been seen in many different ways by many different interpreters. In the preceding paragraphs, I have examined a minimal sampling of what seem to me to be some of the more important perspectives that have been voiced. It is very unlikely that any one of these perspectives is "correct" or even complete. It is equally unlikely that any one of them is flatly false, missing the mark entirely.

In the chapters that follow, I shall try finally to suggest an interpretation which is, as I see it, more complete and less misleading than those so far enumerated. In order to do that, however, it is necessary to postpone sweeping proposals, and begin, even as we did with "knowledge," with some very rudimentary observations about some very basic issues. "What function does this kind of discourse perform?" simply must be preceded by the more basic (and more painstaking) "What sorts of functions can discourse perform?" If we do not enumerate and examine the basic options, we may not even find the neighborhood, much less the address, where religion is "at home."

6

ON THE USE
AND USES
OF LANGUAGE

In the preceding chapter, I have tried to explore a few of the alternative interpretations of religious language-use that have influenced our thinking in recent years. Presently, I shall suggest an alternative interpretation which, I believe, gives a more illuminating account of what is going on when religious people talk. Before I can do that, however, we must briefly examine some of the many sorts of things that can be done in everyday language, independent of any special and "religious" stipulations. If we can get a little feeling for the tremendous variety of games that can be played in language, we can avoid from the start the notion that something is going on only if the game is cognition and assertion (a mistaken positivist view, predicated on a simplistic and excessively narrow notion of what language of any sort amounts to).

SAMPLES OF LANGUAGE USE, TRUTH-CONDITIONED AND OTHERWISE

Reporting/Asserting/Describing (R/A/D)

Perhaps the basic or fundamental language use is one of reporting, asserting, or describing states of affairs (r/a/d). This is the model that the Logical Empiricists wanted all language to emulate. They were mistaken; but we still need to have some idea of how r/a/d language operates. First of all, it has truth conditions. To say that an utterance has truth conditions is not to say that it is true. It is to say that it is either true or false; that there are, at least in principle, discernible circumstances that would count as evidence to support the claim or that would count for evidence to negate it; that its truth or falsity would make a discernible difference in the world. The Logical Empiricists refined this idea to its probably most precise form in attempting to spell out a "criterion of cognitive meaning." The criterion they offered was essentially that in order for a statement to be cognitive(ly meaningful) it must have either formal truth conditions as in logic and mathematics, or empirical truth conditions as in the descriptive statements of natural science; otherwise, the statement is cognitively empty (nonsense).[1]

There is no disputing that this is *a* basic language use. In suggesting some alternatives and additions, we must not make the mistake of thinking that they replace the r/a/d use so analyzed. It is there. It may even be the most frequent. Further, I think that the Logical Empiricists' analysis, for all its flaws in detail, is a reasonably adequate one. That is, if the game one wants to play is the game of asserting facts and describing states of affairs, then he is playing a truth-conditioned game. But we obviously do other things in language, too; and there is no reason to try to discount or ignore them.

Promising

Yesterday my children said they had sore throats and felt too bad to go to Sunday school. We wondered if there might not be less pain and more desire to watch *Super Chicken* than vice versa. However, if they were sick, we didn't want to take them out, thereby contaminating the entire neighborhood. On the other hand, though, if they were too sick for Sunday school (and so stayed home for *Super Chicken*), then they were equally too sick for the Thalhimer's Toy Parade in the afternoon. So we told them, "You can stay home and watch *Super Chicken*, but you will have to stay home this afternoon, too, and miss the Toy Parade." Great dismay! One said, "But you promised we could go!"

As a matter of fact, we had promised, several days previously, and I take promises rather seriously—a promise lays down a moral require-

---

[1] See below, p. 170 ff. and cf. Carl Hempel, "The Empiricist Criterion of Meaning," reprinted in A. J. Ayer's *Logical Positivism* (Glencoe, Ill.: Free Press, 1959), pp. 108–129.

ment on the person who has entered into it. Still, I told the boys that I was very sorry, but if they were sick the promise did not bind. The promise was made under the supposition that they would be well enough to go. With illness, the moral requirement was waived. One said, "You're no good." The other said, "I feel better, let's go to Sunday school." (The point of this is promises, not Sunday school and *Super Chicken*.)

A promise can be broken, surely. But a promise can also be absolved. Also the conditions that would be germane to the proper fulfillment of the promise can fail to obtain, and the promise can then become inconsequential or disconnected. Strictly speaking, however, for all the ways it can fail, a promise is not the sort of thing that can be indicted for being false. (Nor is it the sort of thing that can be endorsed for being true.) The reason for this is that the promising, the uttering of a promise, is not an r/a/d linguistic enterprise to begin with. It is a different kind of maneuver entirely. It can fail, but in a different way.

In promises, then, we note at least one other kind of linguistic maneuver in addition to the r/a/d-variety. I am not suggesting that religious utterances are promises (although it would be interesting to consider many religious utterances as some kind of ritual promise). All I am suggesting is that we can deny that religious utterances are r/a/d, without denying them any rule-governed use whatever—that promising is one alternative role that utterance can perform, and that it is only one of many.

Commanding

This morning the children were still complaining of sore throats, and I am beginning to think that maybe they really were sick yesterday. We decided to keep them home from school, just to be sure. But by ten they were out of bed and running up and down the hall with great gusto, shouting and turning cartwheels. So I came out growling, "You go to your room and close the door; and you go to *your* room and close the door. One more sound out of either one of you, and it's trouble! Move!" So commands are given. Although the boys are too small and too easily intimidated to respond to a command very often with anything other than compliance, from time to time they do try to beg off ("Oh please don't make me do it") or deny grounds ("I haven't done anything, it was him, Daddy"). They will try all kinds of moves to alter the force of the command; and as they grow older and smarter, the moves will become more complex and subtle. The point: they are already aware that there are conditions that have to be satisfied in order for a command to be germane, appropriate, authorized, and so on. Still, these are very different conditions from those that have to be satisfied by assertions and descriptions. One response that you do not make to a command is "That's false" (or "That's true"). Nor do you say, "Prove it!" or "What's your evidence?" Maybe a four-year-old might try that. One such just might be naive enough to say "Prove it" when ordered to his room. But a seven-year-old wouldn't dream of such a thing. He might say "Why?" or "That's not fair," or he might plead or argue or run; but he has better sense than to say "False!" Responding to a command with "True" or "False," or "Evidence, please," or "Prove it," or anything of that sort, just does not make sense. How do you demonstrate an imperative? You don't. So, there is another possible language function in addition to r/a/d and promising. (It might be interesting to consider religious language under the guise of an imperative structure. Surely a significant part of religious discourse is, in fact, imperative in its intent.)

Emotive Expression and Reinforcement

There is an emotive function in language that is of tremendous importance. One thinks of the kinds of things likely to be said by a young man and a young woman "in love." Each of us could supply our own, autobiographical examples of circumstances that have elicited verbal behavior of the sort in question. Consider the words typically exchanged in settings of "romance." Even when they are (mostly) sincere, the last thing in the world that the participants are likely to want is that anyone should take them literally as assertions of fact. Facts have very little to do with it.

A serious sort of game goes on here, the exercise of a variety of ritual. Call it the expression and reinforcement of affection through verbal behavior. It is a linguistic function of high importance.[2] It helps to express, channel, and focus the attitudes, feelings, and empathy between individuals. It plays a crucial role in the development and preservation of people's affective capacities. Because it is ritualized, it functions both as trigger and reinforcement for a wide range of attitudes, motives, and responses. By reinforcing the will (feedback), it provides resolution for intentions and a basis or footing for action.

---

[2] I would not dispense with it for a moment—for the young at any rate. This game is rather too quickly replaced by another, in any case. See Andy Capp. And besides, the exercise is not confined to romance. That, after all, is not the only emotive enterprise in which people engage. Religion may be another.

Now this is clearly not r/a/d language. You do not talk about the truth or falsity of emotive responses and emotive expression. Consider a parallel case: certain passages from the Song of Solomon. They are really rather funny if you try to take them literally or descriptively ("your neck, like David's tower, hung with a thousand bucklers.") Of course, some metaphorical description is going on; but, beyond that, and much more important, the words embody a ritual expression of admiration and devotion which has nothing whatever to do with true or false descriptions of any states of affairs whatever, directly or by metaphor. An accepted, conventional word-pattern gives evidence that certain emotive commitments hold, shows what those commitments are, and reinforces them and certain desired responses to them. Such discourse is the basic stuff of being human, at least as much as asserting and describing are.

Such discourse very rarely occurs "pure" or by itself, it seems to me. It usually is intertwined with some other functions as well. But even in such mixed cases, it makes a difference that we can recognize by taking note of the alternative ways in which one could assert the same state of affairs when colored in different emotive tones through choice of terms, examples and models, ways of speech, intonation, and so on.[3] A person standing on the brink of the Grand Canyon describes what he sees, and in his choice of terms, in his manner of speech, and in all his features, we can discern not only what he asserts but also how he feels about it. It shows in his speech acts and in his surrounding behavior. The emotion-show can be misleading or deliberately deceptive, of course. Just as the r/a/d content can be assessed (on truth conditions), so can the emotion-show be assessed—but on different criteria altogether. Thus, the emotive side or emotive freight of language activity is distinguishable from the straight, cognitive freight-carrying that may be going on.

You might try to merge this back into r/a/d and claim that some expressions of emotion and feeling can be judged true or false. If one says he has a feeling and does not (or pretends), he acts falsely. One can describe one's own emotion readily (and, perhaps, accurately), just as one can describe a street scene or the situation in Munich. Thus, I might say (to anyone interested) that my emotions at this moment consist of a rather choleric dyspepsia and a grim feeling toward the world in general. That is plainly r/a/d, and is truth-conditioned. Thus, one could respond, having examined my whole behavior, "You

[3]Irving Copi, *Introduction to Logic* (4th ed.; New York: Macmillan, 1972), pp. 62-66.

are describing your emotions and feelings accurately" or "You are mis-describing your emotions and feelings grossly." But it still remains true that we can linguistically do something with our emotions beyond describing them, namely, show them, elicit them, practice them, reinforce them. Say we have a young man and a young woman sitting by the edge of a lake and talking. Perhaps, quoting Copi, he says, "Oh, Baby!" (or even something more articulate than that). He is clearly expressing attitudes, feelings, and emotions, and also eliciting attitudes and feelings and emotions on her part at the same time. It may be mis-leading in extreme; but it just isn't true or false. Perhaps he is not interested in the nobler things in the least. Maybe he is just out for a good time and says "Oh, Baby!" just to make her think he really cares. He may lead her down the garden path this way; but it wouldn't be (in this case) by lying. (Lying involves intentional assertions of states of affairs that are not the case in order to deceive.) Rather, he would be leading her down the garden path by pretending, by mimicking the verbal behavior of a man in love when, in fact, he is not a man in love. It is deceit; but not all deceit is false assertion, since one can deceive without asserting or denying anything at all.[4]

Performing

In some of the promises, and imperatives, and emotives of various sorts, promises especially, there are elements of the "performative."[5] Per-formatives comprise a very large family of linguistic maneuvers. A performative expression is one in which something is done rather than one in which something is described. Examples: "I promise," "I par-don," "I christen." In the christening ceremony, the priest is not describing something that has been done or something that is going to be done. He is, through certain conventional and stylized linguistic behaviors, doing something (christening); and the speech acts in which he does it are an essential part of the transaction. It may go awry in

[4]In all of this I have tried to avoid the word "meaning" altogether. I am not arguing that such emotive speech acts have meaning or that they do not. If one wants to say they do, that is fine with me. According to the way I would use the word "meaning," I would say that they do not; I associate the notion of meaning with the transaction of verbal business like asserting and denying states of affairs. But, in a broader sense of "meaning" they have it; i.e., a function is performed. Distinguish expressive meaning and cognitive meaning if you like, or distinguish the meaning function and the expressive function if you prefer. How-ever you call it, there are no truth conditions here.

[5]J. L. Austin, *How to Do Things with Words* (Oxford: Oxford University Press, 1965).

a wide variety of ways, but one would not ordinarily speak of such an expression as being either true or false. Its conditions are not truth conditions. The priest says, "I christen thee Sam," and the mother might say, "No, you have the name wrong—it is Clark"; and that would be an occasion of some distress. Or the mother could take a closer look at the "priest" and realize that it isn't really the priest, it is the mad rabbi from the synagogue on the corner. All kinds of things could happen that would make the "christening" a bad one or no christening at all—render it ineffective, block it, flaw it, or annul it—but it does not make the utterances that occur in it false. It makes them, rather, inadequate, inappropriate, unauthorized, null and void. Not false.

We can already see that the possibilities in language are much broader than mere assertion and denial. Further, all these other uses have their own criteria of "success," distinct from, and often more complex and involved than, truth and falsity. These criteria need exploring. But before exploring such nontruth conditional criteria for non-r/a/d utterances, I want to suggest one more kind of language maneuver for your consideration.

Categorizing

Only one tenth of an iceberg projects above the water. The ice that you see is not the "whole of it," but it *is* a part: evidence of something larger than, but inseparable from, itself. Similarly, in the military, the wearing of the insignia of rank is part of what it is to have rank. Part of the "being a general" that the wearing of stars points to is "being entitled to wear stars." While not the "whole of it," there is some evident self-reference here. Self-reference occurs in language, too, especially in a kind of linguistic operation that is involved in theory formation at the most general and basic level (category formation).

This is the level of talk at which we not only express and use the categorial pigeonholes into which we are sorting occurrent facts, but also actually set up those slots. You can call this category talk, as opposed to r/a/d talk and the other kinds of talk we have mentioned already. It represents a behavior that goes far beyond the overt linguistic operation itself. Still, the overt linguistic operation in which it is done and expressed constitutes a basic and, I will argue, uneliminable part of that complex whole (i.e., categorizing, sorting, and putting a structure on the phenomena—getting the experience that occurs into some array).

We will explore this language use with special care later. I want only to get it on the table at this time. Now I want to examine the notion of felicity conditions for assorted speech acts.

FELICITY CONDITIONS

In the preceding section, I suggested only a few of the many uses to which language can be put besides the ordinary, commonplace description or assertion of states of affairs. In addition, there are instructives (an instructive is a kind of nonimperative direction-giving), ceremonials and transactionals of endless variety, jokes and play, and scores of other kinds as well, the success or failure of which does not depend on the satisfaction of truth conditions by the utterances made.[6] In affirming this, we explicitly reject the early Logical Positivist notion that language has only one ideal function, and we replace it with a more versatile and operational notion of language, one that would determine its success or failure not on its "truth" or "falsity" (its "cognitive" or "strict" meaningfulness), but, rather, in terms of a variety of conditions that are appropriate to the particular use that is actually going on.

Let us now consider some of the kinds of conditions that different varieties of talk need to satisfy in order to be functional and successful. Let us also consider what happens when we try to impose conditions that are appropriate to one kind of talk upon another kind of talk. First, what sorts of conditions do different kinds of language need to satisfy in order to succeed, to be "felicitous"?[7]

For R/A/D Talk

The felicity conditions for r/a/d talk have been worked out in considerably greater detail than those of any other variety of linguistic behavior.[8] There are, of course, difficulties in articulating these conditions with any precision; but it is usually agreed (even if only as a rule of thumb) that there are two levels of conditions that have to be

---

[6]Ludwig Wittgenstein, *Philosophical Investigations* (New York: Macmillan, 1953), pp. 11e–12e.

[7]The notion of "felicity conditions" (which include truth conditions as one variety) is spun off of J. L. Austin's idea of speech-act felicity, which is set out in *How to Do Things with Words*, previously cited.

[8]For this we are indebted to a whole sequence of philosophers, culminating in the twentieth-century Logical Empiricists, that goes back through Hume and lands us in the work of Aristotle and Socrates (as opposed to Plato). I do not want to belabor the historical lineage, but I think that it is worth noting that

satisfied in order for r/a/d talk to be successful. The first is that it
must have truth conditions. It must be truth-conditioned discourse.
This is not to say that a claim of this kind must be true; that comes
later. Rather, there must be conditions which would, were they to
obtain, render the claim true. It is usually further agreed that there
are two main kinds of truth conditions which a statement might satisfy: empirical on the one hand and purely logical or formal on the
other. This allows for a posteriori synthetic statements which are satisfied by empirical truth conditions and also for a priori analytic ones
that are satisfied by logical or formal ones. Seen this way, if a statement is so constructed that it cannot in principle be weighed with
either empirical or formal truth conditions, and yet is advanced for
reportive, assertive, or descriptive purposes, it utterly fails its function.
According to the Logical Empiricists, it would then be said to be
"cognitively meaningless" or "cognitive nonsense"—simply their way
of saying that it fails in this truth-conditioned r/a/d function.

A claim-attempt of this kind can fail to have either empirical or
formal truth conditions in a number of ways. It might be syntactically
ill-formed. If we ask someone, on hearing a great outcry in the street,
"What is going on out there?" and they reply, "The if then than where
is what," no signification or information is directly conveyed in what
is said.[9] While syntactical failure can be merely grammatical, it can be
even more complex. Indeed, we may have a statement-attempt that is
apparently syntactically well formed and shows its lack only upon
careful analysis. A student arrives in class, late and disheveled. We ask,
"What happened to you?" He says, "I was accosted by the Great Pumpkin." Now, if we were agreed that "Great Pumpkin" is a vacuous label
(i.e., that it does not genuinely name any occurrent entity), and if
we further agree that this failure is "in principle" (because of the sense
of "Great Pumpkin"), then we have an utterance ("I was accosted by
the Great Pumpkin") which is apparently syntactically well formed
but which, on closer examination, fails to function since it is incomplete.[10] On this analysis, saying "I was accosted by the Great Pumpkin"
has no more content and is no better formed than "I was accosted by

---

the tradition is not a new one in any sense. See Hempel's "The Empiricist
Criterion of Meaning" and A. J. Ayer's *Language, Truth, and Logic* (New York:
Dover, 1952).

[9]Of course, the actions themselves, the making of noise and the surrounding
behavioral agitation may be somewhat informative; but they are not "telling."
The information is gained by reading symptoms.

[10]Cf. Rudolf Carnap, "The Elimination of Metaphysics Through Logical
Analysis of Language," in *Logical Posivitism,* edited by A. J. Ayer (Glencoe, Ill.:
Free Press, 1959), p. 68.

the." But "I was accosted by the" is neither true nor false. There is no way in which we could articulate truth conditions that, if satisfied, would make it true, or, if not satisfied, would make it false. (If, on the other hand, "Great Pumpkin" is only a contingently vacuous name, the statement is more likely to turn out well formed and truth-conditioned, but false.)

Suppose that instead of saying, "I was accosted by the Great Pumpkin," he says, "I was accosted by the Round Square" or "I was knocked over by the explosion of the Irresistible Force striking the Immovable Object." Now we would have terms that are strictly and necessarily vacuous, due to the self-canceling effect of contradiction. So, we would get, necessarily, "I was accosted by the" or "I was knocked over by the explosion of the," and we would not have a complete (hence, not a functioning) statement.

Of course, there is buried within "I was accosted by the" the constitutent notion "I was accosted," which, barring further difficulties, is intelligible. But the utterance "I was accosted by the," in the way that we are considering it here (taken as a whole), remains incomplete in the very homely sense that if a student turned it in on an English theme it would come back marked, "Not a sentence."

Syntactical failure, obvious or subtle, is only one of the many ways in which an utterance may fail to satisfy the first r/a/d felicity criterion of having truth conditions. Suppose, however, that we have an r/a/d utterance that satisfies this first criterion—there are discernible differences between a world in which it would be true and a world in which it would be false. The utterance is not yet fully successful. It has to succeed not only at being "cognitively meaningful", but it needs to go on and be true, too. The truth conditions that attach to it have to be satisfied themselves. Thus, r/a/d utterances have a two-phase set of criteria that need to be satisfied in order to be fully felicitous. They have to be truth-conditioned, and once that is achieved formally or empirically, the truth conditions themselves demand satisfaction as the price of "happiness." (Note that the latter cannot be an effective occasion of inquiry unless and until the former criterion has been discernibly met.)[11]

---

[11]We cannot talk about the satisfaction of the truth conditions until it has been ascertained that there are truth conditions there to be satisfied. One cannot talk about whether a "cognitively empty" utterance is true (or false). This is one of the reasons why philosophical inquiries, which are essentially inquiries into meaning and use, are logically prior to scientific inquiries, which are essentially inquiries into what is true. Before we can make headway describing the facts, we must frequently spend a little time with semantics. The man in the street may deplore this, but philosophers have known it a long time. Cf. Plato.

For Other Language Use

The other kinds of linguistic moves have their own felicity conditions, quite distinct from those that attach to r/a/d language. Imperative and ceremonial performative utterances, to name two, do not (and need not) satisfy either of the two-step criteria of r/a/d talk. They don't have any truth conditions (that is why they are not r/a/d), and it is consequently absurd to ask whether they are true. They do have conditions of other kinds, and it is consequently appropriate to ask in a given instance just what kinds of conditions are there and, then, whether they are satisfied or not. If there are no conditions at all to be met, then the utterance is not language. Not being rule-governed (by any sort of rules) it reverts to mere noise. Positivists liked to call utterances that lacked truth conditions "nonsense." We will save that label for noises that lack felicity conditions of every kind. What kinds of conditions are there, though, besides truth conditions?

Consider a ceremonial performative, for example. Suppose that I have just tried to perform a marriage between Ted and Alice, using the ordinary ritual. It is a very important question (and becomes more important with passing years) whether the transaction that has been carried out was a legitimate and successful one. You have all read "Blondie," or watched *I Love Lucy,* and have seen Cliché Plot No. 47, in which "husband" and "wife" discover after twenty years that they "are not really married after all"—the minister didn't have a license, or he didn't say the right words, or the license was for the wrong state, or an earlier divorce was not final. Familiar? There are a number of conditions that have to be met in order for the operative clause of the marriage ceremony to be successful. I could utter that clause now ("by virtue of the authority vested in me by the Commonwealth of Virginia, I do hereby pronounce you to be husband and wife"), but you should not become nervous (even if you are reading this with a friend) because the conditions required for it to be operative have not been even remotely satisfied. There are quite a number of them, too. The participating parties need to be willing, for one thing; you cannot, in the U.S. system of law at any rate, line up two unwilling people and transact marriage upon them. The participants also need to be of sound mind and of age. Still other conditions: the sincerity of the transactors, the legal authority of the officer, the presence of legal witnesses—all of this just to make the "I pronounce" binding. Were the conditions not satisfied, it would not matter what is transacted or what words are said—no marriage would occur (at least de jure). So, while "I pronounce thee man and wife" is not (and cannot be) either true or false, it has its governing rules. There are felicity conditions to be satisfied. If these conditions were irrelevant to what was said, the utterance would fail utterly. The minister could report and describe states of affairs at length and there would be no transaction at all. Only if sincerity, authority, and so on, matter is there even an attempt at a wedding. Once they matter, you have to see if they are satisfied. If they matter and are satisfied, the marriage happens; the two levels of conditions are met. It parallels r/a/d nicely. The only difference is in what conditions hold and how they can be satisfied.

Similarly with imperatives. Recall the tragic affair at My Lai, how one sergeant refused to participate in the alleged events on the grounds that the "commands" given were not lawful commands and were, hence, not binding. It is rare to find so clear an example of a philosophical point in the morning news, and grievous to illustrate it with American atrocities; but the example is a clear one. Imperatives or commands have felicity conditions, too. Not truth conditions, of course. Not the conditions of the marriage ceremonial either. Rather, a whole new set of rules that give commands the shape they have. Lacking such, a noise is not a command (*a fortiori* an effective or ineffective one). With the appropriate conditions attached, then commands are tendered and can be appraised as binding, moot, legal or not, enforceable or not—whatever. What sort of conditions are they? Consider a homely case: I tell my neighbor's children not to hit my dog, and they reply, "You're not our boss, we only take orders from Dad" (at which point Dad comes boiling out the back door and gives functioning and binding commands). Here, even a small child is aware that the dimensions of legitimate commands are finite (even if he mislocates them). It is not my intent here to lay out in detail what the felicity conditions of commands might be, but I think that it is obvious, even in this one example, that there are such conditions, that they can sometimes find satisfaction and sometimes not, and that ordinary people are well aware of this context for commands. The Nuremberg trials, too, were based on the notion that there are conditions, even in war, such that people who complied with Nazi "commands" were not absolved from individual responsibility for their acts (and the atrocious consequences of them) by any proper commands from any duly justified authority. Some orders bind, other "orders" don't. Conditions have to be met. (And they have to be germane first.)

Promises, too. There are conditions that have to be satisfied in order for a promise to occur and in order for an occurrent promise to be binding. Some of them are rather matter-of-fact. In order for a person to be bound by a "promise," that which is supposedly promised must fall within the capacity of the individual to enact. Suppose my boys, on seeing the astronauts, say, "We want to go to the moon," and I reply, "Sure, I'll take you there next Saturday." They, cautious, say, "Do you promise?" and I reply, "Sure!" Now, there is something deceptive and immoral in what I am doing-saying here. I am uttering a kind of fraudulent promise—I am deceiving my children into thinking that a promise has been made when in fact no such promise is possible. But the sin here, if it is a sin, occurs in that fraud and not on the weekend following when I do not take them. They may say, "You broke your promise," but I can reply, "Aha! I can't break my 'promise' because the 'promise' I made was not a promise at all." You cannot promise what is beyond your capacity to fulfill, as every politician knows.

Orders and promises, like weddings and assertions, have two rounds of conditions to satisfy. In both cases we can spell out what is required to make a bona fide act-of-the-right-kind, and then spell out what it would take for the act to succeed (in its own way, whatever kind it is). And none of it has to do with truth. The samples given here are only abbreviated notes on a general rule. My immediate point has only been to show that felicity conditions are not all truth conditions.

Later, I want to explore in greater detail the kind of non-truth-conditioned felicity conditions that attach to certain religiously crucial or primitive utterances. Before we get to that, however, I must show what happens when one takes the felicity conditions that belong to one kind of utterance and tries to impose them on another kind. Then we can put together a clear conception of the felicity conditions that belong to religious primitives, and see, finally, what happens when we force the proper felicity conditions of some other kind of talk upon them.

CATEGORY MISTAKES AND FELICITY CRITERIA

You should be more or less familiar with Gilbert Ryle's notion of a "category mistake."[12] A category mistake is what happens when you take something that belongs to one conceptual category and try to cram it into another. This happens rather often in philosophical inquiry because philosophical inquiry has a great deal to do with categorizing (sorting things out).

For instance, the business of metaphysics, as traditionally seen, has largely been to decide how many (and which) categories you need in order to sort out all the things in the world and to discover which are

[12]See Ryle's *The Concept of Mind* (New York: Barnes & Noble, 1949), p. 16 ff.

basic. An example of this is the frequent suggestion that "mind" and "body" are completely independent substances, both of which must be included in any complete list of "what there is." Now, to take everything that happens in the world and sort it into basic categories amounts to finding or imposing some kind or semblance of structure, order, and intelligibility in or on the world. Many philosophers, Descartes for one, have concurred in the "mind/body" categorization and have, consequently, laid out a precise categorial distinction in order to give order to "the appearances."

However, this particular kinds-of-stuff categorial distinction may be entirely wrong-headed. Perhaps "minds" and "bodies" are not usefully distinguished in this way. Isn't the notion of the mental really a kind of behavioral or system-like notion, or a notion based on process? Instead of seeing "mind" as another kind of stuff, can't it be better seen as a particular organization of *ordinary* stuff? After all, in any thorough analysis, must we not take into account not only the stuff of which things are made (the material), but also the structure (the formal)?[13] For, you can obviously take the same material (say, a bunch of clay) and form it differently into walls or pottery. The difference, after all, between an adobe wall and a vase is not a material difference (or, at least, it need not be). It is fundamentally a formal difference— one of structure. Such a wall is not composed of two things. It is not made of clay and structure. It is made of structured clay, and that is quite a different affair. (You cannot take all of the clay away and have eleven baskets of structure left over.)

In parallel fashion, instead of categorizing into bodies and minds, why not set up a substantial category of matter which, when structured in one way, we speak of as body, and, when structured another way, we speak of as mind? Then the mentality or intelligence is not seen as what the mind is "made of"; rather, as the way in which the material, of which everything is made, is, in this case, put together. So seen, looking for mind-stuff and looking for body-stuff and trying to find out their "natures" is an inquiry predicated on a fundamental category confusion, and is doomed to all kinds of absurd answers. We cannot help but wind up with absurdities because our questions are miscast to begin with.

Ryle likens this kind of confusion to that of a man who comes up to Oxford and, having seen Magdalen, Christ Church, and the Bodleian

---

[13]Consider Aristotle. In this light, of course, you must add their capacities (the final), and the actual sequence of events that have brought them about (the efficient).

is upset because he cannot find the university. This is an absurdity because he *has* found the university—not one more building in a row, not another thing among things, but a structure and order imposed upon them.[14] This is a constituent/structure category mistake like the one involved in the body/mind search. Constituent/structure category mistakes are not the only kind there are, however.

You can mix any two categories, and in trying to apply the terms to one that belong to the other, get chaos. Suppose you take some items that belong to the category of "hypothetical constructs" (those marvels which scientists postulate in order to build theories and explanations), maybe "antineutrinos" (used to explain some of the readings on their meters), and treat them as things among things. Then you might ask, "What color are they?" or "Are they round or square?" So doing, you wind up with all kinds of absurdities because you are off on the wrong foot, making a construct/observable mistake at the start.[15]

Or, you can miss a distinction, making your categories much too broad. The Logical Positivists, for example, seemed to suggest that there are really only two categories of language use—scientific description and "nonsense." This is a category mistake of insufficient categories. It occurs most flagrantly when you try to take advantage of the fact that every class and its own complement (taken jointly) exhaust the range of possible facts, without noting the concomitant fact that the complement of a given class may have many important and distinct subclasses. You can, of course, divide everything in language into (a) scientific descriptions, and (b) everything else. X and non-X are always available. But this division is rarely fruitful or useful, and certainly has proved itself to be dysfunctional in this case. (You could, similarly, divide the whole world into paper clips and non–paper clips. That covers everything. I am a non–paper clip. The chessmen on my desk are non–paper clips on a non–paper clip's non–paper clip. God, even. Indeed, everything is a non-paper clip except for the paper clips. Unarguable and utterly fruitless.)

Such categorial lumping need not be this gross or extreme to be dubious, however. It has been suggested, for example, that everything

---

[14]Ryle, p. 16.

[15]The fact that the absurdities that arise out of category confusions are absurd does not prevent them from occurring. The business just cited is not a made-up case. It is one observed in class more than once. "Are electrons green or blue?" But the set of visual color properties just does not apply. And not because we are not able to squinch our eyes up tight enough or get a big enough lens.

that occurs in religion and everything that occurs in the moral enterprise be lumped together. This would be a kind of theoretical economy, making one category do instead of two. But it is ill-advised unless the one category will "do." Examples are abundant: ignoring the distinction between dissent and disloyalty when considering those who disagree with national policy; glossing the separability of those who do not choose to work and those who cannot work when discussing unemployment; and so on, ad infinitum. None of this is aimed at obscuring or ignoring the law of excluded middle. It is simply to say that this law is not the only law we need.

Generally speaking, theoretical (and categorial) economy is desirable; but it is not the only criterion for good categorizing. Theoretical economy at the cost of not being able to get anything done is too frugal. My world theory—that the world is composed of paper clips and non–paper clips—is theoretically very economical—about as economical as you can get. So, on the rule of parsimony, it is a good stroke. If parsimony were the only criterion for such moves, fine; but it is not the only rule. At the very least there are criteria of utility and output as well. Moral utterances and religious utterances are both nondescriptive, perhaps. But they could both be nondescriptive and still be radically different from each other. Ignoring all for the sake of parsimony obscures that fact, with the consequence that we may miss important aspects of our world. Ashtrays and orchids are both non–paper clips, but only a conceptually impoverished observer considers them the same. So, this is another kind of difficulty or price you pay for bad categorizing. You get led into completely stultifying roadblocks when you try to make your categorial divisions too broadly inclusive.

Or again: suppose we decided that numbers really are things, like Pythagoras seems to have thought at one time. Well, if numbers are things, then there are certain enterprises that you ought to be able to carry out with them: stack them end to end, paint them green, and hang them on strings—all sorts of things that one can do with things. But we can't do them with numbers. However, maybe numbers are very teeny-weeny things, so that it is not convenient to stack them, and so on. But then, we can always hypothesize and speculate. If they are teeny-weeny, we can imagine teeny-weeny people (there is nothing logically necessary about people being as big as they are) who use numbers the way we use (say) bricks. Or, maybe, they use two number 8's for snowshoes. We can imagine all sorts of fantastic things, but when we begin to consider such occurrences, we quickly discern the absurdity of it all. "He couldn't find his snowshoes, so he strapped a number 8 on each foot and waded on through the storm." No, that just isn't the kind of thing you do with number 8. With any number. You add, subtract, multiply, divide, extract roots. You do all sorts of things, but you don't put numbers on, carry them around, dig them up, or wear them.[16] Remember the man playing tennis who, after breaking his racket, seized the square root of –2 to make a smashing backhand save? No. The square root of –2 is not something one seizes, quick or slow. You need some sort of object with which to return tennis serves. Numbers aren't objects, and that is that.

Now, when we come into the area of language, it is especially easy to make category mistakes. With linguistic categories, we try to sort out not only the sorts of things that are in the world. We also try, in philosophical inquiry, especially, to sort out the kinds of concepts with which our thought operates, the kinds of thoughts that we can think. And we take note of the differences and similarities among them. In order to do that, we turn a great deal of attention to the language we speak, the kinds of words we can use, the kinds of utterances we can utter. We give very painstaking attention to the patterns of thought and talk that have been developed in natural languages over long periods of time because we find very clear "footprints" of our conceptual endeavors there. Language is constructed in order to carry on concept-moving games and, after long use, it shows the marks of the games played in it. It provides us, uniquely, with a history of conceptual apparatus that, over thousands of years, through trial and error, has been made to fit. So, one way to find out whether a category mistake has occurred in a particular analysis is to see whether the analysis fits the patterns of "ordinary discourse".[17]

So we examine the language and try to sort it out, not just noting the difference between nouns and verbs, but rather, the differences between kinds of speech acts, between the kinds of things that can be done in and with language, and between the kinds of things we have been illustrating—commanding, describing, inquiring, performing, joking, mimicking, reciting—differences which are only sometimes obvious, usually subtle. Such attention to language helps us a great deal in understanding our own concepts and thoughts, and, in turn, in understanding our world as we know it.

[16]Don't confuse numbers with numerals. We can, after all, imagine taking numerals (great big ones) and strapping *them* on our feet; but that is another affair altogether.

[17]Not the discourse of Clyde Clod in the street, but that of an intelligent, reasonably educated person who, in speech, is paying reasonable attention to what he is doing. By "ordinary" what I mean is "nontechnical," "nonprofessional."

There are several ways in which we can make a category mistake in our analysis of language and, hence, in our attempts to understand what occurs. For instance, we may miss a linguistic distinction just as easily as we can miss a thing distinction. Thus, for example, if we fail to note that there is a difference in force between saying "XYZ is round" and saying "QRS is good," and if we, consequently, try to treat statements like the latter as though they were of the former type, disasters quickly ensue. It is a matter of working yourself into an intellectual (philosophical) box and suffering from a kind of cramp as a result. Just as, in the Cartesian case, it took more than a hundred years to get over the structure/substance mistake in the analysis of what there is; so, too, in our analysis of what can be said, when we mis-take normative language as though it were straight empirical description, we engender long-term trouble. (In fact, we have stayed in trouble on this one for several thousand years.)[18]

But the absurdity of linguistic misuse is not always as obvious as that. It may be very subtle. Maybe we take a word like "God" in an utterance like "God exists," and try to assess it in terms of truth conditions: "Is it true that God exists?" But, is it possible that the utterance "God exists" is not an assertion at all? that it was never meant to have truth conditions in the first place? It is just possible that asking, "Is 'God exists' true?" is just as absurd as asking, "Are antineutrinos lavender?" or "Is the square root of −2 too heavy to pick up?"

Consider another case for a moment. Suppose that we are in the process of christening a ship. All is ready. A nuclear submarine, armed with forty-seven Polaris missiles and sixteen vats of essence-of-plague, is to be christened *Olive Branch* by the President's daughter. All of the officials are gathered on the platform at the Newport News Shipbuilding and Dry Dock Company, and just as Irma is ready to smash the bottle of champagne across the bow and say "I christen thee *Olive Branch*," disaster! Marcia Trimble comes leaping out from behind the bunting with a wild, turned-on look. She has a bottle of champagne in her hand, and before Irma can do anything, Marcia smashes her bottle across the bow and says "I christen thee *Capitalist Warmongering Pig-Boat*." Okay, what has happened? What can now be said? All kinds of things, but some of them would be absurd. If someone shouted, "That's not true," it would be folly. "You're not entitled" would be a better fit. The criterion has to fit the case. Someone might really shout, "That's a lie," but if they did, they would be missing a subtlety of

---

[18]This is not my issue, but "XYZ is good" is not a descriptive. It is a verdictive. Even if you don't agree with that, consider the difference that it makes.

some importance. A ceremonial may be incomplete, it might be mis-performed, it might be unauthorized, it might be insincere. A lot of things could go wrong, but none of them would make it "false," any more than the preventive arrest of Marcia would have made the intend-ed and proper christening "true."

Thus, finally, the point of this section. Forcing the wrong felicity conditions upon a locution is a clear and distinct variety of funda-mental category mistake, just as lethal to good sense as any substance/ structure, missed-distinction, construct/observable, or abstraction/ object mistake we have explored. Here, as in those other cases, the seriousness of the error shows in the logical absurdity of "what we would say if."

Presently, I will suggest that the statement "There is a God" is one about which a great many questions may be asked and comments ad-vanced, but not "Is it true" or "Is it false." Here, the category mistake (which amounts to forcing the utterance under the felicity critera of r/a/d talk) is subtle; but I am convinced that it is there and that it is lethal to good sense. I shall try to make it clear. After all, in order for a state-ment to have the status of "true" (or "false"), it has first to come within the arena of either formal truth conditions or empirical, discern-ible, experiential ones. And, if we are uttering something like the noise "There is a God" and have in mind the God-concept that is traditional in the West (remember the knowledge/transcendence cramp?), then there are certainly no empirical truth conditions available. And, if the kind of ontological argumentation Anselm and others tried won't come off (remember that?), then there are not any formal truth conditions either. So the utterance cannot be either formally or empirically true or false. So it cannot fall within the purview of cognitive expression. It isn't an r/a/d that has failed, it just isn't an r/a/d at all; and it is absurd to try to use it in that role. That would be a "wrong conditions" cate-gory mistake. But it would be equally absurd to leave it at that. "Non-cognitive" isn't much more of a label than "non–paper clip." To termi-nate the analysis at this point is a "lumping" category mistake. So we must pursue it further. Precisely what role does such a religious primi-tive perform? Once we have located that, then we must see what condi-tions of felicity obtain there. They will not be truth and falsehood, but there must be conditions of some kind, or else the religious utterance is really "nonsense."

7

CATEGORIZING

Man has classified himself in many different ways—the gregarious animal, the toolmaker, the language-user, the featherless biped. Another, more important way, is indicated by the very fact that he classifies. Given to sorting, organizing, and categorizing everything he observes, man is the classifying animal. He does not seem willing or able simply to observe the stream of events that occur. Rather, he seems impelled to sort and classify it into patterns, structures, classes, kinds, and sets—always trying to find some structure to the world in which he lives.

LEVELS OF CATEGORIZING

Certain levels of categorizing are obvious and fairly empirical. Sorting visible things in terms of their shape is one such. When, for example, biological sorting (taxonomy) began, back around the time of Aristotle, the biological "families" were determined in terms of the gross and overt physiological similarities of individuals, in wider and wider circles of diminishing congruence. Bats, for example, were classified as a kind of bird, and whales as a kind of fish, all because of gross similarities in apparent structure, features, and habit. It was an obvious way to cut the pie.

But as the circles expand, we have to move to finer and subtler bases of classification. Instead of sorting things by external shape and the analysis of gross parts, we soon come to sort them by material and by fine structure. We go from externals to minute and inner organization. This continues until, in the later history of taxonomy, the sorting is done in terms of abstract classes, defined by "fundamental" or "basic" connections which, frequently, are not apparent in direct sensation at all. Thus, analysis can move altogether away from the sensorily accessible, settling on such things as causal (and other) relations and intelligible function.[1] Movement in this direction is usually considered progress, even though it grows ever more subtle and indirect, and ever less obviously empirical. Our set-making has grown more refined, but much less apparent in its instantiations.

As long as we are classifying in terms of directly observable distinctions and similarities, we are going to have many categories. However, the push toward subtlety and abstraction is also a push toward ever more inclusive categorizations (and fewer of them). Not satisfied with sorting the world out into robins and bullfinches, chimeras and kings, we push on to larger and more inclusive kinds. Indeed, we may eventually come (it is the dream of every metaphysician) to some two "sorts" or even a single basic one. Note again, however, that as one presses on for these broader and "more basic" kinds, one is pressing a search for class signals or class characteristics that are distinctly less obvious. Even though it is not easy to find classificatory properties in terms of which amoebae and skyscrapers belong to the same set, it can be done. But you have to look considerably beyond the surface of things.

There is, then, a twofold taxonomic impetus—to find ever finer and subtler distinctions, and to find ever more inclusive and basic kinds. Out of this combined effort, an issue has arisen that is one of the traditionally basic philosophical questions: "How many fundamental or ultimate categories do you have to include in order to take the whole of reality into account while 'saving the appearances'?" Do you need five? or four? or three? or two? Do you need, perhaps, only one?

This is the classic debate between metaphysical dualists (representing

---

[1]Aristotle also did some of the beginning moves on functional classification, suggesting that, in differentiating things, one of the primary matters to take into account is a thing's potential—what it can become (or do). It is in the process of becoming, of fulfilling potential, that "function" is seen. We would not talk anymore in terms of the fulfillment of ends and purposes; but we say much the same thing when we speak of the procedures and functions and operations that a thing can carry out (or be used to carry out).

all pluralists) and the monists, who opt for that last ambitious and glorious alternative. The controversy is the same, whatever particular categories are under debate. How many kinds must you have? To many persons there seems evident need for considerably more than one. Maybe we need a category of "things," (a kind of "physical" set). Most people have agreed to that. But, don't we need some sort of mental or "mind" category, too, to cover phenomena and events that are not easily explicable on physicalistic grounds? A lot of people have accepted that (but not Hobbes). Maybe we need both of these (Descartes). Another approach would suggest that we need two basic categories in order to explain the lot: space-time, as a kind of basic passive category within which events can be transacted; and matter-energy, as a kind of basic active category furnishing both the material and the structure for the transactions that might be carried out. For that matter, it might be suggested that we need a third continuum, too, to cover (using traditional language) the "purpose" and "value" of the transactions that occur in the net.[2]

This is not a book in taxonomic metaphysics, and I really do not want to argue the merits of any particular metaphysical scheme— whether we do or do not need this or that "kind." My point, rather, is simply to note that categorizing is a fundamental human business, that it takes many shapes and forms, and that it can be carried down to a level of generality and abstraction at which the categories mentioned are not in any sense directly discernible entities or processes.

NONEMPIRICAL CATEGORIZATION

Suppose, for the moment, that you have taken the categorial position that analyzes and groups events in terms of space-time, matter-energy, and purpose-value. None of these items are things that one sees, tastes, smells, feels, or hears. Obviously, one does not smell purpose, value, space, or time. You might try to argue that a person can see or smell matter; but that is not at all clear. Matter, the notion of matter or physical stuff, is a way of explaining what we *do* smell—a theoretical move. We smell apples, alfalfa on the summer breeze—that sort of thing; and, if the theory is a good one, smelling apples and alfalfa can

---

[2]That is, that if we try to take the world as it is, explain it, categorize it, and reduce out all of the matter-energy and space-time explainable conditions, there is still a kind of overload left—notions of ends, purposes, potentials, values, the good, and so on.

be explained by appeal to causally structured physical events in the space-time order.

To talk about physical stuff or matter is very much unlike talking about staple guns. To talk about space-time is very much unlike talking about ten miles or Saturday. To talk about purpose-value is very much unlike talking about heroism or a particularly generous act. When we talk about space-time, we are bringing into our language some locutions that are not connected to sensibly verificatory events in any obvious ways. As categorizing presses on, we come to categories that are only theoretically linked to discernibles. This does not entail, however, that the categories are footless or that argument about them is without point.

Consider an argument about the nature of time. (I do not mean to pursue that here, but to look at it on its face for a moment. Maybe someone says, "What is the time?" and you misunderstand him to be asking, "What is time?"—a good Platonic question.) You just don't go looking in the closet or under the rug or at the clock to find out. The question is aimed at a categorial notion that is very abstract and highly ephemeral. Yet I do not think that we can afford to dismiss this kind of categorizing move on the grounds that it enters into the abstract and ephemeral. There is a great deal to be gained in our understanding of our world through the use of just such notions; and if their use is fruitful, their exploration is in order. The danger is not in their use and exploration; it is in their misuse, and that is usually the result of failure to explore with care or, indeed, to explore at all.

But what, precisely, is going on when we say, "Matter is real," or "There is physical stuff at some ultimate or nearly ultimate level in our analysis of the world"? How can we make such noises if "matter" is an abstract, ephemeral, and theoretical notion? Have we abandoned our empiricism altogether?

Begin by considering a homely case: What is going on when we say, "There are dogs"? What is the function and force of any taxonomic utterance? To say "There are dogs" is to say, essentially, that "dogs" is a useful classificatory term for human purposes and, consequently, that this taxonomic notion is a good one. That is, it allows that if we want to come to terms with what is going on all about us, and if we want to make all of the useful classifications that can be made, then this is one that we will want to include. There is a difference between claims like "There is matter" ("Matter is real") and "There are dogs" ("Dogs are real"); but it is only that the utility of the dog classification is immediate, visibly apparent, and narrow. If anyone has doubts about the utility of the latter, he need only walk a few blocks to find some concrete and exemplary instances. But, if the question of the "reality" of matter is in dispute, it is not quite so easily settled. "Matter" is much more inclusive, much more primitive, and much less discernible. But, in either case, the major force of the utterance is that of a pragmatic endorsement of a "way of explaining"—a theoretical move that connects to the empirical in its output and use rather than in its content and source.

This is especially clear in phenomenalist knowledge theory. Phenomenalism is a variety of empiricism which suggests that the content (not the object) of our direct awareness and experience consists of sensations, and that everything else that we have, beyond these sensations themselves, comes either through inference or theory construction.[3] So seen, even a notion as simple as "dogs" is a construct to make sense out of certain patterns of experience. We have our sensations—"woof, woof" noises and so on—and we weave them together and make them intelligible by noting that they fall in certain patterns, explaining this pattern through the use of the classificatory notion "dog." Even for phenomenalists, though, there is a tremendous gap between classificatory notions like "dog," "table," "shoe," "ship," or "sealing wax," on the one hand, and basic and inclusive notions like "matter," "mind," or "time." Still, the latter are every bit as necessary as the others, only more inclusive and abstract. They gain their status by their output, though. They are confirmationally empirical rather than genetically so. So, from

---

[3] I do not think that the traditional phenomenalist theory that we infer objects or categories from our sensations is workable. As observed long ago (Hume), we cannot infer anything out of a set of premises that is not there. If you start with a set of premises about the content of your own sensations, you're not going to be able to infer out of it anything about what causes them. A sensation could be caused, reasonably, by any sort of objective event whatever. There is no necessary causal connection between a sensation of a certain sort and any particular variety of cause. Further, you cannot get around that inductively, as a phenomenalist, because the kinds of things that you must cite to get around it inductively are all circular. You can say, "We can infer that the cause of sensation *Y* is of a certain sort because, in the past, all sensations of the *Y* sort have had such causes." But, in that situation, in referring to all these past sensations being caused in certain ways, you would be begging the very issue that is at stake. If all we have is our sensations, then the causal network that "lies behind" them can be hypothesized and can be offered as an explanation; but it cannot be inferred. So, we might suggest physical matter, extended in space and time, as an intelligible causal hypothesis that would nicely hang our sensations together; and we might then try to decide (on some pragmatic criterion) whether the hypothesis is an attractive one; but we can hardly infer a physical world (or a nonphysical world, for that matter) out of the sensations themselves as they occur.

the phenomenalists' position, it is especially vivid that one of the basic moves that people make (have to make) in coming to terms with their world, consists of constructing (hypothesizing, postulating, or positing) hypothetical *X*'s as explanations for the experiences which they have. It is not, however, confined to this view. Indeed, I am convinced that every description of experience presupposes some such theoretical framing—regardless of the knowledge theory in use. The only option is to claim that we perceive "kinds" directly. But we don't; so the construction maneuver is required. And, besides, so long as confirmable output is available, we have not lost our empirical footing at all.

MAKING, USING, AND REMARKING CATEGORIES

When we try to describe the pattern of experience, we are obliged to assume and use some set of previous categorial constructions. These constructions crop up in our descriptive talk as the frame of reference or set of presumptions within which the descriptions are uttered. Thus, when we talk, in our usual way, of shoes and ships and sealing wax, we are using a wide variety of categories that provide the arena within which the descriptions and assertions are occurring. In statements like "The cat is on the mat" or "Thank God, it's Friday," categories like "physical entities," "structural processes," "time," "space," "matter," and "gods" are employed rather than asserted. They are presumed as the context within which the claims or assertions occur.

Indeed, it is impossible to utter descriptions and assertions except in the arena of some such constructions of basic entities, sets, and kinds. Imagine trying to describe an event without them. One could not even make so simple a claim as "This table is old and brown" because this claim calls upon classificatory notions of color, time, and, if not necessarily of physical entities, at least of a class of kinds called "tables"—all of which are sufficiently abstract to go far beyond the specific content of experience as it occurs. About the best that one could do, if he tried to operate category-free, would be to call out some noise at each event as it occurs. He could not even classify effectively in terms of memory, because classification in terms of memory also depends upon an appeal to some class of a similar sort— comparing the content of the present experience to the content of the present memory and deciding, "They are alike."

My point here is only that some classificatory move is necessary. We could argue a great deal about what classes have to be used, but I do not think that we can argue at all that the classificatory move itself can be eliminated. It is prior to every assertion. All cognitive talk (assertions that are true and assertions that are false) is theory-dependent to the extent that it is impossible to engage in the enterprise of truly or falsely describing unless and until we have posited, stipulated, established, adopted, or supposed some kind of categorial structure which we impose or pattern upon experience so as to make sense out of it and make it describable.[4] Consequently, I think that we are obliged to allow that what is going on in categorizing moves is, necessarily, noncognitive. But it is clearly a special kind of noncognitive. I shall call it "precognitive."

Now, when this constructive maneuver occurs, it is in some linguistic act. Hypothesis formation is a symbolic-linguistic operation. We even do our everyday sorting by naming. We establish categories by reaching linguistic conventions for class names.[5] Certainly, when we move to the level of abstract class formation, the act is a linguistic one. Equally certain, whatever kind of linguistic act it may be, it is not an act of description.

While I do not think that there is anything controversial about the notion that some kind of categorizing maneuver precedes viable description (that descriptive talk depends upon the frame and support of some kind of categorial structure), there certainly is a problem over whether and how this categorial structure which underlies descriptive talk can be linguistically expressed. Even if you grant, for the purpose of argument, that behind every true or false description some supporting categorial structure is presumed, you can (in good company) question whether that structure can be directly affirmed or uttered, and (if it can be) whether it ever needs to be. Of course, when we try to utter it, we are attempting a very different kind of speech act from the one we attempt in the describing game. If we try to utter or express our classifications directly, we are trying to utter or express something that is logically prior to the possibility of truth conditions and, hence, of cognitivity. A cognitive claim, a truth-conditioned claim, occurs within the context of a classification—not vice versa. So, even as categorizing is not a cognitive enterprise, categorial expression is not cognitive talk. It, too, is precognitive or cognitivity-funding.

Consider the kind of utterances we might make in trying to affirm the

[4]I am avoiding words like "ontological" and "metaphysical" here. They suggest a kind of objective, absolute, utter reality or something of the kind, that I try to avoid. By talking categories, I am trying to keep the notion operational and pragmatic.

[5]This is not the whole of it, of course; but it is an uneliminable part of an extremely complicated whole.

advisability of a certain classificatory or categorial move (perhaps "Matter is real" or "Antineutrinos exist"), or to deny the utility of one (maybe "Justice is an illusion" or "There are no demons"). First of all, they are locutions in which some process or event is transacted or carried out. They are not reports or assertions that certain categories occur. (It must be clear that categorizing is something that one does: categories are made, not found.) They are not even reports or assertions that the utterer employs certain categories. Actually, in large part, the very speech act itself, the very uttering, is what one does to set up a categorial structure. Consider a man who takes the position that a large part (if not all) of the events in the world are best seen in terms of the category "matter." If and when he affirms that, he is subscribing to a certain way of classifying and categorizing events. He is not, however, saying, "The way I classify events is in terms of the category 'matter.'" It is not an autobiographical description of some move that he has made at some other time and in some other way. Rather, the utterance is the core of the very making of the move.

This is important, so I want to belabor it a little. We have already agreed, even if only for purpose of argument, that some kind of categorizing move is necessary in order for descriptive locutions to occur meaningfully. We cannot describe except in the structure of some kind of categories; and we are not going to get any categories unless we categorize. What I am now suggesting is that the act of categorizing is essentially a linguistic act. But that means that if we are going to categorize, we have to be able to utter categorials. Because, until we come to the point of uttering something like "There is matter" (or "Matter is real" or "Matter is one of the basics"), we have not operationally set up a physicalistic category for use. It also means that whatever categorials we utter are not (cannot be) "descriptions."

I will grant that the uttering does not have to be audibly vocalized in public; my notion (which may, of course, be wrong) of linguistic behavior is broader than that. It may be a kind of mental act (I think that mental acts are linguistic) in which we decide to use one category or another. But deciding this is tantamount to saying (it *is* saying) "There are physical objects."

What I am suggesting, then, is not only that there must be some kind of categorial structure behind every descriptive utterance, but that in order for someone to engage in descriptive utterance productively, he has to make or accept some categorial moves. In order for him to make these categorial moves (when he cannot simply accept them as already made in the language), he has to utter (audibly or inaudibly), express, constitute, set up, and advance some categorial commitments.

Am I, then, repudiating those who claim that one cannot voice these things, that they are "shown but not said"? Not really. In fact, I think that there are two ways in which these conceptual moves can show up in language. One of them is captured in Wittgenstein's claim that the categorial structure of our thought (and world) is shown— shown in the structure and order of ordinary speech.[6] So seen, we find categorial matters expressed, shown, in the midst of speech, by the range of nouns that are allowed in a language, by the variety of verbal forms that are permitted, by the syntactical structures that are allowed, and so on. Thus, for example, in the ordinary patterns of common English, we find an implicit categorial structure that calls for entities and predicates. The nominal/predicative structure itself reveals the kind of inbuilt ontology which those who share this language utilize. So, one way in which we find categorial structure is in the syntactical and semantic structures of the language itself—shown rather than said.[7] I do not think think that this ends the matter, however.

We cannot depend upon finding every needed categorial move already packed into the structure of the mother tongue. Granted, many are; and, since they are, many have become such second nature to us that we only use (and never utter) them these days. Too, not many occasions are likely to arise when I will need to say anything like "There are subjects, there are attributes, and there are predicative relations." But those categorial moves would not be packed into the language now if someone had not once entertained them and if use had not finally institutionalized them.

So, while we may realize that any time we attempt actually to assert a category we go "beyond the bounds of sense," we can still entertain different categorizings so long as we (a) hold ourselves aware that such categorial trials are not reports or descriptions within some given

[6]See the closing sections of the *Tractatus*. Wittgenstein claims that structures of this kind can only be shown and cannot be said: "Whereof we cannot speak, thereof we must be silent." So seen, the ultimate structure (the atomistic structure, as he saw it then) of both language and the world are finally revealed or shown in our speech acts, and cannot be affirmed or denied meaningfully.

[7]I would agree with the early Wittgenstein that the structure cannot be said if "say" = "assert." But I do not think that it is at all necessary to say that "say" = "assert." Of course, to try to directly assert or deny the categorial structures is a serious mistake, since categorial structure is presumed in any assertion or denial.

structure, and (b) remember that what we are doing cannot, consequently, be weighed for truth or falsehood. The common error here does not reside in making a noncognitive move. It resides in mis-taking a noncognitive move to be cognitive. So, we perfectly well may (and usefully do) come to the point of saying, "things and their attributes are among the ultimate constituents of the world." The utterance isn't cognitive. But it isn't idle either. In it, we are voicing, and thus attempting to show in a way more direct than use, the organizational pattern or the structure in terms of which we desire to carry on our truth-testable discourse. To make such an utterance is to adopt a way of cutting the event-pie. You don't have to do that every day of course; but there are other ways of cutting that pie, and controversy between them, so the enacting phrase does get reiterated from time to time.

Again, to utter such a noise is not to assert that there are objects, predicative relations, et cetera, floating around as objective entities; rather, it is to remark how one structures the occurrent data. The person who says, "There are physical objects," is stipulating or setting up a way of categorizing for himself, or remarking it and urging it upon his hearers. A person who says, "No, there are not any physical objects," is rejecting that categorizing pattern. He is saying, "I won't cut the pie that way"—a refusal rather than a negative assertion.

To recapitulate: We cannot assert[8] these things because they furnish the conceptual apparatus that makes assertion possible. So, when we make this kind of noise, we are not engaging in a speech act that is true or false. It is not cognitive. In this sense, "It cannot be said" is absolutely right. My point, however, is that within the field of noncognitives (which is enormously big), one of the interesting things that occurs is category establishment. It is not cognitive, but it is presupposed by everything that is, and hence is far from silly.

So, when we say, "Matter is real," we are not doing the same kind of thing we are doing when we say, "The cat is on the mat." "The cat is on the mat" already presumes a causal, temporal, physical, spatial, categorial structure in terms of which it ("The cat is on the mat") is a true or false assertion. "There is such a thing as matter," "There are such things as causes," "There is such a thing as space," "Time is real," "Our world is made up of space-time, in which matter-energy is

[8]One could, of course, say "Bishko uses categories *X, Y,* and *Z;* and I don't." That would be a straightforward assertion that would be true or false; and you would have to examine Bishko's behavior to see if he categorizes this way, and examine mine to see if I do not. No problem there; but that is an assertion about Bishko and me, or (perhaps) about our categories. But it is not an assertion of the categories themselves.

arrayed"—these are proposals, not reports. They are rather like suggested rules for playing a game.

Consider: We sit down to play poker (or some variety of poker),
and someone says, "What shall we play?" Someone else replies, "Dealer's choice," and the dealer says, "Okay, fours and one-eyed jacks
wild, seven-card stud." The dealer is not making a report about what is
so; he is saying, "Let's take the world of the poker deck and structure
it this way." The response to this can never be, "That's false." It might
be, "Oh, that's dull, let's don't play that game," or "Only little old
ladies at tea play with that many wild; let's play straight poker instead."
What we would have going on here would be a series of counterpro-
posals, not counterreports. Similarly, when we say such things as
"There is matter," "There is space," "There is time," or "Antineutrinos exist," what we are doing is uttering proposals, or postulating a
way of sorting events; and this is transacted in the very act of utterance.
It will, later on, be captured and incorporated into the structure of
the game we play. (If we decide to play one-eyed jacks wild, and
someone comes along and observes us playing, all that he has to do is
observe the moves that we make in order to discover that we are playing one-eyed jacks wild.) Assertion is a move in a particular rule-governed game. The rules themselves are not moves in that game. In the
process of playing the game the rules are shown. They are not moves;
they are rules. But they have to be established before they can be
shown.

Consider again: There are certain moves that are chess-permissible:
moves that you can make in chess. They are observable in the game.
By observing what is chess-permissible and what is not (i.e., by observing the play at length), we can discover what the rules of chess are.
They are implicit in the play as it is played by people who know what
they are doing.[9] The rules are neither chess-permissible nor not chess-
permissible. Setting them is not a move in chess. The rules stipulate
what moves will be chess-permissible. The rules do not occur as moves
in the game. They occur as the context within which the game is
played.

So, the categorizing moves show when the game is being played. But
the categorizing moves are made before the game is played. When we
categorize, and lay a theoretical foundation for description, it is
essentially like saying, "One-eyed jacks are wild this time." Wittgenstein

---

[9]The rules here are, of course, already set; and they can be reported in the same
way that the categorial commitments of a culture can also be reported. But to
report a chess rule (or to report a categorial move) is quite a different matter
from setting or reaching a rule, positing one, etc.

and the others who say that they can be shown but not said are, then, correct if what they mean is that you cannot utter the rules of the game as one of the moves in the game. But, if what they mean is that you cannot utter the rules of the game at all, then they are mistaken. We can and do utter them. Indeed, we can and we do propose alternatives. You can quit playing one game and play another by changing the rules; you can compare and evaluate alternative games by appraising the rules; and you can also just play the game within the rules. But in every game there must be some rules, which must be arrived at through a linguistic transaction.

WEIGHING CATEGORIAL ALTERNATIVES

To try to assess categorial utterances on direct empirical (or formal) grounds (i.e., to try—without querying whether they have truth conditions at all—to determine whether they are true), is clearly to raise a set of questions that is radically inappropriate. It is just as inappropriate as asking, "Where in the line of march does the parade occur?" or "Where among the refectories, the library, and classroom buildings do you find the university?" For, what is happening here, rather than description or assertion, is the voicing, affirming, or stipulating of the context within which a network of descriptions and assertions is going to be worked out. Consider theories for a moment. The conditions that have to be satisfied in order for a theory or explanation to be accepted as a good theory or explanation are not identical with the conditions that have to be satisfied in order for a description to be accepted as a good description (i.e., as true). We can talk about a theory or an explanation as "adequate," or "productive," or "successful," but unless we can absorb it in the role of an assertion, within the framework of some more basic and inclusive theory (which must, then, be weighed for adequacy itself), we cannot speak of it as either true or false. The adequacy (or inadequacy) of a theory or explanation is determined, to a large extent, by the degree to which the theory or explanation can underwrite and support a network of descriptions that can be true or false—i.e., the degree to which the theory or explanation furnishes a working frame of reference for assertion. Similarly for categorials. They establish the framework within which inquiry into what is true and what is false makes sense.

   At about this point in the argument, I frequently encounter the notion that I am really playing a cheap game. Cheap because, if you take the categorizing move out from under the control of truth conditions (which is exactly what I am doing), you may fall prey to the mistaken notion that one can categorize any old way, without controls of any kind. But this is a mistake. You cannot categorize "any old way" at all. There are felicity conditions for categories and for categorial expressions just as much as there are for category-dependent descriptions. They are just not the same conditions. So, I am not saying, "You can stipulate any category at all." In fact, there are a number of ways of categorizing that can be explicitly (and on good grounds) rejected. But we would never reject a categorizing because it isn't true or doesn't have truth conditions. Categorizings are never true because they never have truth conditions. We might reject a categorizing because it does not furnish any truth conditions for descriptions that might be voiced in terms of it; but to dismiss it for lacking truth conditions itself (or for failing to be true) would be to commit a linguistic category mistake of the grossest sort—attaching the conditions and qualities that belong to one kind of linguistic maneuver to another radically different kind. That would make no more sense than condemning the square root of –2 on the grounds that it is not portable.

There is, after all, a radical difference between deciding whether a given move in a game is permissible within that game, and deciding whether a certain game is a desirable one. Given the rules of seven-card stud, bringing along an extra ace in your trouser cuff and palming it during the game is not rule-permissible. Applying such extant rules is distinctly easy—very different from, and essentially easier than, deciding what to play. The criteria for deciding what to play and the criteria for allowing or barring a move, once we have decided the shape of the game, are different criteria. You find out whether a given move is rule-permissible by laying the move up against the rules and seeing whether it fits. Is there a line in the book that covers palming aces? Yes or no, as the case may be; but deciding what game to play is more complicated.[10] Typically, the sort of thing we try to consider, in deciding what to play, includes such matters as "Is playing according to this set of rules workable?" "Do people enjoy playing this?" Consider a homely example: One of the things I try to do is block out a certain amount of time to play with my children; and one of the great decisions that has to be made each time is what to play. Once we have made up our minds, there is no problem. I can follow the rules, and so can

---

[10]There may be a second set of rules sometimes. For card games, there could be not only rules for poker and rules for pinochle, but also rules for deciding what card game to play under given conditions, etc. There could even be a whole hierarchy of rules upon rules upon rules. But there usually is not.

they, quite well. Whether to play tag, old maid, seven-card stud, toss a football, or ask riddles depends on more tenuous conditions, though. What do they enjoy? What do I enjoy? What is stimulating, fun, productive, educational, relaxing? Right now, the game we play most is passing a basketball. We have reasons for doing that, but you would not find them by going to the basketball rulebook to see if there is a rule that says, "Playing basketball is desirable."

One kind of reason to play or not to play may come down directly to the quality of the rules themselves—I don't like to play games that have inconsistent rules, or that have too many rules, or that don't have enough rules.[11] In order to make this kind of judgment, we need a set of metarules for judging rules: consistency, redundancy-avoidance, and the like.

Now, this is essentially what I have in mind with regard to the describing game. It is funded by some set of categorial maneuvers which, in turn, are weighed by some second set of rule-evaluating principles (usually of pragmatic and operational dimensions). So: suppose Bertocci, Russell, Plato, and Newton say, respectively, "There are persons," "There are logical atoms," "There are Forms," and "There is matter, space, and time." What they are doing is stipulating or setting up the categories in terms of which they are going to play the describing game. This is not a true or false move, but it is not a footless move either because "There are persons," "There are logical atoms," and so on, can be weighed on intelligible grounds. Is categorizing the world in terms of logical atoms a productive way of doing it? Is it an elegant way? Perhaps it is elegant but not productive. But productivity is probably more important than elegance. So perhaps logical atoms will go by the board. If so, then, in the long run people will not say, "There are logical atoms," anymore, and will stop trying to restructure the language so as to reflect them.

So, even if the voicings of categorial patterning cannot be weighed on grounds of truth and falsity, they can be weighed. Many other grounds occur to me. Some may have little merit, but others are crucial. For example, instead of trying to decide whether some categorial affirmation (like "Matter exists") is true or false, we could try to weigh the

[11]This is one of the disadvantages of playing BB Traps (another game my children play). At last count it has about 235 rules, at least 70 of which are inconsistent, and at least 25 of which are replaced from day to day. A game, if you can call it that, so structured, is chaotic. I think that what they are really doing is just hitting each other over the head with pillows off their beds. But "hitting each other over the head with pillows" is not acceptable, while "playing a game" is acceptable. Therefore, it is a game (it has a name and "rules"), but they do not remember from one day to the next what the rules are.

issue on evaluative and moral criteria. We might try to argue that it is more moral to categorize the world this way ("Moral," of course, would need filling in). Perhaps we could then say that a Chinese who does not categorize the world in a thing/attribute way is making a kind of moral mistake in his choice of categories. I do not think that we could get very far with this "moral" criterion because I do not see any particular way of filling in the moral benefits or harms of selecting one particular categorial pattern over another. I do not think that we can get anywhere at all in trying to fill it in in terms of truth conditions, and not very far on virtue conditions. But it seems to me that, in addition to "moral" norms and "representational" norms, there remains at least one other set of norms with which we might make a great deal of headway: pragmatic norms. (If you don't like the word "pragmatic," you may say "utility norms." If you don't like "pragmatic" or "utility," you may say "operational norms" or, simply, "practical norms.")

In order to fill this in, let us turn our attention away from basic conceptual categories for a few lines and look at a much more everyday sort of maneuver—theory-making at a much lower level of abstraction and generality. Suppose that we have a physicist who is trying to decide between several alternative theories for explaining a set of events of a simple sort. He has a meter in front of him, and the meter is connected with wires to an object on his workbench, and the meter reading is +5. He wants to give some intelligible account of what is going on, and he has several alternative theories that he might offer.[12] What he wants to discover, most likely, is some kind of causal connection. (Note this appearance of one of the major categories that he uses in his work— causal connections, which are hardly discernible.) He will hypothesize some such connection that will in some sense "explain" or "illuminate" the occurrent events. Illumination is what theories are for. He certainly wants one that will be successful. On its face, the theory can hardly be accepted or rejected for being true or false.[13] The theory comes in to give him an operating apparatus within which specific

[12]Note how highly unlikely it is that he will deduce any of these theories from the observation data going on before him. It is very difficult to deduce anything useful from a meter reading of +5 on a dial connected to some wires and a thing on a desk.

[13]We might decide that some subtheory is "true" or "false" if it is structured in terms of a more general one; but here we are starting more or less from scratch. So we cannot effectively appraise the theory this way. The data has to be structured and interpreted before we start describing and assessing on truth grounds. The move we are examining here is a move to structure and interpret.

assertions can be so appraised. So, how does he choose between rival theories? He would choose on pragmatic (utility, operational, or practical) grounds. But what does that amount to?

There are probably a dozen or more things involved, but we can enumerate a few of them. First of all, the theory needs to be one from which (when taken in conjunction with certain other hypotheses)[14] the data to be explained can be inferred. (The logical link between the theory and the event runs from the theory to the event, not from the event to the theory.) This is only to say that our theory has to be relevant. It has to connect up. If you cannot infer the data you are trying to explain from the theory with some auxiliary hypotheses, then the theory fails. Not as false, but as irrelevant or "not-connected."

Let us assume that this much has been achieved. Unfortunately, we could probably achieve this much with several different theories. We could have any number of alternative theories, all of which could be "connected" and, thus, shown to be relevant to the data that we are trying to explain. So, relevance is not enough. It is a necessary condition for good theory, but insufficient.

What we badly need is for the theory to mesh or interact effectively with other theories that are in use, already established and employed. Given our choice between two theories, *A* and *B,* both equally relevant to the explanation of event *E,* upon discovery that theory *A* meshes coherently and intelligibly with eleven other theories that are in regular and productive use, and that theory *B* does not, we will go with *A.* But that is still not enough. After all, we might have more than one theory that is not only relevant but also "meshes."

So, a third quality: the coherence or the internal consistency of the theory itself. We need a theory that is not self-negating. That one is so obvious we need not belabor it. A radically inconsistent or contradictory theory, in that it is self-canceling, does not leave us with any explanation to appraise. It leaves us empty-handed.

A fourth needed quality is what I shall call theoretical fertility. This, with the others, will take us a long step toward a good explanation. Not only does the theory need to mesh, be consistent, and be such that we can infer the specific data that we are trying to explain from it (and some auxiliaries); we will, it is hoped, also be able to infer a great deal of additional data from it, too. Our scientist wants to get an explanation of that meter reading; but a theory that explains only

---

[14]The main reason for auxiliary hypotheses is that really basic theories need definitional or bridging rules in order to get from pure mathematical equations to observational descriptives.

that meter reading would not be a very promising one. At least he would want it to explain all meter readings taken under substantially identical circumstances; and he might even want it to explain a great many meter readings taken under very different circumstances. Consider a concrete example: We have a visual event we want to explain. We are standing on U.S. 1, a car goes by, and as it recedes northward it "shrinks." The image gets smaller. This "shrinkage" is what we want to explain. We could hypothesize that machines moving in a northerly direction decrease in physical size. From the hypothesis that objects moving north physically shrink (and the auxiliary hypotheses of ordinary optics), we could deduce the phenomenon in question. But we could also deduce the phenomenon in question without making any assumption about the shrinkage of things moving north. We could simply add some rules about perspective. Indeed, we could come up with any number of alternative hypotheses, all of them compatible with the data, each of them consistent, and each of them meshing with other hypotheses in use. Suppose that, thinking it enough, we adopted the "everything shrinks when it moves north" hypothesis. It says nothing about things going east. It says nothing about things coming toward us. It says nothing about things we are moving away from. (What if the car stood still and we ran south?). It is a narrow, infertile hypothesis. We reject it in favor of one that covers a wider range of more-or-less similar events (and, we hope, even some other events that are not really very similar at all). So, when we adopt our hypothesis-package that has to do with optics and the radiation of light and perspective and all that kind of thing, we adopt a hypothesis that covers not only cars moving north while we stand still, but one that covers an almost infinite range of phenomena neatly and efficiently.

Now, this theoretical "fertility" business is very basic. Its opposite is "sterile" or, at best, "ad hoc."[15] A theory is really fertile if it yields solutions to problems we have not even conceived of at the time the theory is constructed. It anticipates further data. Also under the heading of fertility, we expect a good theory to be useful in the generation of further theory. This further generation of theory is not a marginal criterion of theoretical quality. All else held equal, choice is not difficult between two theories, only one of which opens up new avenues of inquiry and suggests new ways to move.

A fifth quality that is ordinarily included here is theoretical simplicity (parsimony). We don't want any more theory than we need. Nor do

---

[15]A theory that only solves the singular problem for which it was constructed, after the fact, is termed "ad hoc."

we want theoretical explanations that are superfluously complex. The simpler, the better. The more straightforward and uncomplicated, the better. Parsimony has at least two possible grounds. One is simply the inbuilt human affection for elegance, and may not be too important. The other is our desire to reduce the possibility of error. That is important. The more complex a theory becomes (i.e., the less theoretically economical), the wider the variety of ways in which it can go awry— the greater the probability, indeed, that it will go awry (Murphy's law).

One more: the theory should provide in its application some means for its own modification and improvement. This stipulation may merely amount to another subheading under fertility, but however we classify the rule, we do want a theory from which cases can be generated that will put the theory itself to practical test. It must be self-corrective rather than all-adaptable.

Now: if the theory is relevant, meshes with others in use, is internally consistent, fertile, simply structured, and self-testing (and unambiguous, precise, etc.—the list goes on), I think that our scientist is off and running. He has satisfied a basic list of theoretical virtues (virtues for theories), all of which are thoroughly pragmatic. He has weighed the theory on the basis of its likely productivity or usefulness. He has not weighed the theory for truth. He would not reject it, should it be wanting, as false. He would reject it as sterile, ad hoc, superfluous, overcomplex, jarring, inconsistent, and the like. He might also reject it if he found that it could not be assessed in any way. But that would not be because it lacked truth conditions, it would be because it lacks test conditions altogether. A theory like that is not even presystematically viable. (That, as compared to the Logical Empiricists' class of noncognitives, would be full-fledged "nonsense.")

What I want to do now is take these notions, which are common enough in the construction of scientific hypotheses, and extend them to cover what I am calling "category formation." Suppose we were trying to decide into what ultimate constituents to sort our world. Suppose, further, for purposes of argument, that I am right in saying that we cannot decide this on grounds of truth and falsehood. Instead, we can (and I shall now suggest that we do) decide whether to adopt or maintain a category by seeing, in use, whether it is a fertile one, whether it is intelligible, whether it meshes or misses the other categories in use, whether it is ad hoc, whether it has output, whether those who employ it get somewhere (as opposed to those who employ alternatives and don't get anywhere), and so on. For instance, Pythagoras was convinced that the ultimate constituents of the world are geometrical numbers (points, lines, triangles, etc.). Now, his theory was not a completely sterile one. Indeed, aspects of it are rather clever and fruitful. A theory about the ultimate constituents of the world needs connecting to the things you observe. This theory has it (marginally). For instance, it helps us to explain the phenomenon of fire (one of the apparent constituents of the world) by suggesting that fire is composed (beneath the level of observation) of extremely small and extremely acute triangles. Their size and shape "explains" why they "burn." (Visualize an object thrust into the midst of a maelstrom of billions upon billions of extremely tiny and very sharp little triangles rushing pell-mell upwards through space, trying to find their natural habitat. If the triangles were big or blunt, you would have an effect like that of a meat grinder, I suppose; but, being small and sharp, what you get is a kind of corrosion and eating away of what is placed among them. You get burned.) Well, you have to stretch the Pythagorean business pretty far to get much out of it (which is one of the reasons why nobody is a Pythagorean anymore), but it is not absolutely sterile. "Fire is triangles" is a pretty neat move. But if we were trying to choose between a set of "ultimates" like this (one that runs back to little triangles and circles and squares, etc.) and another that runs back to elementary subatomic particles of energy (or wavicles, if you prefer), the choice is not a difficult one to make. The contemporary, physical, building-block story is extremely productive, extremely coherent, highly fertile, and readily yields test conditions in terms of which it can be examined, modified, and improved. In choosing the atomic story rather than the Pythagorean story, we do not say that the Pythagorean one is false and the atomic one is true; rather, we say that as alternative frameworks within which to try to give a significant description of the world, the Pythagorean story is comparatively sterile and much less useful (and that the atomic story is vastly preferable, consequently, on pragmatic grounds). It is on such pragmatic or practical grounds that we adopt the atomic point of view and go on to use it for structuring our descriptions of what occurs in the world. So: why do we get this meter reading? Because when the poles of the battery are connected, a stream of "electrons" moves through the connecting cables, setting up "polarities" of "attraction" and "repulsion" that move the meter's needle. This is an effective explanation. We will stay with it until we get a better one. And we do not object at all to the abstract and ephemeral categories utilized in the account. Further, the move away from Pythagorean geometricalism toward contemporary physicalism is reinforced again and again. It isn't just a nicer way of explaining meter readings. The greater and broader the testing in use, the better the contemporary story carries the freight. But this still does not make the account a "true description," only "effective basic theory." *A fortiori,* the basic categorial moves that underwrite the fundamental world view are not rendered "true descriptions" by the world view's success.

In all of our utterances we are making some basic categorial presumptions which we will either maintain or discard, depending on the success or failure of the ways of talk that we are able to construct in terms of them. If we found that structuring our talk in physicalistic language was not successful, we would eventually drop physicalism. If we found that Berkeley's phenomenalism was a more productive and efficient model with which to work, we would find that the language would gradually become more and more phenomenalistic, and eventually, phenomenalism would be the implicit categorial posture of the language that we talk (just as physicalism is today).[16] Every utterance is categorially structured; and, if we search the utterances we make with any care at all, we can find that structure (whatever particular shape it may take) there.

Then, if and when there is any reason to do so, we can go ahead and affirm the categories themselves or alternatives to them. "There are causal connections." "Physical matter is fundamentally real." "Space and time are objective structures of reality." We can go ahead and affirm them, so long as we remember that in affirming them we are not making a claim to be weighed as true or false within the framework of space, time, causality, and physical-matter categories. Rather, we are making, in the uttering itself, a framework in terms of which descriptions will be weighed, and which must itself, consequently, be either maintained or rejected on grounds as simple as utility, productivity or output, simplicity, scope, and the like.

SUMMARY

I have argued that our thinking has an essential and basic part that I am calling the categorizing maneuver—sorting out, classifying, and tying together the events that occur within our experience into a pattern of intelligible order. I have argued, further, that intelligible thought and speech inevitably presume some kind of categorial structure within which they are arranged. Free of such categorial structure,

[16]The very fact that phenomenalism is *not* is rather substantial evidence that it is categorially inadequate and that physicalism has been found better in use. I must admit that I prefer phenomenalism on grounds of elegance; but elegance must come much later on the list of categorial virtues, and take a subordinate place when compared to things like output.

there would be no intelligible order to any noise we might make, or to any other kind of would-be-semantic operation we might attempt.

I have also argued that there is a fundamental error involved in trying to apply criteria which are themselves predicated on a set of categories to the categories on which they are predicated, and that this error is committed when we try to take a set of categorial expressions and assess them as "true" or "false." Trueness and falseness are properties of assertions that we make; assertions can only intelligibly be made within a categorial structure; consequently, trueness and falseness (indeed, the very possibility of trueness and falseness) are contingent upon the prior occurrence of some such categorial apparatus. This is why I have said that the categories and their expression are *pre*-cognitive. That means that they are noncognitive, but draws a distinction between the many sorts of noncognitives there are.

Utterances like "The square root of −2 is lavender except on Thursdays" or "The fourth of July got tired and went to bed" are cognitively quite empty. An utterance in which we attempt to allude to or point out some of the basic categories in which we form our thought (and, even, consequently, some of the basic structures of the world in which the thought is occurring), while also cognitively empty, is a special kind of noncognitive utterance. It is special because it is a kind of utterance that is presumed, and must have occurred, before any cognitive (descriptive) success can occur.

Now, not every locution of the form "There are *X*'s" is fundamentally categorial. You have to look at the context to decide whether the speech act that is occurring is a categorizing operation.[17] Consider an example, however. It seems clear that if someone says, "There are quanta," he is uttering an existential (categorial) at a very inclusive and basic level.[18] Suppose, then, that some such categories are put in use and found to be operationally acceptable. The output of that network would be standard scientific descriptive locutions. And the

[17]It may be categorizing at a much less basic level. In a sense, "There are bears, kangaroos, and lions in the zoo" is a kind of categorizing move. But it is not a basic one. What is going on here is really the application of a set of categories (and not a very basic set at that) to a particular situation. Only when the categorizing has been pushed down to some very inclusive and very basic level, and is being entertained (rather than merely employed), do we really want to say that we have genuine existentials (existence affirmations, categorials) occurring.

[18]Of course, locutions like "There are quanta" do not exhaust the range of scientific discourse. It is the function of a very few locutions to underwrite and fund a whole descriptive network articulated in terms of them. Most of what the scientist has to say is description of what is going on in the world, structured according to his categorial commitment to interpret the data-stream in terms of some previously constructed apparatus (like matter, time, and/or quanta).

output would be cognitive. That is, the output descriptions are underwritten or funded by the categorial moves, which makes them subject, within that framework, to tests of truth and falsehood. Next, of course, we would want to determine, as best we can, which ones are true and which ones are false—within the frame. If, on the other hand, the categorizing moves are themselves bad moves (not false but dysfunctional), they will not effectively underwrite such a network of descriptive language. At the very least, the network will founder in use.

Here we have a distinction which is rather like (not identical to) the distinction between validity and soundness. Any set of premises will underwrite valid conclusions. As soon as we have a set of premises, we can assess whether the conclusions drawn from them are drawn validly or not. But only if the premises with which we begin are themselves well drawn are we in business. If they are not, then our conclusions may still be valid, but the whole apparatus is of little descriptive merit. It is not sound. Similarly, with categorizing, any sorting will underwrite linguistic descriptions of some kind, and (within the framework) it is possible for them to be "true"; but if the framework itself is misdrawn in some way, then (even though the descriptions issued may be true-in-context), the whole enterprise is without force.

Do not let this relativizing of the notion of truth slip by you. Truth or falsity, so seen, can only be discussed in context. No description (descriptive utterance) is in any sense "absolutely" true or "absolutely" false. It is only true or false as a function of its satisfaction of a set of conditions within the frame of reference within which it is articulated.[19] And the frame of reference is, itself, never true and never false. At best it is useful. At worst it is barren.

But, do not let this relativizing of the notion of truth mislead you, either. After all, isn't the quest for truth-independent-of-any-frame a Quixotic endeavor anyway? And frame-defined description is not footless. It *is* frame-defined, and the frame itself can be painstakingly weighed. That keeps the system testable and self-corrective, and (at the same time) keeps us able to differentiate weighing a frame of reference and weighing within one—no small thing.

---

[19]Note, by the way, that from this perspective, inconsistency can occur only within a frame, strictly speaking. So one kind of apparent inconsistency we frequently encounter is really not inconsistency at all. It is just the chaos you get when you try to weigh against one another some claims that are articulated in different frames. It is like quoting Saint Peter to show a Moslem that he is wrong. Not inconsistent, just absurd. That is the kind of thing that happens when you forget that truth (and evidence) is frame-defined.

8

THE PRIMITIVE
DISCOURSE
OF THEISM

In the preceding chapter, I have tried to show that there is a language function that comes prior to, and, indeed, sets the limits of, truth-conditioned description. It is rather like the formulation of theory; yet it is more basic than ordinary theorizing. I have described it as the vocalization of a most basic "way of taking" events and have called it "categorizing." I have tried to show that some such categorizing lies behind all description, and that rival categorizations frequently lie behind conflicting descriptions. And, finally, I have tried to show how this categorizing is done by linguistic act—semantic in its outreach, a performative speech act in its implementation, and testable.

I am convinced that a very important and basic part of religious discourse is the expression of "categorials." I have called attention in an earlier chapter to the apparent fact that religious discourse occurs at two levels—religious primitives and, in turn, religious derivatives that are formulated in terms of the primitives. That early suggestion can now be reformulated according to the theory of linguistic-category construction and expression. The religious primitives, from this vantage point, are those fundamental or categorizing expressions in terms of which a person views the world "theistically" (i.e., sorts events in terms of a theistic model). The religious derivatives, from this perspective, are those innumerable and assorted descriptions that are uttered within the framework of theistic categories—those that utilize the entities and processes that are constructed, posited, postulated, or evoked in the primitive uttering.

I suggested early on that the very paradigm of a religious primitive is the theistic existential, the "God affirmation"—the avowal, the way-of-taking construction, "God exists."[1] We must now explore the force of this most primitive theistic move *qua* categorial; most primitive because the derivative statements that may be constructed in terms of it will stand or fall with it. Note that we do not now ask, "What does 'God exists' mean?" or "Is 'God exists' true?" Rather, "What is the distinct character of categorizing the world theistically?" or "What are we doing when we say 'God exists'?" or "Whatever it is we are doing here, is it worth doing?" Thus, we recognize "God exists" as precognitive, and avoid the category mistake of trying to force it into the cognitive mold. We do not look for its truth conditions, *a fortiori* for its satisfying some truth conditions. Nor do we, on the other hand, liberate the move from all restraint or suggest that it is "above logic," "above reason," "above analysis," or "above appraisal." We try, rather, to bring it under analysis and appraise it with legitimate and linguistic–categorially appropriate appraisal rules. Is it fertile? Is it ad hoc? Does it mesh? And so on. While this notion of theism as a "way of taking" is reminiscent of the views of Hare and Wisdom, it goes beyond those views in making explicit provision for weighing a "way of taking," for determining whether a blik is a *right* blik.

THE FORCE OF THE THEISTS' WAY OF TAKING

Let us consider the force or character of this way of taking events. It is, first of all, to impose a purposive or telic structure upon them. It is to arrange the data under a rubric of ends. This is not to say that in the basic theistic move one asserts, "There are ends in the world to be seen, tasted, smelled, felt, or heard." It is to sort the data, not describe them. Even as the physicalist makes his basic moves, imposing a material and causal structure upon what he observes, without suggesting for a moment that we can gather a pocket full of causes or taste a soupçon of matter, so the theist structures the world telicly without asserting the sensory discernibility of purpose "writ large in the sky."

[1]We should remind ourselves again that not every religion is theistic; not every religious way of taking is predicated on a categorial voiced in these terms. But, theism is the variety of religion that concerns us; theistic discourse is the kind of religious talk we are trying to analyze. Hence, the God affirmation is the religious primitive with which we must begin.

What he is doing is perceiving the events of the natural order under the model of intention. Such a perceiving may be fruitful or it may be sterile; but, either way, it is prior to description and its truth conditions.

Second, given taking the world under the model of intention, the theist takes the world as in some sense the output of an intender. This is not to say that he infers a designer from events observed. It is not to reinstitute some latter-day teleological argument for the existence of God. Rather, it is to project upon events as they occur a parameter of intention, and within that, to construct an "author" of intention for their support. This is exemplified in Wisdom's story of the "garden," in which we can readily see such rival categorizations of the same events "taken" in different ways. Consider an example: A man has hoped and dreamed of having a certain job in a certain place, of living in a particular town and pursuing a special lifestyle—a hope and a dream that have not materialized, and which, as he reads his future, he doubts ever will materialize. But time passes and events mesh. "Out of the blue" an opportunity arises; he is offered, and takes a job; and his dream is fulfilled. He could take these events in several ways—as coincidence, fate, divine guidance, luck. One man might say, "God works in mysterious ways His wonders to perform." Another might say, "Wow! What good luck!" Both are amazed and both are gratified, but each sorts out the occasion of his amazement and gratification in different patterns, neither of which is either demonstrable or defeasible by an appeal to the individual occurrent facts. Consider again: A child dies. One man says, "God knows His own and called her home." Someone else says, "What a tragic and insensitive, inhuman world we live in—even the innocent are struck down!" Still another sighs, "We live, we die, the grass flourishes and withers away, and what is man?" These, too, are ways of taking or structuring the event into the total perspective on the world that is held by the different individuals as they confront it— not descriptions that are testable in a common framework in even the most detailed examination of living and dying. One might even say, "We pass from nonbeing into being and back into nonbeing again"; and while his statement may be obscure to the point of pain, it still must be weighed within its own frame of reference, and not be condemned for the inapplicability of inappropriate criteria.

So the theist is taking the world purposively, seeing it under the model of intention, arranging it (and eventually describing it) under a projected rubric of intender (designer, God) and plan. But that is only part of the force of the basic theistic move.

The theist is also taking the world under the model of norms and

values. In bringing a rubric of intention to bear upon events, he also
imposes a rubric of values which brings the events under judgment.
This is not to say that the theist claims to be able to perceive "the
good" or "the bad" (or anything in between) festooned upon the events
of the natural order. It is not to say that the theist claims to recollect
communion with the form of the good in some prior life, or to taste
the flavor of virtue in the events that surround him. Rather, it is to say
that, prior to his description of individual events, he sees them as under
a pattern of appraisal. Most emphatically, he sees his own life and the
lives of his fellows under such a pattern. Thus he brings to bear upon
all that he does and all that they do a normative model—articulated
in terms of the fulfillment or defeat of those intentions in terms of
which he reads his whole world. The normative model, too, may be
useful or it may be utterly sterile or even corrosively dysfunctional. But
it is neither a true way nor a false way, for ways of taking are neither
true nor false.

   Taking the world under the model of intention, seeing the world
under a rubric of norms, and seeing man and all his enterprise as subject
to judgment, meld together into a taking of life, especially man's life,
as (at least in potential) "meaningful" and "worthwhile." In this way,
the theist brings to bear upon human history a frame of reference that
forces each act, both grand and hidden, into the winnowing of purposive appraisal. This finds its sharpest focus, I believe, in the theists'
way of taking their own lives—in their appraising the success or failure
of their own endeavors as part of the working out of history (which
they see as working toward a goal and, eventually, to be measured in
detail for its success). The crucial status of this particular aspect of a
theistic way of taking is often ignored in the rather more Pollyanna
views of "life-morale" and "escape"; but a basic and fundamental part
of it is that they take the world (and themselves) as under the rubric,
and in dread, of judgment. Consider, again, an example: A youth goes
to college, and out of the combined resources of family and the larger
society, he is provided with multiple opportunities for the fulfillment
of whatever capacities and potentials he has. But each day he confronts
the option between the hard labor and enterprise that is a necessary
condition of fulfillment, and the frittering away of energies and capacities in the idylls of "good times." Anyone, whatever his way of taking
the world, can feel the crunch of that. But the theist feels that crunch
in a distinctive way. As he considers the options before him (and the
options of earlier days long gone), he constantly brings to bear upon
himself the notion of what he ought to do to fulfill what he sees as
"gifts" and to answer what he hears as "calls." The nontheist in the

same circumstances can readily feel the press of human needs answered or unanswered, but he does not feel that press as one of "vocation" met or unmet: he does not perceive the world "that way." Thus it is that the theist, as he takes his world, takes it in fear or dread of judgment. But that is not the end of it.

The basic theistic move also involves taking the world as an occasion of joy. It is no accident that the notion of "celebration" lies close to the heart of so much recent theistic talk. This is not to say that the theist ignores or blinks at the tragedies and adversities of his own or others' lives. Rather, it is to say that the theist sees and interprets the pattern of his life as a working out in the midst of struggle—as a fulfillment in which there is joy like that of an artist producing a work out of an intractable medium. Consider, again, a way of taking a given case: An individual's ambition and labor are met by frustration. "Doors are closed." Hopes are dashed. What are the reaction options? To take the events as the occasion for redoubled commitment and increased investment of time and labor is, I think, the theists' way. For, he takes and sees his world (in Hick's terms) as an arena for the "making of souls." This is not to suggest that all theists necessarily respond to adverse circumstances in precisely this way, although I would suggest that this is a common theistic pattern. A theist may also, upon confronting adverse events (the frustration of his interests and desires), read those events (again under the rubric of intention) as an indication that his desires and interests are "unworthy." Bringing himself and his interests thus under judgment, he may read events that are adverse to his own inclinations as portents of what ought (not) to be, and modify his behavior accordingly.[2]

This taking of events as reinforcement or chastisement (a dialectic of anguish, celebration, judgment, and affirmation) does not, however, exhaust the forces at work in this way of taking. Taking the events of the world as a perfectly general disclosure (when seen and read correctly) of both what is and what is said "ought to be," is, of course,

[2]There is, of course, danger in the possibility of equivocating between the two options. If the theist's interpretation and perspective is to be a fruitful and useful one, he must find some basis on which a consistent choice can be made between redoubled efforts in the face of adversity (seen under the pattern of reinforcement), and closure of effort in the face of adversity (seen under the pattern of judgment). If care is not exercised, if the theist vacillates too readily between the two, the perspective which he occupies seems to reveal itself as formless and indeterminate. We shall consider such problems presently, when we try to assess the whole theistic way of taking (on categorially appropriate grounds). I call this example to your attention at this time simply to indicate the kind of problem which the theist faces.

to take events—individual and specific as well as collectively—as "revelatory."[3] But, quite in contrast to this, we must also note that taking the world theistically also involves taking it as in some sense "unfathomable." The theist's perspective on the world very clearly involves the allowance that, whatever the extent of his particular knowledge (or, for that matter, whatever the extent of the knowledge of all men combined), there remains a vast quantity of data unknown and unknowable. The former does not, by itself, distinguish his view from that of any reasonable scientist, but the added supposition means that the world is seen under the rubric of mystery as well as under the pattern of disclosure.[4]

Here, then, is a sample of some of the forces and effects of seeing the world the theists' way. Perhaps enough samples have been given that we can perceive the general character of their particular perspective on events. The theist and the nontheist are not in dispute about the facts or events themselves. The events are there; but they are there to be arranged, to be grasped, to be comprehended under a structure. There is where the conflict arises. For, our theist sees the world as mysterious, as disclosure, as intended, as normatively structured, as challenge and arena, and as ruled.

But can a man see the world all these ways and be seeing the world *a* way? That is, does such a collection of vantage points come clear as *a* vantage point—does the collection, taken collectively, pass the criteria of clarity and internal coherence? Further, if my analysis of the difference between primitive and derivative levels of religious discourse (between categorials and descriptions formulated in terms of them) is correct, and if my analysis of the enterprise of weighing categorial structures and expressions is correct, then we ought to be able to bring the basics of the theistic way of taking under appraisal in terms of the whole array of these weighing criteria. How does it fare?

WEIGHING THE THEISTIC WAY OF TAKING

I think it almost inevitable that the verdict on the theistic way of conceptualizing the world is mixed when we weigh it on the kind of

[3]There are dangers here, as there were dangers above, of slipperiness: dangers attendant upon the difficulty of specifying concretely what is disclosed in some specific event or in all history.

[4]And, thus, again, a problem is posed as the perspective incorporates into itself a divergent set of viewpoints, and runs the consequent risk of sheer and designed inconsistency at worst, or inattentive and undisciplined equivocation at best.

categorial criteria we have discussed before. I have already indicated, in notes, several points at which it seems to me that the theistic way seems to run afoul of the criterion of internal coherence. But what verdicts can be reached on the basis of a wider array of categorial standards?

Consider the criterion of inclusiveness or scope. By design or definition, the theistic perspective is "all-inclusive." Indeed, it may be altogether too amenable and adaptable. One might try to dismiss this criticism on the grounds that it is typically aimed at some specific theistic utterance taken as an assertion. (The charge is that an assertion equally compatible with all states of affairs is assertively empty—the Positivists' "nonsense" again.) One could claim, viewing the basic move as we are now (as an attempt at categorially structuring the full array of events), that this is not a cogent criticism. If it were cogent, it would capture all ways of taking, not just this one. So, one could claim that this criticism boils down to the claim "The expression of a way of taking is not a successful assertion." But, if it is not an assertion at all, then *a fortiori* it is not a successful one; so the "lack" of success should be no occasion of dismay. But, we cannot dismiss the charge of overdone amiability quite so lightly. There is something odd about a view that takes success and frustration as equally disclosing the same ultimate structure of events. Although it is not operative at the same level of abstraction, it is reminiscent of the systematic amiability of Freudian theory, which has so often earned it the label of "self-fulfilling." If the theistic way of taking is this amiable, then it might succeed on a criterion of inclusiveness or scope, but in the very overdoing of that success, it would fail quite wretchedly on the criterion of self-correction or modification. In my opinion, however, the basic theistic move is not necessarily this slippery. Rather, this tendency is something that we find generated ad hoc in the face of circumstances which the theists' way of taking (taken at face value) does not seem to cover. Even as, at the descriptive level, theists (under pressure) can flee to transcendence, so too, at this categorizational level, they can (under pressure) flee to overamiability. But this is more of a tactical or strategic error than it is a basic or inherent flaw in the fundamental perspective. What the theist needs to do is refine and sharpen the dimensions of his view in the face of data that are adverse, rather than diluting or watering it down to the point of all-inclusiveness. And he can do this. On the other hand, this "trimming" can itself pose genuine problems for the theist because, as indicated, his perspective is calculated by design and definition to be all-inclusive. So the verdict here is "very broad" and sometimes "too broad." If scope were the only criterion, this verdict would not be too bad. There are others, however. Consider "simplicity."

Here the theist does rather well, it would seem. His basic vantage point involves vast theoretical economy; for it offers, as the ultimate explanatory ground of all that he observes, one principle being (force, process, entity, or construct). However, this virtue, like broad scope, can also become a significant vice: for all its parsimony, it views the world in a way that can obscure rather than illumine useful distinctions that could be drawn among the events that occur. The danger, when bringing a parsimonious conceptual apparatus to bear on the world and examining hard data, is of smearing disparate data together. All things held equal, parsimony is a good thing. All things are hard to hold equal, though; with the consequence that, on this ground, we may again say that theism often does too well. Consider: There is a war between some society and its enemies. One of the items that the society needs to explain is how and on what grounds its enemies are counterposing their collective will against the will of "God's elect." Granted that the theists' way is more parsimonious than that of some theological pluralist (say a Zoroastrian); but, in that very increase of parsimony, there is an implicit inability to explain conflict. Our Zoroastrian, who sees the world under the aspect of titanic struggle, has a much easier time coming to terms with this case than does our standard theist, who, in the very economy of his theory, locks himself into a narrowness of explanation that brings him to the brink of self-contradiction. The net effect of this kind of difficulty is, usually, that the parsimony survives only at the apparent level; and that the necessary complicating factors are imported into the system in some rather devious or roundabout way. Thus, our standard Western theists have incorporated all the difficulties of Satan theory in trying to bring their very parsimonious world view to bear upon a set of intractably conflicting events. As a result, the apparent simplicity conceals actual complexity; and what seems to be parsimony may be, in fact, a cover-up. Nevertheless, *prima facie,* the theists' world view is about as parsimonious as can be. So, on theoretical simplicity as on scope, there is at least an initial strength in this way of taking. But it is a strength which has inherent in it, given the data to be arranged under the system, debilitating weakness and, possibly, defeat.

When assessing theories, one of the criteria we are concerned with is the extent to which the theory under appraisal meshes with other theories in use. When assessing ways of taking the world, it is not possible to cast this criterion in quite the same terms. "How well does this way of taking the world mesh with other ways of taking it?" is,

at best, obscure. And yet it has its point. For assorted men do take
the world in different ways, and the compatibility or incompatibility
of their ways of taking may determine the dimensions and success
of their assorted interactions and, especially, the possibility of com-
munication between them. Further, theories do occur at different
levels of generality and inclusiveness. So, while we would not ordinarily
ask how well two alternative same-level ways of theorizing the same
event mesh (whatever their mutual level of abstraction), we certainly
do ask about the mesh or failure to mesh between some general theory
and other theories, of less abstraction and greater particularity, that are
well established in use and are supposedly subsumed beneath it. For,
given two alternative theories at the same level of abstraction, one of
the most straightforward methods we have of deciding between them is
in terms of their comparative success at accommodating or subsuming
this array of less general theories in common use. When we ask whether
the theists' way of taking can or does succeed in subsuming the vast
array of more particular theories and explanations to which men subscribe, the answer in principle and the answer in practice are again quite
divergent. The answer in principle is quite similar to the one we get on
the criteria of scope and simplicity. In principle and by definition, the
theists' way of taking subsumes all lesser theories as special cases and
applications of its generality to the individual instance. As any contemporary theist will tell us, "Truth is one, there is only one kind of
facts, and our view has nothing to fear from genuine scientific discovery." What the theist is trying to say, as he juxtaposes his way of taking
and particular descriptions and accounts of things that happen in the
world, is that these lesser and common theories may be seen simply as
a set of bridging hypotheses between his general blik and the particular data themselves. So, in principle, by definition and necessarily,
the theists' way of taking subsumes all others and "meshes" very
well indeed.

To leave the matter here, however, is misleading in the extreme.
For, when we are weighing theories in this way, we are less concerned about matters of principle and definition than we are about
the actual and practical melding of explanatory force. Thus, when
a physicist tells us that Einstein's general theory in mechanics subsumes
assorted other theories as special cases, our interest is in the confirmation he provides with detailed accounts of exactly how the theories
relate. And the confirmation is readily provided. But this is not at all
apparent in the instance of theism. We are told that the theists' general
view subsumes all lesser and useful views compatibly; but we are not
shown. Indeed, we have some ground for suspecting that we cannot be

shown. For example: In common use, and at a level of considerably greater particularity than the theists' general blik, is the theory of adaptation and/or modification of life forms, and of survival in the competition for living space and resources of those that happen to modify in ways that fit (evolution). Theists will, generally, deal with this more particular theory in one of two ways: they will say either that it is false and therefore does not have to be subsumed under their world view (since that only subsumes theories that are fruitful and, ultimately, descriptions that are true); or they will say, "Yes, this set of claims is acceptable and subsumes; that is how God did it." But how much of a demonstration of subsumption is this? It is not a demonstration of any kind. It is, rather, a blanket assertion of the very matter at issue. When we consider Einstein's general theory of mechanics, and are informed that for particles of moderate size Newtonian mechanics can be subsumed as a special case, a genuine demonstration is readily forthcoming with all of the auxiliary hypotheses needed to show precisely how this set of general laws works out in this specific area in this precise (subsidiary) way. This example illustrates the difference between evidence and question-begging. So, in spite of the fact that the theist can claim, in principle, total mesh, there is extreme difficulty in showing just how that mesh does, in fact, occur at the level of practicality.

Indeed, there is even some question about the possibility in principle of tying this particular way of taking together with certain theories of less generality and, particularly, with certain descriptive statements about events in the world that are articulated in terms of less all-subsuming theories. For example: We have stated previously that part of the theistic way of taking amounts to seeing the world under the aspect of intention and appraisal. Bearing this in mind, it is only with great difficulty, if at all, that the theists' way can subsume as special cases all of the data that we have discussed in earlier chapters under the heading "the problem of evil." The theist can, of course, reply, "These statements in terms of which the problem of evil are articulated are statements which are formulated in terms of a rival (and sterile, wrongheaded) way of taking the world; and there is no necessity, consequently, for our way of taking to mesh with them (or it)." To a very limited extent, that is correct. But it misses the cutting edge of the issue, for these rival ways of taking the world *both* see the world under the aspect of intentionality. The concept of evil finds its home base in such a framework, just as does the theists' concept of good. So, the rival ways of taking must be rivals on grounds other than that. The problem of evil is a problem for the theist *because* he sees the world under the aspect of intentionality. If he did not look at the world this way, there would be no problem. So, it is not a matter that the theist can dismiss as "something we don't need to mesh into our system." It is a problem that is generated and issued by the very fabric and character of his system, and which he must meet head on.

Now, this is not to say that he must meet it on the grounds on which arguments from evil are ordinarily stated. For, if we are considering his view as a way of taking, rather than as a set of descriptions, the grounds have shifted. However, while the grounds have shifted, the grounds have not been altogether erased. The problem assumes a new aspect, but it does not disappear; and it remains for the theist, even under this new aspect, central and crucial to the viability of his way of taking. It would be folly, if my appraisal of the force of the basic theistic move is correct, to think that it is true or false (and proved to be false on the basis of the events described as evil when seen under the aspect of intentionality that is used by both the theist and his non-theistic rival). It would be equally foolish, however, to think that the theist can simply escape scot-free without subjecting his way of taking to this test in application. It must be so subjected, and it is in this sub-jection that the theistic way of taking finds its most crucial testing. Basically, it amounts to this: The theist takes the world under the aspect of intention and purpose, and this necessitates that he interpret the events that occur in evaluative terms. But, would it not appear that in interpeting the events that actually occur in this world, in these evaluative terms, one is obliged to see many of them under the aspect of negative value? If one did not choose to interpret the world under the aspect of evaluative terms at all, then, of course, there would be no use in his perspective for either the term "evil" or the term "good." But, having chosen to work from this evaluative vantage point, and given the events that are indeed transpiring before him, he confronts the difficulty of being unable in good conscience to deem them all "good." But, if he is not able to deem all events "good" (i.e., as the fulfillment of purpose), it is because he sees many of them as "bad" (i.e., as the counterfulfillment of purpose). But what is it to see events as the counterfulfillment of purpose? It is to see them either as the fulfillment of counterpurpose, or as in some intractable medium that works against purpose's fulfillment. In either case, however, this jars sharply against the basic character and thrust of taking the world *sub specie* theism. Thus it is that the theist finds himself enmeshed again in the problem of evil, even when we endeavor to interpret the force of his enterprise in what I take to be the most illuminating way: as a way of taking the world, rather than as an attempt at the

enumeration of specific facts. So, even on these shifted grounds, the problem of evil is not to be dismissed or ignored, for it still confronts theism
as a problem of substance (and, perhaps, as its point of defeat).[5]

These are, I think, the primary weaknesses of theism as a way of
taking the world: overamiability and distinction-hiding. Another basic
difficulty might be expected to arise when we recall the primary source
of the trouble we had bringing truth-conditioned appraisal to bear
upon primitive religious utterance; that is, the affirmed transcendence (and, thus, inaccessibility to test) of that "Being" to Whom
attributions were being made in the talk so understood. But this difficulty in appraising religious discourse when seen as r/a/d comes to
be no difficulty at all when that discourse is seen as the expression and
constitution of a way of taking. The reason for this is apparent at even
much lower levels of abstraction and generality where theories of explanation are constructed. There is nothing insuperably problematic
in the unobservable status of those entities imported into the technique
of description by a particular "way of taking," whether the entities
thus imported are unobservable "physical" mites dispersed in the
universe of space and time, or are some family of Grand Intenders
against Whom all notions of facts and structures are appraised. It may
be offensive to some to speak of God as a Hypothetical Construction;
but if the god-notion can be seen as a notion analogous in its operation
to those notions that are imported into the theories of less abstraction
and scope as "constructs," I think we may then see in clear terms why
the notion of a God can operate quite effectively in the theistic way
of taking without having to be assigned to some specific discernible
event. This is not to deny the notion any kind of workable and working status within the way of taking; rather, it is to assign to it a bona
fide position within that way which, if not assigned, would leave the
notion substantially footless and without discernible impact.

MEASURING THE UTILITY OF THEISM

A famous (and notoriously bad) argument has been used on occasion
to "prove" that theism is "true": so many people have believed it that

[5]Note, however, that even if theism meets defeat at this point and on these
grounds, the verdict will still not be "false." The verdict will be "inadequate"
or, perhaps, "confused." With that in mind, and realizing that adequacy and confusion occur in greater and lesser degree, we may find a leverage on the rehabili-
tation of the theistic view that is impossible when we try to force it into the
all-or-nothing mold of "true" and "false."

it must be true. That is a howler as it stands, and no one with any measurable amount of judgment would accept it. However, a promising analogue of that argument is available once the ground shift has occurred and we are considering theism a way of taking (weighing it on the felicity criteria that belong to ways of taking). For, while we cannot say that theism is true because so many people have believed it,[6] we do have evidence that it is useful in that so many people have for so long employed it with apparent satisfaction.[7] This argument is somewhat misleading, though. It does not take into account the necessity of specifying objective criteria for "usefulness," it does not take into account the inherent difficulty of making any such utility appraisal from within a frame of reference, and it does not take into account possible alternative reasons for a view's survival besides systematic usefulness (inertia, for example).

There is an old argument about equivocation on "desirable." It ought to be kept in mind when we talk about the application of "useful," too. There may be some basis in extended use for affirming genuine usefulness (at any rate, there is if we are willing to affirm the general good sense of people). But there are just too many reinforcing factors that can preserve a totally dysfunctional institution or view to feel at all secure in the "used"/"useful" inference.

Further, we must remember that a frame of reference, as a way of taking, imposes itself upon or is imposed upon all of the data received within it, and thus engulfs and surrounds the taker in the taking. To think that the taker can simply step back and appraise the utility of his way of taking, so dispassionately and with such ease, is analogous to Braithwaite's notion that "stories" are efficacious even when not believed. If a way of taking *is* a way of taking, and if the data are filtered

---

[6]There are two things wrong with this view: (a) the truth of assertions is governed by truth conditions, not votes; and (b) if our early analysis of knowledge and belief is correct, then so many people have not really *believed* it, however frequent its ritual utterance.

[7]On the same grounds, of course, we could conclude that many religions (both theistic and otherwise) are defensible, for many show the same record of apparently satisfactory use over long periods of time. In making this statement, we are not confronted with the same constraining law of contraries that governs weighing competing claims on grounds of truth and falsity. For, while two rival descriptive claims cannot both be true (but could, of course, both be false), it is quite possible for two rival ways of taking both to be useful (or, of course, both to be useless). It is, consequently, possible to reach the judgment that several alternative religious ways of taking are equally useful, or that they are arrayed on some continuum of utility, and so on. All of this presumes, of course, that this notion of utility can be made intelligible in the individual case.

and structured from the vantage point of that posture, then the enterprise of appraisal is one that can be carried on by the taker only with
severe and burdensome difficulty. It is highly unlikely that he will find
his way of taking anything but useful (and others' ways anything but
useless). It is unlikely in the extreme that a taker will be able to say,
"These rival ways of taking array themselves in a continuum of utility,
useful in varying degrees and interchangeable as a function of their
testable utility," for he sees the world *this* way, not *that* way. So, such
an easy verdict is not readily open to him. He is much more likely to
say, "My way of taking is obviously superior to all others," if, indeed,
he is able to recognize that his way of taking is a way of taking to
begin with. Even that is not too likely.

Finally, we must recognize that apparent success in a way of taking
(and consequent satisfaction in it) can be the product of an almost
limitless variety of extrinsic factors. Not only do ways of taking tend
to be self-fulfilling, and takers tend to be blinkered by their stance
(whatever stance it be), other factors like institutionalization and cultural inertia impede appraisal too. In fact, these impediments may be
so great as to bind an individual and a whole culture into a perspective
on their world that is so inadequate that it is painfully obvious to
anyone "on the outside." On a much lower level, we see this regularly
in such externally perplexing phenomena as jingoistic patriotism, per-
fervid national pursuit of demonstrably lost political causes, calf-eyed
devotion to totally corrosive and destructive romantic interests, and
dogged preservation of catastrophic marriages. So we cannot be satisfied with the verdict "lots of people have used this conceptual boat
for a long time, so it must be seaworthy."

This is not to say, however, that endurance value can be entirely
ignored. Primarily, it is to assert that endurance value is best appraised
from outside. But am I, then, suggesting that once within a frame
of reference there is no possibility of utility appraisal? Am I disconnect-
ing ways of taking from all means of such appraisal by the ones who
"take"? No. I am only suggesting that it does not commonly (and
cannot most effectively) occur in this way. I think, in fact, that the
appraisal from within occurs chiefly at the level of feeling—specifically,
that negative appraisal from within comes chiefly in a feeling of frustration and consternation in attempts to cope with events, and that
affirmative appraisal from within comes chiefly in a feeling of success
in such attempts. It is clear, then, that the kind of verdict reached
through feeling by one within the frame, and the kind of verdict that
is reached by pragmatic appraisal by one who stands outside the frame
and appraises it in a more detached way, may quite commonly disagree.

But, utility appraisal is possible from within. It is usually negative. For frustration can and does arise within a way of taking; and, in that, ways of taking undergo change and revolutions occur. The world may be seen in a new way when old ways have proved themselves to be inadequate in the working.

There is another notorious move, sometimes made when trying to appraise theism on criteria of truth or falsity. It can be suggested that while, in some grand sense or to an outsider, theism is "false," it is still "true for the believer." This, too, is a howler: given the nature of the assertion-verdict "true," such notions as "true for me" and "true for you" are bankrupt on their face. However, there is, again, a move analogous to this which, when viewing theism as a way of taking, has point: an individual can reasonably say that while a certain way of taking has not proved itself adequate for the world at large and mankind in general, it is nevertheless quite adequate (and has, thus, "proved" itself) for him. Indeed, that verdict can sometimes be confirmed "from the outside": we can occasionally see that a way of taking has been an effective synthesizer within an individual's life, without being obliged to reach the same conclusion about its effectiveness in every life (or even in most lives). Thus we may quite reasonably reach the conclusion that the verdict on theism as a way of taking must vary as a function of the utility of that way for each of the individuals who so take.

Wider appraisals are also possible "from the outside," too. For, just as we may appraise the effectiveness and success of a theistic way of taking in an individual's life, so we may weigh the effectiveness and success of that way in a given culture in which it has been dominant, or in an array of cultures in whose history it has been evident. There is no necessity at all that the appraisal reached at each of these levels be the same. It may be found that what is successful, synthesizing, and productive at the level of many individuals is, at an all-inclusive or social level, inadequate on some objective grounds. In precisely this fashion, one could concur in Bertrand Russell's negative overall appraisal of the effectiveness of the theists' way of taking (and, especially, of the Christian theists' way of taking), without being obliged to abandon or deny the independent appraisal that may be reached about the effectiveness of that way in some individual's life. One is not obliged to conclude that this way has been dysfunctional in each of its individual takings in order to confirm Russell's general appraisal of its social and historical merits. (Of course, one is not obliged to concur with Russell at all.)

In this section, I have tried to sketch out the ways in which a theistic

way of taking can be appraised with sufficient clarity to show that it
can, in fact, be appraised. I think it has been effectively shown that
taking the endeavor as an enterprise of description is a serious mistake.
I think it has also been shown that taking it as an appraisable "way of
taking the world" is a more illuminating approach. I have tried to carry
through beyond the substantial insight of Hare and Wisdom to a
fuller account of what a "way of seeing things" amounts to (and how
theism amounts to a way of seeing things). And I have tried to lock this
firmly into a level of appraisal that is appropriate to it—examining it
under the assorted felicity conditions of most abstract and inclusive
theory. In this way—weighing mesh, weighing scope, weighing internal
consistency, weighing fertility, weighing individual and social utility,
and so on—we can come eventually to some verdict that the theists'
way of taking is either mostly adequate, mostly inadequate, basically
useful and illuminating, or basically sterile and pointless.

Carrying through on that appraisal itself, we must consider the "way
of taking" at both public and individual levels.

1. It is not difficult to appraise the collective or public effectiveness
of the theistic way of taking. Nor should it be difficult to obtain general
agreement on the verdict, if we are at all open and free in our application of reasonable criteria to this categorial structure. I think that it
is virtually inevitable that the verdict be "less than adequate" for the
world community taken as a whole, on the grounds that this way of
taking has stood in the way of clear and fruitful understanding of
events that occur in the world, and has been diversionary by transplanting the focal point of human concern from problems that immediately confront us (and are open to our manipulation) to "problems"
that are vastly removed from any possibility of human input or correc-
tion. On the other hand, when we attempt to measure the collective
and historical adequacy of the theistic way of taking things, we are
equally obliged to recognize that it is not totally useless. For, it has
been, and continues to be, a focal point and rallying ground for many
endeavors that are genuinely humane. Seeing the world *sub specie*
"intentionality," etc., yields to men a way of bringing their own am-
bitions and activities (individually and culturally) under judgment; and,
bringing them under judgment, it provides an apparatus to reform them.

It seems to me that the inadequacies of the theistic way of seeing
things show themselves primarily in the face of recalcitrant data, when
the enterprise either flees into transcendence and illogic, or proposes
to deny the observables. In both these "solutions" theism detaches
a person from events rather than assisting him in coming to grips with
them. For all its underwriting of judgment and possible-reform, then,

there is a threat of diversion and purposeful irrelevance. It seems to me that in both forms the trouble arises from a serious unwillingness to alter or adapt the frame of reference itself. This is to say, simply, that the key dysfunction of the theistic categorial frame is that it is resistant to self-correction.

2. The appraisal of the way of taking for an individual is not so easily done. To begin with, it is quite unlikely that any adequate judgment can be made at a "deduction-from-the-universal" level, given the simple and apparent fact that the life events to be synthesized by different individuals *differ*. Further, the way of taking is, itself, flexible enough that it does not make the interpreted data "come out the same way" every time. Second, it is equally unlikely that any adequate judgment can be made by the individual (by and for) himself. For, as indicated before, such self-judgment operates chiefly at the level of feelings (of frustration or success), and feelings are notoriously slippery and difficult to articulate with any specificity. But this is not to say that judgment(s) cannot be reached. It is, rather, only to say that judgment(s) can be best reached neither on a "universal" scale by some grand appraiser nor by the individual from within. There remains the possibility that the best source of judgment is some other individual, close at hand, who can see all the specific nuances of conduct, and of success and failure, as they are worked out in the behavior of one whom he knowledgeably and perceptively observes. It should hardly be startling that this is the best shot. Wherever the subtleties of human intention and conduct are being appraised, they find their best appraisal in such hands (familiar with the dimensions of the individual's feelings and conduct, yet sufficiently detached from them to see them in an independent and dispassionate light). For this reason, whatever we may conclude about the adequacy of the theistic frame of reference in its social and historical impact, the appraisal of it in individual lives remains an open question. Thus, a final utility verdict cannot be given here, even though the apparatus for reaching that verdict *for each individual case* should now be clear.

SUMMARY

I have shown in this chapter that the force of the theists' way of taking the world is to see it under the aspect of intention; to take it as, in some sense, the output of an Intender; to perceive it as under the model of norms and values; to take life (especially man's life) as "meaningful" and "under judgment"; to see history as a disclosure of what ought and ought not to be; and to see events as both revelatory and yet unfathomable.

I have argued, further, that taking the world this way passes categorial criteria of scope and parsimony almost too well; and that, consequently, the theist encounters genuine difficulties with his schema on matters of internal consistency, overamiability with conflicting sets of data, and with blurring or ignoring distinctions that can usefully be drawn between kinds of facts. I have argued, however, that the problems generated by "transcendence" have been eased somewhat by shifting the assessment from truth-conditioned appraisal of descriptions to pragmatic-conditioned appraisals of categorials (which allows the inclusion of constructs). And I have argued that the chief difficulties of the perspective arise in the area of "collective utility," due to its non-self-corrective inertia. And I have argued, finally, that on individual utility-appraisal, the theists' blik *must* receive mixed reviews, and have indicated what would clearly seem to be the best place to go to obtain a review in an individual case.

CONCLUSION

UNDERSTANDING
THE LANGUAGE
OF ZION

I would not claim that the view I have presented here about the use of
religious language (and the conclusions that it entails about the status
of religious belief and knowledge) should replace all the others I have
mentioned. I do think that it supplements them because it takes into
account a very basic language function that they do not. If you should
come to the conclusion that an adequate analysis of the language of
Zion would involve part of the view that I am espousing and part of
the others we have seen, well and good. You may even come to the
conclusion that it would involve a lot of things that my notions do not
spell out and that none of the others spell out. Doubtless, many significant aspects of religious discourse did get left out. You may even
come to the conclusion that some of the views I have examined (and
even the one I advance) attribute some features and uses to religious
language that are absolutely illegitimate—features that do not occur in
it at all. It is far more likely, however, that I have left something out
than that I have suggested too much.

The feature of the theory that I have advanced, about which I expect the most quarrel, is the claim that this "categorial" use of language
is the basic theistic use. For, I have not suggested that you merely add
this use to the list. You must make your own appraisal here, as you
consider the implications of what I have claimed.

I have argued that when we first talk about locating religious language (figuring out what language is religious and what language is not), we must make a sharp distinction between two kinds of discourse. Both of them are religious, but they have entirely different status within the total system. A great deal of language is clearly and obviously religious that consists of claims like,"At the ringing of the bell, the host transubstantiates into the mystical embodiment of the body and blood of Christ." The list of claims is a long one, and you can add to it by consulting your own experience, religious practices, literature, and the like. Claim after claim is straightforwardly "religious" and straightforwardly "descriptive." When the priest says to me, *sotto voce,* in the midst of the mass, "The host is transubstantiating now," I take him to mean what he says. I take him to be making an assertion which, for good or ill, rightly or wrongly, truely or falsely, is being voiced in a thoroughly descriptive way. It is religious in its import and use, but still a description.

It seems to me that the majority of claims that occur in religious discourse are of this descriptive sort. The question to raise about them, in an appropriate context and with appropriate tests, is "Are they true or are they false?" Did the host really transubstantiate? Did the water really become wine, or was it a trick? Did the sun stand still, or were we all hypnotized?[1] So I am claiming that one whole family of clearly religious language is clearly descriptive, clearly true or false as the case may be (but not, as far as I can see it, *necessarily* false), to be weighed for truth and falsity on grounds that are appropriate to the data that is being talked about (i.e., appropriate to the frame of reference within which the descriptions occur).

I have argued that you cannot profitably weigh a descriptive claim in terms of criteria that are germane only to some frame of reference other than the one in which the given claim occurs, any more than you can weigh a move in chess on the rules of bridge. If it is a different

---

[1]Recall what Carnap said, that the great bulk of it is myth: perfectly straightforward, descriptive, etc., but 99 percent false. I don't know whether such a large majority of the claims are false or not. I am perfectly willing to entertain the hypothesis that some of them are true. I am convinced, beyond doubt, that it is impossible for *all* of them to be true, however, because they occur in different contexts and they occur in competing frames of reference, and (even in the same frame of reference) they assert incompatible things on occasion. There are others that I think highly unlikely because it seems to me that if they were true, they would have had natural implications of sufficient complication and size that we would have noticed them. Since we haven't, then by negative inference we have some reason to say that they are not very likely. But some may be true; and the only way to settle it is by examining them in their own categorial frame.

game, it is perfectly appropriate to expect that the rules will be different. That in no way suggests the notion of a game without rules. I have not tried to remove descriptive religious discourse from all check and restraint. Not at all. To do that would be unthinkable because it would so completely disembowel the religious enterprise as to make it completely irrelevant to any human concern. It would purchase safety for religious claims by guaranteeing their irrelevance to all human affairs. Rather, I have insisted only that the tests that are appropriate to the weighing of religious claims must be tests that fit the frame of reference in which those claims arise and occur.

So, I have affirmed that one kind of religious discourse is descriptive (i.e., cognitive—truth testable with conditions that are appropriate to the enterprise). But how do you get truth conditions, rules, for a language game? You get them through certain stipulations that set up the game and get it moving. You achieve tactical rules for chess only in the context of the invention and establishment of the game of chess. You achieve tactical rules for descriptive talk only in the context of stipulations and postulations which establish and give fuel to the game of describing. Independent of these supporting or foundation moves, you do not have an enterprise; and, having no enterprise, then you obviously do not have any tactical rules to govern the enterprise, and there is no "sense" going on in the enterprise. So, I have argued that *any* descriptive language game must have some kind of underwriting support, some set of stipulations which give content to the descriptions that are going on. If engaged in the "physical description" game (which would involve the utterance of claims like "The cat is on the mat" or "And day's at the morn" plus everything down to but not including "God's in His heaven"), then there is a necessary set of stipulations underlying it to provide us with the raw material for the enterprise. We are obliged to stipulate or postulate, in some way, the occurrence or the fundamental reality (call it what you will) of physical entities, of space and time, and of causal relationships—none of which are describable or affirmable within the framework of physical description. If they were describable within the context of the physical description game, then they, like physical descriptions, would presume some kind of underwriting moves. That is to say that in order to make them workable within the frame of reference, they would have to abandon their role of establishing the frame of reference to some other postulational moves; and these, in turn, would be independent and would call for their own presystematic justification. Thus I have argued that there have to be *underwriting* moves to get the game of describing under way. The notion of an "ontology-free" descriptive enterprise is folly. It makes just about as much sense as a "rule-free" game. (A rule-free pastime, maybe; but games have rules, and descriptions have underwriting ontologies expressed in categorials.)

I have suggested that these underwriting moves amount, for the physicalist, to a set of stipulations about matter, space, time, and causation. (With suitable modifications to keep the set of stipulations current, that should be enough.) Religious descriptions might be expected to have some underwriting ontology, too. There is no reason a priori that we should expect physical description and religious description to be underwritten by the same postulate set. But, whatever postulates underwrite religious description, they have to pass the same kind of second-order tests that are passed by the postulates that underwrite the physical (or any other) description game. You are not free to "make up" any set of postulate moves, free of all control and/or test. (You can; but then you have no guarantee that the set will underwrite any useful enterprise.)

So, in differentiating between descriptive discourse within a frame of reference (that is governed by the rules that establish the frame), and discourse that voices the rules or categories themselves, I have not suggested that the rules or categories are subjective or private. The kind of criteria that such moves must pass must themselves be clear, objective, and "standard": fertility, output, mesh, consistency, and so on.

Thus, I have argued that there is a second set of moves—some basic linguistic acts that do for religious description the same sorts of things that the theoretical construction of "space," "matter," "time," and "causation" do for physical description; and have argued that these items must pass muster on these pragmatic second-level or categorial criteria. Thus, we have an image of the whole enterprise of religious discourse: rule-governed description within a frame of reference, and second-level rule-governed categorial moves that set up the frame of reference. This is a notion of the enterprise as a working and, at least conceivably, productive one, instead of as a network of footless or sheerly mistaken descriptions that are falsely and fraudulently forced upon an ill-fitting physicalism. Instead of nonsense, instead of auto-encouraging hoopla, we have a notion of religious discourse as a working enterprise which at least possibly has some discernible testable, and even useful output. (On its own terms.)

I have argued that this second-order religious discourse presents itself as categorial affirmations that set up the religious description context, exactly parallel to the way in which the second-order categorial affirmations of the physicalist set up the apparatus for his world view. It consists of what I have called "existentials." Existence claims. Straight ontological affirmations. These do not have to be made very often. (We do not find the scientist going around saying, "There is matter, there is space, there is time.") It is much more frequently implicit in the syntax and vocabulary of the descriptions uttered, than it is explicit in a categorial voicing. But they can be uttered. You can ask the scientist, "What is basic to your operational system of definitions as you present it?" and he may reply, "The notion of a system, the notion of a function, and the notion of a process." All of this may be implicit in the descriptions that he does utter; but it can all be "said" if the occasion arises. And, these notions can be shown to be useful. "If you make these moves and construct your descriptions in terms of them, it all bears fruit—it gets jobs done. It enables you to run predictions, anticipate facts, and control events." It has pragmatic and empirical output tests. Granted, if he says, "Process and operational system are fundamental constituents of the world," he is making a claim that is "metaphysical"—in the sense that it is not provable in any direct or genetically empirical fashion, and in the sense that it is not testable in the description-system that it underwrites. But it is confirmable in the very fact that it underwrites a network of descriptions, funding them with useful entities, and making their truth-testing possible.

So, for the person who says, "The host just transubstantiated," or "The sun stood still" (in the right context), or "On an as-yet-unspecified date in the future, the bones and dust of the departed will rise again and move around," or "The new Jerusalem will descend from the sky and the mountain will open up like a flower, and the city (jade, alabaster, gold bricks, and all) will settle in," there is an implicit ontological schema that can perfectly well be weighed. Of course it is metaphysical. Of course it (and any utterance of it) is noncognitive, in exactly the same way that any underwriting system (or utterance of one) is noncognitive.[2] But its funded descriptions are cognitive,[3] and the frame itself is appraisable.

The categorials that express what underwrites the family of religious descriptions must be weighed for output, to see whether it is a productive way of taking the world. I have indicated how this can be done. The descriptions that are voiced in terms of them must be weighed

---

[2]This is not to say (this is the last time) that any old ontological system will do. Rather, that ruling out an ontological schema because it is not a description is obtuse. It misses an important distinction between describing and f•nding descriptions. You cannot take money out of the bank if none is there. The categorial/o...ological moves set up the account on which description draws.

[3]These impress me as false.

for truth, to see whether events (seen this way) will bear them out. That, too, is perfectly straightforward.

There is a remaining force in theistic talk, over and above this frame-making, frame-expressing, and asserting-within-a-frame. It resides in that attitudinal and emotive reinforcement emphasized in Braithwaite's account of the enterprise. When persons participate in worship, for example, saying the various sorts of things that are said, the uttering regularly performs this function, strengthened by the weight of ritual. The words used there are strung into strings that look very much like report, assertion, and description. An element of that function is, no doubt, present. Perhaps they were, at one time, entirely of such force. But they have come to acquire, over, above, and even independent of that, the "Braithwaite factor." Consider the Shema. It certainly contains, at least, a vestigial assertive content and force framed in the categorial structure of intent. But, equally clear, there is also the ritual reinforcement of a set of feelings toward the world, man, and man's place in the world. The same for Christian credals; the recitation has very little, if anything, to do with the accurate (or inaccurate) autobiographical description of the cognitive beliefs the reciter holds. It has, rather (or at least chiefly) to do with the ritual preparation of the reciter for the experience at hand, performing some kind of largely self-directed emotive function to put him in the right frame of mind and set of attitudes for the experience of the mass (or whatever).

Thus: frame-making, frame-expressing, asserting-within-a-frame, and affective/conative expression and reinforcement—and all of it testable, each part at its own level and in its proper way.

SUMMARY

I have argued for a strict differentiation between the religious voicings that establish a "way of taking" events, the specific assertions that are formulated within the way of taking so established, and the ritual utterance that surrounds it all. I have shown how the theist, working within his frame of reference, comes to describe a state of affairs in terms quite different from those of his rivals who take events in other "ways," as he brings the given under the aspect of intention, judgment, and the like; and I have argued that everyone has a "way of taking" (some religious and some not); and I have argued that these "ways" are not footless, being obliged to stand the test of pragmatic appraisal.

Thus I have argued that the basic theistic enterprise is not separable from the endeavors of other men by the falseness of a set of descriptions which the theists cast in the same common framework shared by all; but, rather, by the distinctness of the framework which they establish which is *not* shared by all. Thus, I have incorporated the notions of religious belief and knowledge firmly within the apparatus of religious categorization. It all stands or falls there. The question becomes, not "Do I know God exists?" or even "Do I believe God exists?" Rather: "Does taking the world under the rubric of theism illuminate or darken my perception and understanding? Does seeing events as in a network of intention, fulfillment, and frustration, achieve anything?" If and only if the framework is found secure can we talk about whether specific descriptions, cast in terms of it, are "true" or "false."

The folly of much recent theism has been to flee the arena of test, evidence, and argument (with appeals to transcendence, paradox, and mystery) when their claims are questioned. The parallel folly of much other recent theism has been to hold mulishly (with appeals to "special" evidence) to assertions that are palpably gratuitous in anybody's frame of reference. But, I have contended, there is a third parallel folly located in condemning the whole conceptual apparatus on the grounds that it is, in part, not a package of assertions.

The folly of ignoring the fact that the theists' way of taking *is* a way of taking commits one to a category mistake (conceptual) of enormous proportions and consequences. On the other hand, though, pointing out that ways of taking are never packages of assertions is not even to suggest that a particular way of taking is successful. (I have pointed out numerous reasons why the theistic way of seeing things falls short of success.) But it is to suggest that its dismissal (if it is to be dismissed) must be on fitting grounds.

Even with all of its (demonstrable) shortcomings as a way of seeing things, the theistic perspective on events survives. Inertia is, no doubt, one major part of the reason; but I have shown that a careful analysis of the framework-in-use will illuminate both strengths and weakness. Finally, I have shown where some cogent strengths and weaknesses lie.

There then remains only the question of weighing the frame of reference for its utility for the individual, *in situ.* I have shown why that can only be done case by case, and I have shown "how." That leaves a worthwhile (and achievable) task for you.

INDEX

DATE DUE